Operations Research/Computer Science Interfaces Series

Volume 56

More information about this series at http://www.springer.com/series/6375

The development, analysis, solution, and delivery of Operations Research/Management Science models has changed dramatically due to the phenomenal improvements in computer technology. At the same time, disciplines from computer science have benefitted from the advances achieved by operations researchers. The *Operations Research/Computer Science Interfaces Series* is devoted to the advances at the interfaces of Operations Research and Computer Science. Published volumes may study topics at this interface from the computer science and/or operations research perspective.

The series features three types of books at the Operations Research/Computer Science (OR/CS) interfaces:

Monographs written by recognized authorities.

Handbooks on a specific topic.

Edited volumes prepared by experts in specific areas serving as guest editors. These volumes are collections of papers selected after a rigorous refereeing process, with some volumes based upon papers presented at major professional conferences. These are not proceedings volumes, but they may represent a group of papers that were presented at a meeting and then selected for publication through a comprehensive review process.

Because of the depth and breadth of both operations research and computer science topics, the *Operations Research/Computer Science Interfaces Series* publishes volumes on a wide range of topics. Please browse the titles to appreciate this breadth of coverage. You are invited to submit a proposal for developing a book project in this series.

Vasileios Zeimpekis • George Kaimakamis
Nicholas J. Daras
Editors

Military Logistics

Research Advances and Future Trends

Springer

Editors
Vasileios Zeimpekis
Department of Financial & Management Engineering
University of the Aegean
Chios
Greece

Nicholas J. Daras
Department of Military Science
Hellenic Army Academy
Vari
Attiki
Greece

George Kaimakamis
Department of Military Science
Hellenic Army Academy
Vari
Attiki
Greece

ISSN 1387-666X
Operations Research/Computer Science Interfaces Series
ISBN 978-3-319-12074-4 ISBN 978-3-319-12075-1 (eBook)
DOI 10.1007/978-3-319-12075-1

Library of Congress Control Number: 2014957539

Springer Cham Heidelberg New York Dordrecht London

Printed on acid-free paper

Springer is part of Springer Science+Business Media (www.springer.com)

Preface

In the past few years, there has been an increased interest in the planning and execution of military logistics operations. Military logistics is the basic supporter responsible for sourcing and providing nearly every consumable item used by military forces worldwide. The latter is also responsible for providing the Department of Defense and other governmental agencies with comprehensive solutions in procurement, demand forecasting, inventory control, warehousing, and transportation operations in the most effective and efficient manner possible.

Military logistics operations are essential for armed forces to be able to support an ongoing deployment or respond effectively to emergent threats or natural disasters. For that reason, the military segment aims at accelerating logistics improvement, as the latter may enhance the support to the war fighter and tackle accordingly operational demands.

This edited volume is aimed at highlighting recent advances in the development of effective modeling and solution approaches to enhance the performance of military logistics. The objectives of this edited volume can be summarized as follows:

- conduct advance research in global defense-related topics, including military operations, governmental operations and security, as well as nation support
- foster high standards in the practice of military operations research
- promote the global exchange of information and ideas amongst developers and users of military operations research tools and techniques

Significant issues in military logistics that are addressed include the following: (a) Restructuring processes via OR methods aimed at improving the efficiency and effectiveness of the military logistics, (b) Sense-and-Respond logistics prediction and coordination techniques that provide competitive advantage, spanning the full range of military operations across the strategic, operational and tactical levels of war, (c) Procurement and auctioning, (d) Inventory and stock control theories and applications, (e) Military transport and logistical equipment, and, (f) Maintenance, repair and overhaul on operational capability in general and equipment availability.

To this end, the nine (9) chapters included in this edited volume aim towards:

- the provision of a relevant platform for the latest contributions of operations management, operations research, and computational intelligence towards the enhancement of military logistics,
- the creation of a reference for practitioners and army related personnel interested in integrating scientific rigor to improve logistics management within defense organizations & agencies,
- the collection of useful insights into new trends and interesting research avenues that promote the contribution of operations research, computational intelligence and operations management to the improvement of defense logistics,
- the bridging of the gap between the abundant literature on commercial logistics and its scarce defense & combat counterpart.

Chapter 1 deals with Unmanned Aerial Vehicles (UAVs) planning techniques. The latter are important assets for information gathering in Intelligence Surveillance and Reconnaissance (ISR) missions. Depending on the uncertainty in the planning parameters as well as the complexity of the mission and its constraints and requirements, different planning methods might be preferred. The first two planning approaches presented in this chapter, deal with uncertainty in fuel consumption of the UAV. The third planning approach is designed for an even more uncertain and dynamic situation in which travel and recording times are stochastic, time windows are associated to target locations and new targets become of interest during the flight of the UAV.

Chapter 2 presents a supplier selection methodology for Military Critical Items (MCI). A Fuzzy Analytic Hierarchy Procedure (FAHP) is developed in the supplier selection area of MCIs. Furthermore, Principal Components Analysis (PCA) is applied into real-life data, related to MCIs, collected within members of the Hellenic Armed Forces. Competitive Intelligence (CI) oriented mostly to financial data is also used to assist in shaping the supplier selection model.

Chapter 3 describes demand estimation methodologies of repairable items for the F-16 aircraft. The flight hour parameter is used for computing the initial support requirements of repairable items in the United States of Air Force (USAF) whereas the usage parameter is used in that of repairable items in Turkey. Based on these calculations, a new parameter called SORTIE, which is the one cycle of take-off and landing, is generated. Taking into consideration the flight hour, usage and SORTIE parameters, 24 scenarios (8 for each parameter) are created by using real data set of F-16 with a quantity of 894 repairable items. In addition to the traditional approach that tries to find the best parameter common for all data, two new approaches are formed up. The first approach requires grouping the repairable items according to the supply group corresponding to the first two digits of NATO Stock Number (NSN). The other approach treats each NSN independent from each other.

Chapter 4 presents a combined inventory and lateral re-supply model for repairable items. This chapter focuses on the first part of the proposed model that deals with the modeling of an Air Force Logistics problem. The authors consider a network model composed of multiple depots that face uncertain demands for repairable items. The chapter describes the joint problem of determining how many units to repair locally, hold in inventory, and how many to ship to other depots, so as to minimize system-wide inventory storage, shortage and delivery costs. The formulation of the problem extends the Federgruen & Zipkin's combined vehicle-routing and inventory-allocation model by including local repair and lateral resupply capability.

Chapter 5 presents the solution of the problem presented in Chapter 4 by using the generalized Benders' decomposition technique. The results show that the additional Benders' cuts generated by this formulation significantly save the total operational cost, consisting of inventory, shortage and delivery cost. The authors, through five propositions and sample runs, show that Benders' decomposition algorithm is one of the most effective methods in solving these types of problems even in real-life military scenarios.

Chapter 6 deals with the critical role of armed forces in natural disasters especially in transportation of relief material. Indeed, their involvement in disaster response and relief actions is significant as their role is primarily in response to the immediate requirement of human resources and technical equipment for rescue and relief operations of the affected area. While commercial freight transport operations typically focus on minimizing costs, moving relief material is more concerned about satisfying demand for emergency supplies and saving lives. This task is particularly challenging given that emergency managers must operate under strict budget restrictions. To this end, this chapter presents the design, implementation and testing of a web tool that supports armed forces in freight transport planning during natural disaster relief operations. The proposed system is tested and the results show an increased performance in service provision with parallel reduction in administrative and transportation cost.

Chapter 7 describes the use of plane tessellation algorithms to optimize military resource allocation. Voronoi Tessellations are one of the most common approaches to divide a plane into cells such that parts of the plane closest to specific points belong to each cell. Using the cell areas to determine resource optimization is a powerful logistics tool. The aim of this chapter is to describe a method to use a weighted Voronoi diagram to allocate resources efficiently. The method can be used for any number of resources including, but not limited to, troops, ammunitions or medical supplies.

Chapter 8 presents a metaheuristic reconstruction algorithm for solving bi-level vehicle routing problems with backhauls for army rapid fielding. The latter is the process by which new equipment is distributed to soldiers either at dispersed homeland or theatre of operations units. To this end, this chapter addresses Vehicle Routing Problems with Backhauls and Time Windows (VRPBTW) with linehaul and backhaul military units in the context of military operations. The primary objective is the minimization of the required number of vehicles and the secondary objective is the minimization of the total cost of the routes. First a mixed integer programming formulation of the problem is analyzed. Since the VRPBTW is NP-Hard, a metaheuristic algorithm is proposed for the solution. Initial solutions are produced through a tour construction heuristic scheme and evolve through a variation of the

Threshold Accepting method, which is based on a special destruction-reconstruction scheme. The method has been tested on numerous problem instances with favorable results.

Finally, Chapter 9 presents a reliability study of several speculative military scenarios and some initial results concerning well-known reliability systems. More specifically, four different consecutive type of systems are investigated and treated as operational tactics of defensive or offensive military schemes. Structural properties of these scenarios, such as the signature vector or the reliability function, are studied in details and several conclusions concerning the effectiveness of the aforementioned military operations are deduced. In addition, some recursive relations for the calculation of the signature coordinates of well-known reliability structures are also proved. Finally, for illustrative purposes some figures are also displayed in order to depict the operation rules of the reliability structures that are under investigation.

Contents

Contributors

Ana Isabel Barros TNO, Zeist, The Netherlands

Faculty of Military Sciences, Netherlands Defence Academy, Breda, The Netherlands

Yupo Chan Department of Systems Engineering, University of Arkansas at Little Rock, Little Rock, AR, USA

Bahtiyar Eren Hv.K.K.ligi Karargahi Harekat Baskanligi, Bakanliklar-Ankara, Turkey

Serpil Erol Gazi Universitesi Endustri Muhendisligi Bolumu, Ankara, Turkey

Lanah Evers Quintiq, Den Bosch, The Netherlands

Suchisman Sandipan Gangopadhyay University of Illinois at Urbana Champaign, Urbana, IL, USA

Herman Monsuur Faculty of Military Sciences, Netherlands Defence Academy, Breda, The Netherlands

Socrates J. Moschuris Department of Industrial Management and Technology, University of Piraeus, Piraeus, Greece

Athanassios Nikolakopoulos National Technical University of Athens, School of Chemical Engineering, Zografou Campus Athens, Greece

Hellenic Military Academy, Sector of Mathematics and Engineering, Leoforos Varis Koropiou, Vari Attikis, Athens, Greece

Christodoulos Nikou Department of Industrial Management and Technology, University of Piraeus, Greece, Athens, Greece

Ioannis S. Triantafyllou Department of Statistics and Insurance Science, University of Piraeus, Piraeus, Greece

Albert Wagelmans Econometric Institute, Erasmus University Rotterdam, Rotterdam, The Netherlands

Vasileios Zeimpekis Design, Operations and Production Systems Lab, Department of Financial & Management Engineering, University of the Aegean, Chios, Greece

Chapter 1
UAV Mission Planning: From Robust to Agile

Lanah Evers, Ana Isabel Barros, Herman Monsuur and Albert Wagelmans

1.1 Introduction

1.1.1 Background

Current military operations have grown increasingly complex over the past several years as described by Barros and Monsuur (2009). Due to the rapidly changing environment, quick reaction times and increasing uncertainty in the military environment, traditional military planning does not offer the required solutions.

New military planning approaches should be able to deal with these issues by providing solutions that are robust against deviations from expected circumstances and/or easily adaptable (agile) to new information that becomes known during the execution of a plan, increasing therefore the effectiveness and efficiency of military operations. Robust planning seeks solutions that require minimal amount of re-planning during the execution stage. Construction of the associated initial plan

The chapter is based on research that was sponsored by TNO, under a grant of the Netherlands MOD, in cooperation with the Netherlands Defence Academy (NLDA) and Erasmus University Rotterdam.

L. Evers (✉)
Quintiq, P.O. Box 264, 5201 AG Den Bosch, The Netherlands
e-mail: lanah.evers@quintiq.com

A. I. Barros
TNO, Zeist, The Netherlands
e-mail: ana.barros@tno.nl

H. Monsuur · A. I. Barros
Faculty of Military Sciences, Netherlands Defence Academy, Breda, The Netherlands
e-mail: h.monsuur@mindef.nl

A. Wagelmans
Econometric Institute, Erasmus University Rotterdam, Rotterdam, The Netherlands
e-mail: wagelmans@ese.eur.nl

V. Zeimpekis et al. (eds.), *Military Logistics,* Operations Research/Computer Science Interfaces Series 56, DOI 10.1007/978-3-319-12075-1_1

may require relatively large computation time. Agile planning on the other hand, requires fast re-planning solutions to anticipate on events and information that become known during the execution stage, and is usually based on so-called online planning approaches.

A military planning problem for which robust and agile mathematical approaches can be very beneficial, is routing Unmanned Aerial Vehicles (UAVs) in Intelligence Surveillance Reconnaissance (ISR) missions. UAVs are often used in reconnaissance missions to capture both motion and still imagery of potential 'targets' on which up-to-date information is required. Such targets might include important infrastructure, possible locations of Improvised Explosive Devices (IEDs), and insurgent locations. The goal of the UAV mission is to gather as much information as possible given operational constraints related to the UAV endurance capabilities. Obviously, some locations might be more relevant than others in terms of information gathering supporting the military objective. In order to optimize data collection, the UAV mission should include targets of higher relevance, starting and ending at the UAV recovery point. Existing mathematical models could be used to optimize this UAV mission planning problem. However, the existing models do not take the uncertainty and dynamics of the problem into account in the planning and execution stage, and might therefore result in infeasible or suboptimal flight plans.

Although the planning approaches that will be presented in this chapter were originally designed for UAV mission planning, these approaches can also be adjusted and/or extended to fit other (routing) problems in uncertain and complex military environments.

1.1.2 Chapter Purpose and Outline

The purpose of this chapter is to describe different approaches that can be used to handle the uncertainty and dynamicity encountered in UAV mission planning. We will first shortly provide some background on deterministic mathematical models that could be used to determine the route the UAV should fly. This will be done in Sect 1.3.

In Sect. 2 we will consider uncertainty in fuel consumption of the UAV, one of the elements that is ignored when deterministic models are used. We will describe how this uncertainty can be dealt with, using techniques from robust optimization and stochastic programming, introduced by Evers et al. (2012) and Evers et al. (2014a) respectively. We will illustrate these two approaches and also compare them to a more traditional approach.

In Sect. 3, we will focus on an even more uncertain and dynamic situation where travel and recording times are stochastic, time windows are associated to target locations and new targets become of interest during the flight of the UAV. We will describe a very fast problem specific online planning approach to fit this problem situation, which can be used at several moments during the flight to re-plan the route based on all information known so far. Section 3 is based on Evers et al. (2014b).

In Sect. 4 we will conclude this chapter by summarizing the main findings.

1.1.3 Deterministic Models for UAV Mission Planning

In order to improve the effectiveness of a UAV reconnaissance mission, the planned route should contain target locations of higher relevance, taking into consideration operational constraints, such as the fuel capacity and the endurance of the UAV. This planning problem can be modeled by the Orienteering Problem (OP) (see Vansteenwegen (2012) for a survey), wherein the target locations correspond to nodes, profits are associated to the nodes to model the importance of the targets, and arcs between the nodes are used to represent the flight path from one target location to the other. Weights on the arcs between the nodes can be used to model the fuel consumption or the time required to fly from one target to the other. This generalization of the well-known Traveling Salesman Problem (TSP) does not require all nodes to be visited. The goal of the OP is to find a tour or path of maximum profit, feasible with respect to a capacity constraint that restricts the total weight of the arcs that are included in the path or tour. Note that the term 'tour' is used in mathematical modeling when describing a route for which the begin and end point are the same.

Mathematically, this comes down to the following. The OP is defined on a graph that connects all nodes in set N, representing the set of all potentially interesting targets, and one node that represents the UAV recovery point, called 'the depot'. The flight path between each two nodes i and j is modeled by an arc $(i, j) \in A$, where A contains all connections between the locations. The fuel (or time) consumption between each two locations is represented by a parameter, say f_{ij}. The total fuel (or time) used during the mission may not exceed the available capacity F. The value of the information that can be obtained at target i is represented by a profit value p_i. This notation will be used throughout this chapter. The objective of the OP is to select and sequence targets such that the sum of the profit value of the targets included in the tour, is maximized.

Royset and Reber (2009) use the OP to plan UAV missions, aiming to locate insurgents placing IEDs and already placed IEDs. To obtain the target profit values, they use the data from an IED prediction tool. The tool provides the expected number of IEDs for each grid location. All input parameters, like the fuel consumption, are assumed to be deterministic. An extension of this problem was introduced by Mufalli et al. (2012), who propose a generalization of the OP in order to model simultaneous sensor selection and route planning of UAVs. Different sensors can be attached to the UAV before its flight. The choice of the sensor to be used (e.g. electro optical and infrared), depends on the information requirements of the targets and the type of targets. As such, a specific profit value is associated to each combination of target and sensor. Also, due to the weight of the sensors, attaching a sensor results in a sensor specific decrease in the travel range of the UAV. Even though travel 'cost' and profit values are variable depending on the associated sensors, these parameters are all assumed to be deterministic.

In reality however, the input parameters and even the set of targets in a UAV planning problem may be uncertain. Since UAVs operate in a dynamic and uncertain environment, effective UAV mission plans should be able to deal with uncertainty and changing expectations.

1.2 Uncertainty in Fuel Consumption of the UAV

Uncertainty in fuel consumption of the UAV is caused for example by unexpected weather circumstances, uncertainty in the times required to obtain the desired quality of the recorded imagery, combined with efficiency of the individual UAV operator. That is, the level of experience of each operator will differ. For example, if imagery of a specific target is required, a more experienced operator may require less time to record good quality imagery, while an inexperienced operator may need to loiter near the target for a longer amount of time to achieve the same result. Since recording a target may take longer or shorter than expected, the UAV may require another amount of fuel than expected.

We will describe how this uncertainty can be dealt with using techniques from robust optimization and stochastic programming respectively. Each of these two approaches provide an initial plan, accompanied by a policy that describes how to use, and if possible, how to extend the initial plan during the actual flight of the UAV. While robust optimization only requires general assumptions on the behavior of uncertain parameters, in stochastic programming these parameters are assumed to follow a predefined probability distribution. We will end this section by comparing these two approaches, together with a more traditional, deterministic approach.

1.2.1 Robust UAV Mission Planning

In military UAV mission planning, often sustainability (robustness) of an initial plan is highly valued. More specifically, the flight plan that is constructed before the actual start of the UAV flight should be designed in such a way that the probability of being able to record all planned targets is sufficiently high. In constructing the initial plan in such a way, the mission planner can communicate to the commander which information requirements are likely to be fulfilled within the coming mission. The commander can then design his/her future tactics by knowing beforehand which information will become available during or at the end of the UAV mission. Designing the initial route of the UAV based on the so-called Robust Orienteering Problem (ROP) can help the mission planner in balancing the probability of feasibility of the initial plan, against the value of the information to be obtained in the planned tour.

Note that the actual fuel realizations are not known at the planning stage. It will depend on these fuel realizations whether or not all planned targets can be recorded during the actual flight of the UAV. To operationalize the ROP plan, the ROP can be extended with agility principles. These agility principles are used to make decisions during the flight of the UAV, in which all fuel realizations that have been revealed so far are taken into account. First, given the fuel realizations, the initial tour will be followed as long as possible. In case of unbeneficial fuel realizations, this might imply that the UAV has to return to its recovery point before all planned targets are recorded. In case of beneficial fuel realizations on the other hand, the resulting extra fuel capacity can be exploited to increase the total profit value obtained during the entire mission. Since visiting the planned targets is of primary interest, additional targets are considered only after reaching the final target of the planned tour. The total expected profit to be obtained during the mission can be estimated beforehand by using the ROP tour as an initial plan and by correcting its profit by the estimated effect of the agile strategy. This new planning approach combines the benefits of both robustness and agility: With high probability all targets of the initial tour will be visited and, if possible, at the end of the initial tour all available real-time information will be exploited.

1.2.1.1 Modeling the ROP

In Evers et al. (2012) the Robust Orienteering Problem (ROP) was introduced to deal with uncertainty in the fuel usage of the UAV. The ROP is defined on a graph, where weights on the arcs are used to represent the fuel consumption between each two targets, required both to fly from one target to the other and to record the target. Contrary to the OP, in the ROP these weights are each modeled as an uncertain parameter, of which the realization is assumed to be bounded by a predefined upper and lower bound. The goal of the ROP is to find a maximum profit tour (representing the value of the information to be obtained at the targets) that remains feasible for all realizations of the uncertain parameters in a so-called 'uncertainty set'. By varying the uncertainty set, a balance can be achieved between the probability that a tour remains feasible and the objective value of such a feasible tour. Before further addressing the ROP, we will briefly describe the robust optimization framework designed by Ben-Tal et al. (2009).

Ben-Tal et al. (2009) define a solution to be 'robust feasible' if the solution remains feasible for all realizations of the uncertain parameters within a predefined uncertainty set. The uncertainty set can for example be defined using norms. Special cases of such uncertainty sets may lead to intuitively easy to understand requirements on the robust feasible solutions. The use of the L_∞-norm for example, where the uncertainty set has a certain size (say ρ), leads to a solution that remains feasible if all uncertain parameters differ at most ρ times their maximum deviation from their expected value.

The framework of Ben-Tal et al. (2009) was used to introduce the ROP. In the ROP we denote the expected fuel consumption from target i to j by $\overline{f_{ij}}$. The realizations of the fuel consumption f_{ij} are assumed to lie in the following predefined interval:

$$f_{ij} \in \left[\overline{f_{ij}} - \sigma_{ij}, \overline{f_{ij}} + \sigma_{ij} \right],$$

where, σ_{ij} represents the maximum absolute deviation from $\overline{f_{ij}}$. Notice that no extra assumptions on these realizations is required, contrary to the two-stage approach described in the next section. For later convenience, the realizations of the fuel consumption can be rewritten as $f_{ij}=\overline{f_{ij}}+\zeta_{ij}\sigma_{ij}$, where the expected deviation from $\overline{f_{ij}}$ is given by $E(\zeta_{ij})=0$, with $\zeta_{ij}\epsilon[-1,1]$. We can now define the uncertainty set Z as the set of realizations of the uncertain parameters ζ_{ij} against which we want the solution to be protected. The larger this uncertainty set is chosen, the larger the probability will be that the solution will remain feasible under the realizations of the uncertain parameters. A large uncertainty set on the other hand, might lead to a relatively conservative solution. As such, by varying the size and shape of the uncertainty set, a balance can be found between feasibility and the objective value that will be obtained in case the solution is feasible. This set Z, can be mathematically defined as an intersection of balls $B_s^{|A|}(\rho_s)$:

$$Z=\left\{\zeta_{ij}\in R^{|A|}:\|\zeta\|_s\leq\rho_s\forall s\in S\right\}=\bigcap_{s\in S}B_s^{|A|}(\rho_s),$$

where A is the set of arcs, the norm $\|\zeta\|_s=\left(\sum_{(i,j)\in A}|\zeta|^s\right)^{1/s}$ defines the shape of the ball, while ρ_s defines its size and the finite set $S\subset[1,\infty]$ determines which balls are used in the intersection. To simplify notation we defined,

$$B_s^{|A|}(\rho_s)=\left\{\zeta\in R^{|A|}:\|\zeta\|_s\leq\rho_s\right\}.$$

When modeling the UAV mission planning problem, we should take into account that the total fuel consumption may not exceed the total fuel capacity of the UAV, say F. Suppose that x_{ij} represents a decision variable in the model, which will be 1 in case a direct flight from target i to target j is part of the tour. If all fuel realizations would be known in advance (which unfortunately is not the case) the tour should satisfy

$$\sum_{(i,j)\in A}f_{ij}x_{ij}\leq F.$$

The ROP provides a way to design an initial tour, taking the uncertainty in fuel consumption into account, already at the planning stage. A solution to the ROP is robust against the uncertainty in fuel consumption, if it satisfies

$$\sum_{(i,j)\in A}\left(\overline{f_{ij}}+\zeta_{ij}\sigma_{ij}\right)x_{ij}\leq F\forall\zeta\in Z.$$

Note that the above equation contains infinitely many constraints, but it is shown in Evers at al. (2012) that the problem can be rewritten such that the associated robust counterpart only contains a finite number of constraints.

1.2.1.2 Adding Agility Principles

As just described, by the use of uncertainty sets the robust counterpart takes uncertainty into account already in the modeling stage. The resulting solution is an initial tour plan, i.e. a solution to a static problem. Note though, that at the execution phase the actual fuel realizations will determine whether or not this tour can be completed. In other words, if the fuel consumption turns out to be higher than accounted for, the tour has to be aborted and potential profit of the unvisited nodes will not be obtained. In such a case, the sum of the profit of the nodes that cannot be visited is referred to as the *profit shortage*. On the other hand, when the realizations of the weights turn out to be relatively low, at the end of the tour the remaining capacity may be exploited to expand the initial tour with additional nodes. The sum of the profit of the additional the nodes that can be visited in such a case, is referred to as the *profit surplus*. To this end, it is discussed in Evers et al. (2012) how the initial ROP tour can be executed based on agility principles. The agility principles describe policies on when to abort the tour and how to extend the tour for relatively high or low realizations of the weights, respectively. For details on defining such agility principles we refer to Evers et al. (2012). A disadvantage of this approach is that it does not take the consequence of the realizations and these policies on the total obtained profit into account in advance. In constructing the initial tour, it only balances feasibility against the planned objective value. We will now discuss how stochastic programming can help overcome this issue.

1.2.2 Two-Stage UAV Mission Planning

In this sub section we will present a two-stage stochastic programming approach to the UAV mission planning problem, where we assume that the fuel parameters follow a certain probability distribution: the Two-Stage Orienteering Problem (TSOP). Note that this assumption is more specific than the assumption about the uncertain parameters used in robust optimization. Contrary to what is done in the ROP, the TSOP incorporates the effect of the fuel realizations on the profit value that will actually be obtained. More specifically, the TSOP takes into account that nodes situated further ahead in the planned tour, are less likely to be reached due to uncertainty in fuel consumption.

The first stage decision is the construction of the tour. In the second stage it is determined, based on the realizations of the uncertain parameters, how many of the nodes in the planned tour can actually be visited (by also considering that one should return to the depot on time, before running out of fuel). The so-called 'second stage' cost is the sum of the nodes in the planned tour that cannot be reached. The objective is to maximize the total profit of the first stage tour, minus the expected second stage cost, based on the probability distributions. Based on the previously defined notation, the TSOP objective can be expressed as

$$\max \sum_{(i,j)\in A} p_i x_{ij} - E_f\left(g(x,f)\right),$$

where $g(x, f)$ is a function that expresses the sum of the profits of the nodes in the tour described by x, that cannot be visited as a result of a given vector of fuel realizations f. The function $E_f(\cdot)$ is used to calculate the expected profit that is unobtainable due to travel and recording time uncertainty, based on the probability distributions of f. Although this objective function is in general nonlinear, it is possible to linearize this function as shown in Evers et al. (2014a). In the second stage, both x and the realizations f are known and thus $g(x, f)$ provides the profit shortage resulting from the targets in the tour x that cannot be reached for that specific f. Therefore, the profit shortage can be modeled as a second-stage mixed integer program (MIP).

The approach used to solve the TSOP is the Sample Average Approximation (SAA), which is a well-known solution technique from stochastic programming for solving stochastic optimization problems through the use of Monte Carlo simulation, see Norkin et al. (1998).

Note that the TSOP captures the expected effect of the actual fuel realizations on the total profit to be obtained by the second term of the objective. This formulation will produce long planned tours, since a tour will not be optimal as long as nodes exist with a positive probability of being reached, and since adding one of those nodes to the tour increases the TSOP objective. Hence, the first stage decision is constructing a tour described by x, before the actual travel and recording time realizations are known. However, this first stage decision is based on the expected effect that the realizations in the second stage will have on the total profit to be obtained.

1.2.3 Comparing Planning Approaches

Based on an illustrative example, we will discuss the differences between the ROP and the TSOP. Furthermore, we will compare these two approaches to a more traditional approach: using the expected value for the uncertain fuel parameters and as deterministic parameters in the OP.

Real instances of UAV planning problems are, due to security reasons, restricted. Therefore we use representative data to illustrate the different planning approaches. We use Tsiligirides' problem set 1, with a capacity constraint set to 65 (Tsiligirides 1984). Since only data sets were available for the deterministic OP, Evers et al. (2012) and Evers et al. (2014a) added data on the distribution of the uncertainty to the test instances. In this example, we assume that fuel consumption is normally distributed. To test the performance of the different planning approaches, 1000 scenarios were used repeatedly (the same ones for every tour that is tested), where one scenario contains one fuel realization for each arc, each drawn from the associated normal distribution. We used Eclipse 3.6 for the implementation of both approaches. The ROP formulation as well as the MIPs related to the SAA approach for the two-stage problem were solved by CPLEX 12.1 (IBM 2009).

1.2.3.1 The ROP Combined with Agility Principles

Table 1.1 shows results of the ROP, using a so-called 'budget uncertainty set'. This uncertainty set corresponds to the intersection of the $B_1^{|A|}$ and $B_\infty^{|A|}$ balls defined by L^1 and L^∞ norm s, as explained in Sect. 1.2.1.1: $Z = B_\infty^{|A|}(1) \cap B_1^{|A|}(\rho)$.

The first column indicates the size of the budget uncertainty set *Z*. The second column contains the total profit of the targets in the planned tour. The average shortage in the third column represents the profit of the targets that were unobtainable due to high fuel realizations, averaged over the 1000 scenarios. The average surplus on the other hand, represents the average profit of the targets that were added to the tour in case of low fuel realizations, based on the predefined agile policy. The last column contains the expected profit, which is the planned profit, adjusted by the shortage and surplus.

Note that selecting the budget uncertainty set *Z* with size $\rho = 0$ equals solving the deterministic OP, where the solution is only protected against realizations that equal the expected fuel parameters. Note also that the OP solution often results in a tour that cannot be completely finished, as the average shortage is relatively high. When tours are planned a bit more conservative, by increasing the size of the uncertainty set, the planned routes will get shorter and will thus contain less profit. Consequently, the average shortage tends to decrease, while the average surplus tends to increase. For this instance, the solution to the Agile ROP with $\rho = 2$ gives the highest expected profit.

Table 1.1 Results of the ROP with budget uncertainty for different sizes

ρ	Planned	Av. shortage	Av. surplus	Expected profit
0	245	13.28	0.19	231.91
1	240	6.16	0.55	234.39
2	240	6.53	3.88	*235.35*
3	235	1.46	1.73	235.27
4	235	1.72	1.64	234.92
5	230	0.58	2.55	231.97
6	230	0.20	2.01	231.81
7	225	0.44	8.73	233.29
8	225	0.11	3.78	228.67
9	225	0.02	4.66	229.64
10	225	0.04	4.30	229.26

1.2.3.2 The TSOP

When using the TSOP model, we find a tour for this instance which results in an expected profit of 239.13. Hence, even though the TSOP only takes shortages into account and disregards the possibility of adding targets to the initial tour, the TSOP finds a tour which has a higher expected profit than all of the tours found by the Agile ROP.

1.2.3.3 Comparison

When comparing the structure of the tours resulting from the deterministic OP, the ROP and TSOP, the main differences are found often at the beginning and/or the end of the tour. Figure 1.1 shows the ROP tour, the OP tour and the TSOP tour respectively.

The ROP plans most conservatively and thus provides the shortest initially planned tour. The TSOP provides the longest tour and it contains several targets with low profit at the end of the tour.

Both the ROP and the TSOP provide a predictable tour in their own way. The expected profit is not the optimization criterion of the ROP. Instead, it optimizes a guaranteed profit value for a given certainty level (represented by the uncertainty set), without requiring explicit assumptions on the probability distributions of the uncertain fuel parameters. The new targets that are possibly selected and added after the final target in the ROP tour however, depend on scenario-specific fuel realizations. In the TSOP on the other hand, all targets that will be recorded in any scenario are already part of the planned TSOP tour. A recourse action ensures that the UAV has enough fuel to return to the depot in any scenario. The optimal TSOP tour is determined by maximizing the expected profit, based on predefined probability distributions of fuel consumption, combined with the recourse action.

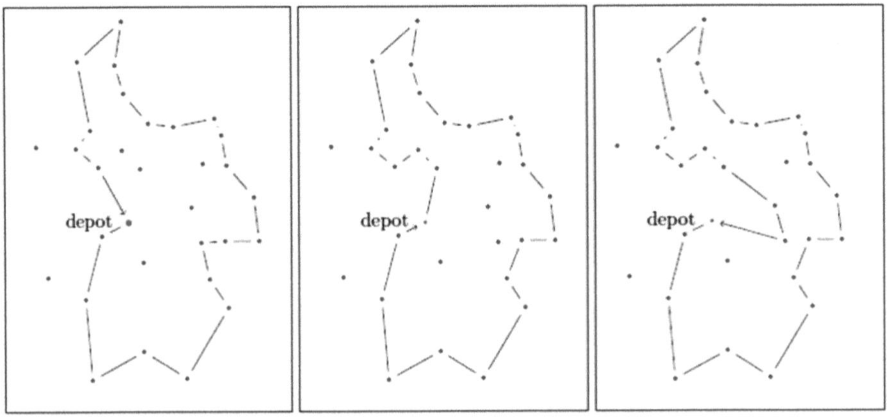

Fig. 1.1 ROP tour, OP tour, TSOP tour

The probability of reaching each consecutive target in the TSOP tour decreases as targets are located further ahead in the planned tour. The absence of a predefined certainty level in the TSOP may allow for tours with a higher expected profit than the ROP, as just illustrated.

Both approaches outperform the deterministic OP (see the expected profit for $\rho = 0$ in Table 1.1), by taking uncertainty into account already in the planning stage. Each of these two approaches have their own advantages. Depending on the mission characteristics, either robustness of the initial tour or maximizing the expected profit may be preferred.

1.3 Uncertainty, Time Windows and New Targets

For some targets, or for specific missions, the information about a target can only be obtained within a certain predefined time window. Detection of IEDs for example can be done by comparing imagery of a specific area, taken on different days, and by examining whether significant changes in the surface are visible. In order to enable a meaningful imagery comparison, imagery should be collected in similar circumstances and time periods, i.e. time windows, in order to reduce the influence of other effects, like shadows. Moreover, there is often the need to collect information on given time windows due to activities that are more likely to take place within given time windows. Uncertainty in travel and recording times (which is related to the uncertainty in fuel consumption, discussed in the previous section) might cause the UAV to arrive late at a target, and consequently, to be unable to obtain the desired information.

While time windows add additional complexity to the planning problem, certain missions might also require coping with dynamicity in the problem definition. More specifically, it might be desirable to re-route the UAV to a new location that was not yet known at the start of the flight. This is for example the case when urgent information requirements on 'time-sensitive targets' become relevant during the flight of the UAV. In this section we will describe an online planning approach, in which the tour may be re-planned repeatedly based on real-time information on the past flight and recording time realizations and the current available set of unrecorded targets.

1.3.1 Weighted Location Coverage

The approach the we will describe, does not only incorporate all currently known information when recalculating the planned UAV tour, but it also takes locations where new targets may appear into account in advance. This will be done based on the 'Weighted Location Coverage' (WLC).

In the previous models, optimization was based on a profit parameter p_i representing the information value of a target. We will now add one parameter to each of the arcs in the model, which will also be part of the objective that we aim to maximize. We want to encourage that the planned route of the UAV goes through areas, close to locations where new targets are expected to appear.

Suppose the UAV is on its way from target i to target j as depicted in Fig. 1.2. Locations 1, 2 and 3 are identified beforehand as locations where new targets might appear during the flight. A predefined parameter U denotes the maximum expected response time within which new targets should be reached, from the moment they become known. In case the UAV is located within a radius for which the expected time would be at most U time units to reach a potential location of a new target, we define that potential location to be 'covered' by the UAV at that point in time.

For each arc $(i, j) \in A$, and for each potential location $k \in N'$ where new targets may appear, we denote the fraction of the arc during which k is covered by b_{ijk}. Additionally, when the UAV is located at target j, each potential location $k \in N'$ is either covered or not covered, which will be denoted by indicator variable b_{jk}. When the UAV arrives at target j from target i, several time realizations will become available: the observed travel time realization t_{ij}, the observed recording time realization r_i and the 'waiting time' realization w_j observed when the UAV arrives at target j before the beginning of its time window. Using these realizations we can define the WLC of arc (i, j) as:

$$c_{ij}\left(t_{ij}, w_j, r_j\right) = \sum_{k \in N'} \left(t_{ij} b_{ijk} + \left(w_j + r_j\right) b_{jk}\right) \lambda_k,$$

where λ_k is a weight which expresses the expected number of new targets to appear during the flight at location k and/or their importance.

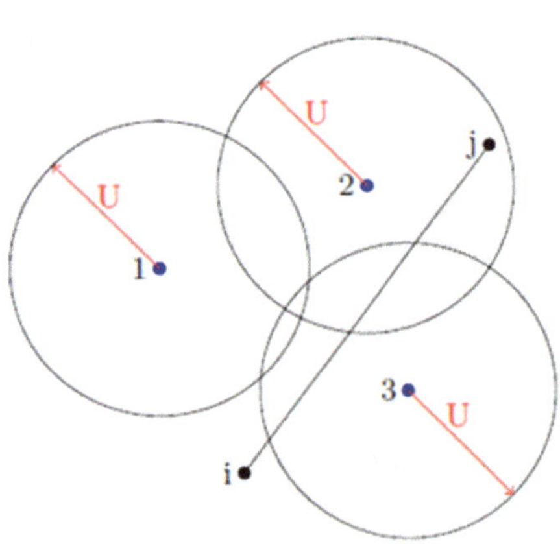

Fig. 1.2 Locations 2 and 3 are covered for a fraction of the arc from i to j

1.3.2 Online Planning Approach

The model that will be used to re-calculate the planned route, each time new information becomes available, is called the Maximum Coverage Stochastic Orienteering Problem with Time Windows (MCS-OPTW). This re-calculation will be performed, each time just before the UAV leaves a target location, as well as each time a new target has appeared. In the first case, re-planning could be beneficial due to deviations of previous travel and recording time realizations from their expected value. In the second case, we evaluate if the new target should be included in a newly planned route. Note that allowing re-planning will likely result in less predictable routes than the routes that will result from the robust and two-stage approach described in Sect. 1.2.2. However, the dynamicity encountered when new targets become of interest during the flight, makes such a re-planning approach desirable.

1.3.2.1 Balancing Objectives

The MCS-OPTW balances two objectives. The first objective is to maximize the expected profit that could be obtained by recording a subset out of all targets known so far which have not been recorded yet, based on the probability distributions of the travel and recording times, if the tour would be executed as planned. This first objective relates to the known deterministic Orienteering Problem with Time Windows (OPTW) (see Vansteenwegen (2012) for an overview of the OPTW and related problems), but we will extend this part of the problem by taking travel and recording time uncertainty into account. Note that this objective alone does not take possible future appearances of new targets into account in advance. However, these possibilities are dealt with in the second objective of the MCS-OPTW, which is to maximize the expected WLC of the planned tour, based on the probability distributions of the travel and recording times. Note that the waiting times also influence the WLC, but for a given tour, the waiting time realizations follow directly from the travel and recording time realizations and the lower bounds of the time windows. By maximizing the WLC, the planned tour will be directed close to areas where new targets are expected to appear. In doing so, we aim to improve the ability to timely reach new targets. These two objectives are weighted by the parameters α and β. The objective function of the MCS-OPTW is the following:

$$\max \alpha E_{tr}\left(\sum_{(i,j)MA} p_i x_{ij} I_{ixtr}\right) + \beta E_{tr}\left(\sum_{(i,j)MA} c_{ij}\left(t_{ij}, w_j, r_j\right) x_{ij}\right),$$

where $E_{tr}(\cdot)$ expresses the expected value based on the probability distributions of the vectors of travel time parameters t and recording time parameters r. Note that E_{tr} does not include an index for the waiting times w, since for a given tour, the waiting time realizations follow directly from the travel and recording time realizations and the start of the time windows. The indicator variable I_{ixtr} is assigned the value 1 if target i can be reached before the end of its time window for a given tour described by x and for given travel and recording time realizations t and r respectively, and 0 otherwise. To determine the values I_{ixtr} we take into account that when the UAV arrives late, no recording will take place and the UAV will continue to the next target. On the other hand, if the UAV arrives before the start of the time window, some waiting time is required before the UAV can start recording. Furthermore, we take into account that a return policy will be applied to ensure that the UAV will return to the depot in time. Therefore, for the targets selected in the tour, I_{ixtr} might be assigned the value 0 as a result of either late arrival or early abortion of the tour.

These issues and the dependence between the values I_{ixtr} of consecutive targets in the tour, prevent the possibility of expressing $E_{tr}(\cdot)$ analytically. However, for a given scenario of realizations containing one realization of t_{ij} for each arc $(i, j) \in A$, and one realization r_j for each target $j \in N$, all values of I_{ixtr} and all waiting times w_j can be determined easily. That is, taking into account all assumptions related to waiting, recording and returning to the depot, we can determine a scenario-specific arrival time at each target in the given tour (assuming that the tour will be performed as planned), and consequently we can determine if the profit of the target can or cannot be obtained in the given scenario. As such, for a specific scenario, the total obtainable profit value can be determined. Similarly, for a specific scenario, the WLC of a tour can be determined, based also on the resulting waiting times and by taking the return policy into account. In case one or more of the final arcs in the tour would be skipped due to the return policy, these arcs will not contribute to the WLC of the tour.

1.3.2.2 Fast Re-planning Solutions

A fast heuristic that finds good solutions to the MCS-OPTW was proposed in Evers et al. (2014b). For the instances tested in Evers et al. (2014b), the maximum computation time is 1–3 s, depending on the test instance. When constructing and evaluating solutions, a large number of scenarios is used to calculate the average profit obtainable from visiting a subset of the known targets and the average WLC of the planned tour over all scenarios, to obtain a good approximation of the value of the MCS-OPTW objective. This evaluation is not computationally expensive, since it is linear in the number of scenarios. These computational results were obtained using an Intel(R) Core(TM) i7 CPU, 8.00 GB of RAM.

1.3.3 Re-planning Illustration

Figure 1.3 illustrates how the planned tour can change during the flight of the UAV, based on current information on flight and recording times, as well as on the current set of targets. For this purpose, we use the test instance Solomon r108 (Solomon 1987), where we assume travel and recording times to be normally distributed. The

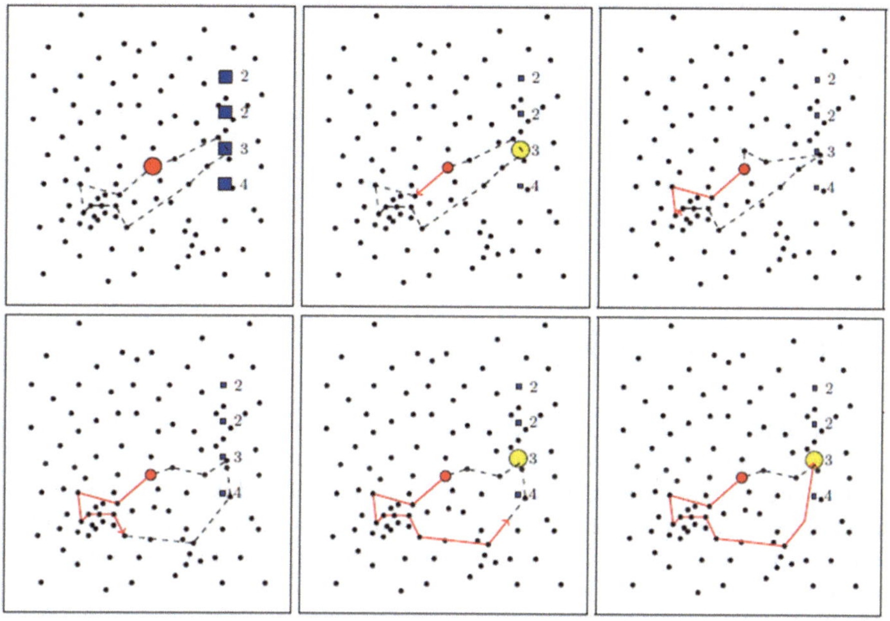

Fig 1.3 The tour is re-planned at several moments based on time realizations and new targets

blue squares in Fig. 1.3 represent locations where new targets might appear. The planned tours were obtained by solving the MCS-OPTW heuristic with $\alpha = 0.8$ and $\beta = 0.2$.

The current location of the UAV is depicted at several consecutive moments during the flight (denoted by the point of the red arrow), as well as the planned route for the remaining time capacity (denoted by the dashed line). In this illustrative scenario, two time-sensitive targets appear during the flight of the UAV (represented by the yellow circles). For the first, the UAV is located too far away from the location of the time-sensitive target. The second time-sensitive target appears at a later moment at which the UAV is close enough to be re-tasked to the time-sensitive target and to timely reach it. Also, at two moments after recording a target, the planned tour was adjusted based on previous travel and recording time realizations.

Finally, we will illustrate how the parameter β associated to the WLC influences the planned tour. Recall that the WLC was introduced to direct the planned tour to areas where new targets are expected to appear, such that the number of timely reached new targets can be increased. Figure 1.4 depicts the initial tour for increasing values of β. Note that an initial tour might be adjusted after the first re-planning step, but depicting these tours will provide insight in how the planned tour is situated relative to the areas where time-sensitive targets are expected to appear. Figure 1.4 illustrates how the value of β directs the UAV towards the potential locations where time-sensitive targets are expected to appear.

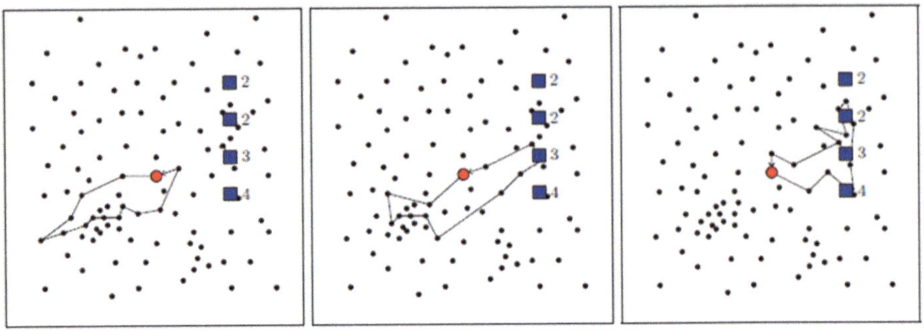

Fig. 1.4. The initial MCS-OPTW tour, for $\beta = 0, \beta = 0.2$ *and* $\beta = 1$

Concluding, we have illustrated an online planning approach, which takes uncertainty in travel and recording times, time windows as well as potential locations of new targets into account, already in the planning stage. Taking uncertainty into account in advance provides solutions that dominate a deterministic OPTW planning approach (Evers et al. 2014b), and taking potential new targets into account in advance increases the number of new targets that can be reached on time.

1.4 Conclusions

Current military operations require coping with new challenges like rapid reaction time, extremely stringent limiting conditions, and uncertainty in the operating environment or at theater level. New military planning approaches should be able to deal with these issues by providing solutions that are robust against deviations from expected circumstances and/or easily adaptable (agile) to new information that becomes known during the execution of a plan. This chapter described such robust and agile planning approaches, applied to a tactical military planning problem: Unmanned Aerial Vehicle (UAV) mission planning. The new models and planning approaches can also be adjusted and extended the other military applications to develop plans that can better deal with the increasingly complex, uncertain and rapidly changing environment.

References

Barros, A.I, Monsuur, H.: New trends in military planning: Agility and robustness. Proceedings of the 1st conference of the International Society of Military Sciences, 2009

Ben-Tal, A., Ghaoui, L.El, Nemirovski, A.: Robust Optimization. Princeton UniversityPress, Princeton (2009)

Evers, L., Dollevoet, T., Barros, A.I., Monsuur, H.: Robust UAV mission planning. Ann. Oper. Res. **222**(1):293–315 (2014). doi: 10.1007/s10479-012-1261-8

Evers, L., Glorie, K., van der Ster, S., Barros, A.I., Monsuur, H.: A two-stage approach to the orienteering problem with stochastic weights. Comput. Oper. Res. **43**, 248–260 (2014a)
Evers, L., Barros, A.I., Monsuur, H., Wagelmans, A.P.M.: Online stochastic UAV mission planning with time windows and time-sensitive targets. Eur. J. Oper. Res. **238**(1):348–362 (2014). doi:10.1016/j.ejor.2014.03.014
IBM. IBM ILOG CPLEX V12.1 user manual for CPLEX (2009)
Mufalli, F., Batta, R., Nagi, R.: Simultaneous sensor selection and routing of unmanned aerial vehicles for complex mission plans. Comput. Oper. Res. **39**(11):2787–2799 (2012)
Norkin, V.I., Pug, G.C., Ruszcynski, A.: A branch and bound method for stochastic global optimization. Math. Program. **83**, 425–450 (1998)
Royset, J.O., Reber, D.N.: Optimized routing of unmanned aerial systems for the interdiction of improvised explosive devices. Mil. Oper. Res. **14**(4):5–19 (2009)
Solomon, M.: Algorithms for the vehicle routing and scheduling problem with time window constraints. Oper. Res. **35**, 254–265 (1987)
Tsiligirides, T.: Heuristic methods applied to orienteering. J. Oper. Res. Soc. **35**, 797–809 (1984)
Vansteenwegen, P., Souffria, W., van Oudheusden, D.: The orienteering problem: A survey. Eur. J. Oper. Res. **209**(1):1–10 (2011)

Chapter 2
Supplier Selection Procedure of Military Critical Items: Mutivariate, Fuzzy, Analytical Hierarchy Procedures

Christodoulos Nikou and Socrates J. Moschuris

2.1 Introduction

In the US Department of Defense (DoD) whose budgets over defense related products and services are immense, procurement functions gain status and importance as it is acknowledged that they can contribute significantly in achieving its strategic objectives (Apte et al. 2011). One major aspect of the procurement procedure is the supplier/vendor selection (Weber et al. 1991). In the armed forces area, the same importance is appointed to supplier selection as it is stated that Military Logistics include, among others, aspects of military operations that deal with the acquisition of parts, materials and services, and act as a force multiplier that attains the advantage from a given force configuration by increasing the timeliness and endurance of the force (DCDC 2007). US DoD considers as Military Critical Items (MCI) supplies vital to the support of operations that are in short supply or are expected to be in short supply and mission-essential items that are available but require intense management to ensure more rapid supply for mission success (USADoD JP4-00 2000). Consequently, MCIs supplies do play a vital role in Armed Forces capability to fulfill a mission.

The objective of this paper is to present a methodology that is able to identify a supplier who meets an agency's need in the military procurement area, by

C. Nikou (✉)
Department of Industrial Management and Technology, University of Piraeus, Greece, 17th Serifou Street, 13561 Athens, Greece
e-mail: chrisnikou@gmail.com; cnikou@unipi.gr

S. J. Moschuris
Department of Industrial Management and Technology, University of Piraeus, 80 Karaoli and Dimitriou Street, 18534 Piraeus, Greece
e-mail: smosx@unipi.gr

V. Zeimpekis et al. (eds.), *Military Logistics*, Operations Research/Computer Science Interfaces Series 56, DOI 10.1007/978-3-319-12075-1_2

avoiding crisp data in decision making process, which (data) may be insufficient to model real life situations (Kahraman et al. 2003; Shen et al. 2013). Thus, Fuzzy logic theory, proposed by Zadeh (1965), is used hereinafter to deal with the vagueness/subjectivity of human thoughts and expressions and therefore, it strengthens the comprehensiveness and reasonableness of the decision making process (Shen et al. 2013). It is applied on Analytic Hierarchy Process, which is a widely accepted method in the supplier selection area (Liu and Hai 2005; Ho et al. 2010).

For the score of this paper, real data were collected through confidential questionnaires of members of the Hellenic armed forces. To these data, we applied some descriptive statistics, as part of a usual statistical analysis that provides the necessary feedback for someone to decide if a statistical method may be applied, i.e. if it requires normality assumptions. Confidence intervals were also calculated, since they provide estimation on the data population's answers and can assist in its simplified graphical depiction. Additionally, Competitive Intelligence (CI) was put to the cadre, as there is a growing interest in that area (Rouach and Santi 2001; Blenkhorn and Fleisher 2005). CI is conducted by an organized competitive intelligence system in 60 % of companies with revenues of more than $ 1 billion (Miller 2001). PCA, aims to reduce in an efficient way, the number of data/variables under study since MCDM methods, when applied to a large number of alternatives, may generate inconsistencies (Zanakis et al. 1998).

The main contribution of this paper, in our humble opinion, is located in the methodology proposed in the military procurement area. It combines methods that confront subjectivity of human judgment and modern statistical ones that allow the efficient identification of a small set of variables from the original group of variables of the collected data. This combination is done in a professional area where to the best of our knowledge there is still work to be done with that kind of methods. Additionally, this paper suggests the use of a CI process as a tool that may increase the transparency of the supplier selection procedure.

The rest of the paper is organized as follows: In the next section we review parts of relevant literature and present our conceptual integrated framework. Then, the phases that comprise the evaluation procedure based on real data are described, and conclusions, limitations and directions for future research are cited.

2.2 Literature Review

The problem of supplier selection/evaluation is not new and a great number of conceptual and practical studies have been reported so far, since it is an area of purchasing function (Sen et al. 2010) which is increasingly seen as a strategic issue in various organizations (De Boer et al. 2001). A short review of various evaluation techniques, applied to cope with aforementioned problem, is presented in Table 2.1.

Supplier selection plays a critical role and has a significant impact on purchasing management in supply chain (Amin and Razmi 2011;Omurca 2013). Several financial data verify the importance of purchasing into the defense area. In fiscal

Table 2.1 A short review of supplier evaluation and techniques

Supplier evaluation methods/techniques	
Evaluation technique	Authors
Weighted linear models	Lamberson et al. (1976); Timmerman (1986); Wind and Robinson (1968)
Linear programming	Pan (1989); Turner (1988)
Mixed integer programming	Weber and Current (1993)
Grouping methods	Hinkle et al. (1969); Muralidharan et al. (2002)
Analytical hierarchy process	Nydick and Hill (1992); Mohanty and Deshmukh (1993); Barbarosoglu and Yazgac (1997); Cheng et al. (1996) Akakarte et al. (2001); Lee et al. 2001 Muralidharan et al. (2002); Chan and Chan (2004); Liu and Hai (2005); Chan et al. (2007); Hou and Su (2007); Guler (2008); Dagdeviren et al. (2009)
Simple multi attribute rating technique	Barka (2003); Huang and Keska (2007)
Case-based reasoning	Ng and Skitmore (1995); Choy et al. (2002); Choy and Lee (203); Choy et al. (2005)
Genetic algorithm	Ding et al. (2005)
Analytical network process	Hill and Nydick (1992); Narasimhan (1983); Sarkis and Talluri (2002); Bayazit (2006); Gencer and Gurpinar (2007)
Matrix method	Gregory (1986)
Multi-objective programming	Weber and Ellram (1993); Narasisimhan et al. (2006); Wadhwa and Ravindran (2007)
Total cost of ownership	Smytka and Clemens (1993); Degraeve and Roodhooft (1999); Degraeve et al. (2000); Bhutta and Huq (2002)
Human judgment models	Ellram (1995); Patton (1996)
Principal component analysis	Petroni and Braglia (2000); Amiri et al. (2008); Lasch and Janker (2005); Sheng and Lan (2009); Lin and Song (2009); Sen et al. (2010); Surjandari et al. (2010)
Data envelopment analysis	Narasimhan et al. (2001); Talluri (2002a); Weber and Desai (1996); Weber et al. (1998); Liu et al. (2000)
Interpret. structural modeling	Mandal and Deshmukh (1994)
Game models	Talluri (2002b)
Statistical analysis	Ronen an Trietsch (1988); Mummalaneni et al. (1996); Verna and Pullman (1998)
Discrete choice analysis exp.	Verma and Pullman (1998)
Neural networks	Siying et al. (1997)
Semi-structural questionnaire	Schmitz and Platts (2004)
Max-Min approach	Talluri and Narasimhan (2003)
Vendor performance index	Willis et al. (1993)
Standardized unitless rating	Li et al. (1997)
Outranking methods	De Boer et al. (2001)
Mathematical models	Weber and Elram (1993); Sadrian and Yoon (1994); Rosental et al. (1995); Ghodyspour and O' brien (1998)

Table 2.1 (continued)

Supplier evaluation methods/techniques	
Evaluation technique	Authors
Thurstone scaling techniques	Thompson (1991)
Vendor survey plan	Lee and Welln (1993)
Integrated fuzzy AHP	Kahraman et al. (2003); Bottani and Rizzi (2005); Bozdag et al. (2005); Haq and Kannan (2006); Chan and Kumar (2007); Kunadhamraks and Hanaoka (2008); Kong et al. (2008); Pang (2008); Sen et al. (2010); Lee (2009) Ku et al. (2009); Chamodrakas et al. (2010)
Fuzzy PCA	Lam et al. (2010)
Integrated AHP and DEA	Ramanathan (2007); Saen (2007); Sevkli (2007)
Integrated AHP and GP	Cebi and Bayractar (2003); Peercin (2006); Kull and Talluri (2008); Mendoza (2008)
Integrated fuzzy and cluster analysis	Bottani and Rizzi (2008)
Integrated fuzzy and GA	Jain et al. (2004)
Integrated fuzzy and multi objective programming	Amid et al. (2006)
Integrated fuzzy and quality function deployment	Bevilacqua et al. (2006)
Integrate fuzzy and smart	Kwong et al. (2002); Chou and Chang (2008)

year (FY) 2007, US DOD's contract obligations included $ 330 billion for defense-related supplies and services (FPR 2007). In FY 2010, US DOD estimated that overall spending on logistics, including supply chain management, mounted to more than $ 210 billion (GAO-11-569 2007). Hellenic MoD's budget calculations for FYs 2013 and 2014, in spite of the ongoing financial crisis, were of 3.36 € and 2.9 billion € respectively (PGD 2012, 2013). Suppliers, in defense area, account for 50–80% of a major item's value (GAO-98-87 1998) and Beil (2010) reports that average US manufacturer spends roughly half of its revenue to purchase goods and services. Consequently, selecting suppliers with solid and modernized criteria could be a secure way for reducing defense budgets, in an effective and transparent way.

In this paper, we focus on a supplier selection methodology of MCIs, otherwise seen as critical safety items. The aspects that may categorize an item as an MCI relate to the safety of the personnel that uses it and its capability to fulfill the mission assigned (JLC ACSIMH 2005; DAGuidebook 2010; UK JSP 886 2010). Briefly, the lack or the malfunction of an MCI will have a major impact to the safety and accomplishment of a mission. Laios (2010) uses the portfolio analysis (supply positioning model) to classify items depending on the risk of supply, i.e. consequences from their shortage and the volume/expenditure of purchase they represent. By that MCIs may be corresponded to critical and bottleneck items, since in both cases the risk of supply is high and may jeopardize the success of a mission.

Our literature review of the relevant area in defense procurement, indicated that no single, widely accepted, approach exists for supplier selection that can fit in every case, and that supply managers may adopt different selection criteria, each time a procurement need arises (kanan and Tan 2002; Hsu et al. 2006; Ho et al. 2010; Degraeve et al. 2000). By reviewing Ware (2012), it seems that the application of fuzzy logic in supplier selection issues is something relatively new. More specifically, in the majority of the papers mentioned by Ware (2012), fuzzy AHP and Multivariate Statistical Analysis (MSA) were not applied to a significant extent. Ho et al. (2010) provide only one paper (Bottani and Rizzi 2008) as an integration of Fuzzy AHP with Cluster Analysis (a MSA sub-area). Studying uncertainty in supplier selection decisions that involve strategic (critical) and bottleneck items, is something that needs to be seriously considered (De Boer 2001). Competitive Intelligence (CI) may be used as an extra tool to reduce that uncertainty, as it could serve to highlight the critical gaps in the knowledge of decision makers and illuminate the key uncertainties (Hopple 1984).

NATO Support Agency (NSPA) procurement regulation (FD251-01 2012) states that supplier's eligibility will be based on the following factors: residency, national eligibility status, present capability and past performance, and that in vendor evaluation procedure, the Source Identification Section shall maintain a database containing information on the performance of suppliers with whom NSPA has concluded contracts, which should as a minimum cover cases of late delivery and discrepancies. No clear use of Fuzzy Logic and MSA is observed therein, while other defense related editions urge to deal with uncertainty in procurement decisions (DoD 2003; DAG 2010). Past performance is included in Bernhardt's (1994) working definition for CI. Lysons and Farrington (2006) provided a list of common vendor rating methods, where no Multivariate Statistical Methods exist. Furthermore, indicative criteria for supplier selection are referred in the regulatory for the public defense procurement, European Directive 2009/81/EC (Greek Law 3978/11 2011) which also covers procurement functions with non-EU members. By following the provisions of that Directive and the respective procedures, transnational agreements for reasons of national security/defense may be reached such as the USA/Foreign Military Sales contracts. The existence of indicative criteria allows suggestions for the public procurement supplier selection process, of methods and tools seen in the private section relevant literature, as long as the suppliers under evaluation cover the basic prerequisites set by that Directive. Public/private sector cooperation and exchange of knowledge to resolve procurement issues is a growing tendency in many countries and various public/private partnership arrangements replace conventional purchasing (Thai 2004; Choi 2010).

2.2.1 An Integrated Approach for MCI Supplier Selection

Figure 2.1 shows the steps of our methodology within the frame of a defense agency under public procurement law and the positioning of the suggested decision tools. Due to the specialized nature of the data (Armed Forces Data) the application of the framework required a panel of experts operating in military procurement area. For

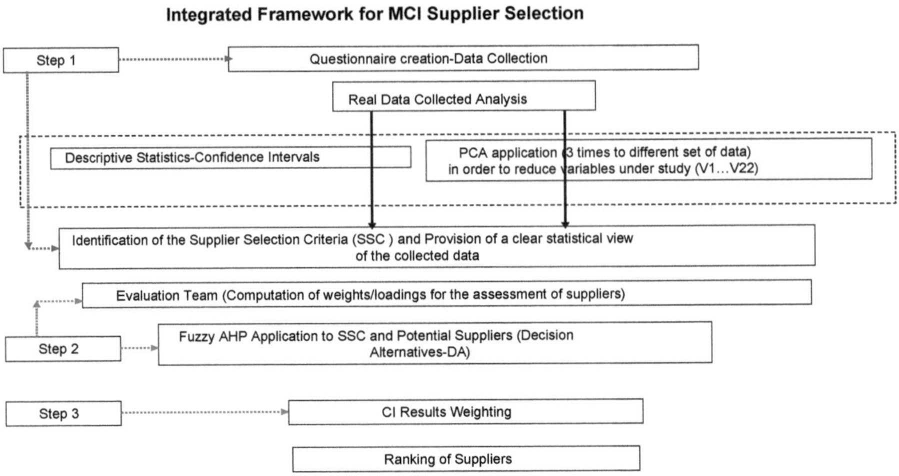

Fig. 2.1 Steps of the methodology for an integrated approach of MCI supplier selection

that scope, an Evaluation Team was created by two senior managers with a lot of experience in military procurement and the authors of this article, in order to embed every day experience in our approach. In addition to that, we took into account that multiple decision makers are often preferred in order to minimize partiality of a decision process (Bilsel et al. 2006) and the increasing importance of group decision making (Ahn 2000). The tools used to develop the suggested methodology are analyzed hereinafter.

2.2.2 *Competitive Intelligence*

Intelligence issues also appear in Logistics. Greek Intelligence Doctrine for land forces (GID 2005) urges for the use of a C4ISR system (Command, Control, Communications, Computers, Intelligence, Surveillance and Reconnaissance) in order to obtain intelligence that will drive, among others, to successful military logistics. Porteus (1994) provides examples of obtaining information on military procurement and Lee et al. (2009) suggest a procurement system that includes supplier selection, to enhance Business Intelligence (BI). BI includes competitive intelligence (Negash 2004). Competitive Intelligence (CI) is a systematic program for gathering and analyzing information about competitor's activities and general business trends to further a company's goals (Kahaner 1996). There is a positive relationship between CI and successful financial performance (Miller 2001) and Bernhardt (1994) reports that one of the usual CI objectives is financial issues. SWOT and financial analysis are the most used and effective tools of CI analysis (Miller 2001). In addition to that, SWOT analysis is often used to identify internal and external factors that may influence the fulfillment of strategy goals (Jiang et al. 2011).A failure to monitor supplier financial performance can result in interruptions in supply, if a financially troubled supplier is unable to deliver goods and services as agreed (Cancro and McGinnis 2003). Laios (2010) states that evaluating financial issues of a potential supplier is a demanding process and may become very important in cases of critical and bottleneck items (MCIs). In UK 2010 Bribery Act Adequate Procedures for corporate anti-bribery programs, indices 199–206 suggest the existence of an anti-bribery procedure. In the research study "Identifying and reducing corruption in public procurement in the EU" commissioned by the European Commission and conducted by PwC EU Services and Ecorys in 2013, the use of intelligence methods is suggested as a mean to reduce corruption. Consequently, we suggest that a CI system of MCIs could assist in securing the transparency of procurement actions and focusing on financial objectives, SWOT information and Corporate Trends of the potential suppliers. Therefore the key points of an MCI CI system may be the following, for each one of the potential suppliers that reached the final selection phase:

a. Its current corporate strategy and the possibility of a forthcoming change in it.
b. Its anti-corruption policy.
c. SWOT analysis for each one.
d. Financial Health information.

Ascertaining the financial health of a supplier can be subtle and challenging, because the signs of financial distress often emerge slowly and because financial data may not be publicly available or masked under the financial reports of larger firms that individual operating units belong to (Cancro and McGinnis 2004). If the Management decides to use as a CI sole source the financial statements of, balance sheet and the profit and loss statement [they provide the basic financial information for an enterprise/agency (Laios 2010)], then we suggest the evaluation of three ratios of solvency and one of profitability, derived from the abovementioned financial statements. Solvency ratios are more significant than profitability ratios (Inman 1991; Cancro and McGinnis 2003) and below-mentioned specific ratios are considered to be important for supply managers to understand basic financial information of a company and for the evaluation of potential supplier (Laios 2010; Cancro and McGinnis 2003).

e. Solvency-Current Ratio = Current Assets/Current Liabilities. A value grater than 1 may imply that the firm can cover its short-term debts.
f. Solvency-Acid Ratio = Current Assets –Inventory/ Current Liabilities. This ratio, although similar to Current Ratio, it provides a more direct estimation for the supplier's liquidity since it takes into account the time for the inventory to be turned into liquid assets. A value grater than 1 may implies a sufficient liquidity.
g. Solvency-Inventory Turnover = Cost of Gods sold/Average Inventory. A low value may imply high operating cost and inefficient inventory management.
h. Profitability-Operating Margin = Operating Income/ Net sales. It provides the net profit that derives from each $ of sales.

Possible CI objectives could also be other, hard to quantify, information. In Ware (2012) supplier loyalty is mentioned as a selection criterion that may reduce the supplier selection risks. A good reputation of a supplier in the market may ease contracting in peacetime conditions (CSI Proceedings 2006). Chan (2007) provides risk factors that strongly affect global supplier selection, such as geographical location, political stability, economy and terrorism. All this, could be a part of the SWOT analysis of each candidate supplier for a study of the influence on the contractual fulfilment of his obligations and the risk of interrupting supply. For example, political stability enhances long-term relations with suppliers which is a part of a supply strategy for critical items (Laios 2010). Conclusively, the establishment of a CI system does not imply the existence of corruption phenomena in any defense acquisition practise. It aims at reducing procurement risks that may occur throughout the life cycle of a weapon system f.e. It is more likely to support it in a long-term period a financially viable supplier with good reputation in the market.

2.2.3 Principal Components Analysis

Xia and Wu (2007), report that there is a large part of procurement experts that consider supplier selection as the most important function of a purchasing department and that decision makers cannot handle simultaneously many factors/parameters of decision. Miller (1956) stated that most decision makers cannot simultaneously handle more than 7–9 factors when it comes to decide. Consequently, it would be wise to use a reliable solution towards the direction of reducing decisional factors. Principal Component Analysis (PCA) is not new in the supplier selection area (Table 2.1) because it is considered to be an efficient way to reduce data and simplify the model under study without losing valuable information (Johnson and Wichern 2007). Algebraically, PCs are particular linear combinations of p random variables ($X_1, X_2, \ldots, X_p$) that explain most of the variability of the original variable set. Geometrically, PCs are linear combinations that represent the selection of a new coordinate system obtained by rotating the original system with $X_1, X_2, \ldots, X_p$ as the coordinate axes. The new axes represent the direction of the maximum variability and provide a simpler and more parsimonious description of the covariance structure (Jhonson and Wichern 2007). Let the random vector $X' = \left[X_1, X_2, \ldots, X_p\right]$ have the covariance matrix Σ with eigen values $\lambda_1 \geq \lambda_2 \geq \ldots.. \geq \lambda_p \geq 0$. Consider the following linear combinations:

$$\psi_1 = a_1' X = a_{11} X_1 + a_{12} X_2 + \ldots..a_{1p} X_p$$
$$\psi_2 = a_2' X = a_{21} X_1 + a_{22} X_2 + \ldots..a_{2p} X_p$$
$$\vdots$$
$$\psi_p = a_p' X = a_{p1} X_1 + a_{p2} X_2 + \ldots..a_{pp} X_p$$

These linear combinations $\Psi = CX$ have $\mu_\psi = E(\Psi) = E(CX) = C\mu_\chi$ and $\Sigma_\psi = Cov(\Psi) = Cov(CX) = C\Sigma_\psi C'$, where $\mu\psi$ and $\Sigma\psi$ are the mean vector and

	Supplier Quality indicators
1.Testing Capability	V1
2. Scope of resources	V2
3. Technical Expertise	V3
4. Industry knowledge	V4
5. Commitment to Quality	V5
6. Supplier's Process Capability	V6
7. Commitment tot continuous improvement	V7
8. Visionary Leadership	V8
9. Employee Fulfilment	V9

	Supplier Service Indicators
1. Ability to meet delivery due dates	V10
2. Price of materials, parts and services	V11
3. Flexible contract terms and conditions	V12
4. Geographical compatibility/proximity	V13
5. Reserve Capacity	V14

	Buyer- Supplier Strategic/Management Fit Indicators
1. Open to site evaluation	V15
2. Supplier's reputation	V16
3. Financial stability and staying power	V17
4. Honest and frequently communications	V18
5. Cultural match with Supplier	V19
6. Past and current relationship with the supplier	V20
7. Supplier is strategically Important	V21
8. Supplier's willingness to share confidential information	V22

Footnote: V means Variable

Fig. 2.2 Supplier quality, Service/delivery and stgic/mgmt fit indicators

variance-covariance matrix of *Xp* respectively. Finally we obtain $Var(\psi_i) = \alpha_i' \Sigma \alpha_i$ and $Cov(\psi_i, \psi_k) = \alpha_1' \Sigma \alpha_k$ with *I, k* = *1, 2....p*. The PCs are those uncorrelated linear combinations $\Psi_1, \Psi_2, ..., \Psi_P$ whose variances are as large as possible and the first PC is the linear combination with maximum variance. There are various statistical softwares such as SPSS, MINITAB that perform PCA calculations. In this paper we used the MINITAB statistical software. Cheraghi (2004) concluded that supplier selection dominant criteria were aspects of quality, delivery, price and service and Ho et al. (2010) mentioned that the three most popular evaluating criteria are those related to aspects of quality, delivery and price/cost. Ongoing importance of quality delivery and cost aspects enhanced us to use the supplier selection construct suggested by Hsu et al. (2006) and investigate the importance attributed to indicators mentioned therein and related to quality, service, delivery, cost and buyer-supplier management fit. Real data were evaluated from questionnaires where members of the armed forces were asked to rate the importance of above-mentioned indicators, in cases of MCIs, by their importance and rate of appearance on a five point Likert scale (Indicators depicted in Fig. 2.2). The number of questionnaires constituted the sample size (N=30) where PCA was applied (see Fig. 2.1). Each set of indicators was a different question in the same questionnaire.

Analytically, PCA was applied three times, one in each subgroup i.e. Supplier Quality, Service/Delivery and Stgic/Mgmt Fit subgroups, in an attempt to reduce indicators/Variables under study so that they reach the number suggested by Miller (1956) and therefore be made easier for a decision maker to handle. Some indicators of the 3rd subgroup, such as supplier reputation and financial stability may be important objectives of a CI system, as shown in previous subsection.

2.2.4 Fuzzy Sets Theory and Fuzzy AHP

Fuzzy logic deals with the vagueness of human thought (Zadeh 1965) which is usually an outcome of the majority of the real world situations where most decision environments are characterized by complex and imprecise information (Aggarwal and Singh 2013). Supply Chain Management issues could not be an exemption. According to Ho et al. (2010) the most well known method to operationalize supplier selection decision making is the Analytic Hierarchy Procedure (AHP). AHP includes subjective judgments, thus a fuzzy approach on that issue can overcome the possible uncertainty of these judgments (Tang and Beynon 2005) and fuzzy logic allows numerical values to belong in two categories with a different extent (Bottani and Rizzi 2008). Fuzzy AHP (FAHP) is developed from the AHP and integrates fuzzy logic into AHP, making it able to provide more sufficient information (Aggarwal and Singh 2013).

The Basic Concepts of fuzzy logic adopted in this paper are cited below and can be viewed in detail in Chang (1992, 1996), Tang and Beynon (2005), and Theodorou (2012). Triangular Fuzzy Numbers (TFNs) were selected since they are the most popular ones (Amin and Razmi 2011) and easy to handle (Lam 2010).

Definition 1 Let M E F(R) be called a fuzzy number if: (1) exists $x_o \in$ such that $\mu_M(\chi_0) = 1$ and (2) For any $a \in [0, 1]$, $A_a = [x, \mu_{Aa}(x) \geq a]$ is a closed interval. *F(R)* represents all fuzzy sets, and *R* is the set of real numbers.

$$\mu_M(x) = \begin{bmatrix} \dfrac{x}{m-l} - \dfrac{l}{m-l}, x \in [l, m], \\ \dfrac{x}{m-u} - \dfrac{u}{m-u}, x \in [m, u], \\ 0, if \quad otherwise \end{bmatrix} \tag{2.1}$$

Definition 2 A fuzzy number *M* on *R* is defined to be a triangular fuzzy number if its membership function $\mu_M(\chi): R \rightarrow [0, 1]$ equals to equation (1). *1* and *u* are the lower and upper values of the support of M respectively and *m* the modal value. The triangular fuzzy number can be denoted by *(l, m, u)*. The support of M is the set of elements $\{x \in R \,[\, l < x < u\}$.

Their operational laws used in this paper are the following:

$$(l_1, m_{1,}u_1) \oplus (l_2, m_{2,}u_2) = (l_1 + l_2, m_1 + m_2, u_1 + u_2) \tag{2.2}$$

$$(l_1, m_{1,}u_1) \otimes (l_2, m_{2,}u_2) = (l_1 * l_2, m_1 * m_2, u_1 * u_2) \tag{2.3}$$

$$(l_1^{-1}, m_1^{-1}u_1^{-1}) \approx (1/l_1, 1/m_1, 1/u_1) \tag{2.4}$$

To continue with the next basic definitions, some hypotheses should be stated. Let $X = [x_1, x_2 \ldots, x_n]$ be an object set and $U = [u_1, u_2 \ldots, u_m]$ be a goal set. According to Chang (1992, 1996) each object is taken and extent analysis for each goal is performed therefore, m extent analysis values from each object may be obtained, $M_{g_i}^1, M_{g_i}^2, \ldots, M_{g_i}^m, i = 1, \ldots, n$.

Definition 3 The value of Fuzzy Synthetic Extent (*Si*) with respect of the *ith* object equals to

$$S_i = \sum_{j=1}^{m} M_{g_i}^j \otimes \left[\sum_{i=1}^{n} \sum_{j=1}^{m} M_{g_i}^j \right]^{-1} \tag{2.5}$$

where $M_{g_i}^j$ are TFNs.

Definition 4 For 2 convex fuzzy numbers M_1, M_2 the possibility of $M_1 \geq M_2$ is $V(M_1 \geq M_2) = \frac{\sup}{x \geq \psi} \left[\mu_{M_1}(x), \mu_{M2}(\psi) \right]$, where x and ψ are values on the axis of membership function of each criterion.

$$M1,\ M2, V(M1 \geq M2) = 1 \, iff \ m_1 \geq m_2 \quad and \quad V(M_2 \geq M_1) = hgt(M_1 \cap M_2) = \mu_{M1}(d) \tag{2.6}$$

where d is the ordinate of the highest intersection point D between μ_{M1} and μ_{M2}. When $M_1 = (l_1, m_1, u_1)$ *and* $M_2 = (l_2, m_2, u_2)$ the ordinate of D is

$$V(M_2 \geq M_1) = hgt(M_1 \cap M_2) = \frac{l_1 - u_2}{(m_2 - u_2) - (m_1 - l_1)} \tag{2.7}$$

Definition 5 The degree of possibility for a convex fuzzy number to be greater than K convex fuzzy numbers Mi (i=1…k) is:

$$V(M \geq M_1,\ M_2 \ldots, M_k) = V\left[(M \geq M_1,)\ and\ (M \geq M_2) and \ldots and (M \geq M_k)\right] = min V(M \geq M_i). \tag{2.8}$$

To get the estimates for the weights under each criterion (weight vector) it is assumed that

$$d'(Ai) = min\ V(S_i \geq S_k) \tag{2.9}$$

Table 2.2 Saaty's (2000) scale and correspondent fuzzy numbers

Definition	Intensity of importance	Triangular fuzzy numbers	Explanation
Equally important	1	(1, 1, 1)	2 activities contribute equally to the objective
Weak importance of one over another	3	(3, 4, 5)	Experience or judgment slightly favor one activity over another
Essential or strong importance	5	(5, 6, 7)	Experience and judgment strongly favor one activity over another
Demonstrated importance	7	(6, 7, 8)	An activity is strongly favored and its dominance is demonstrated in practice
Absolute importance	9	(8, 9, 10)	The evidence favoring one activity over another is of the highest possible order of affirmation
Intermediate values between the two adjacent judgments	2, 4, 6, 8	(1, 2, 3),(3, 4, 5), (5, 6, 7) (7, 8, 9)	When compromise is needed intermediate Values
Reciprocals of above nonzero	If an element *i* has one of the above numbers assigned to it when compared with element *j*, then *j* has the reciprocal value when compared with *i*		
Ratios	Ratios arising from the scale		If consistency were to be forced by obtaining *n* numerical values to span the matrix

k = 1, 2… n, k $\neq$ i. The weight vector is given *by* $W' = [(d'(A1), d'(A_2) \dots d'(A_m)]$, where A_i (i = 1, 2…m) are m elements. Via normalization, the normalized weight Vector $W = [(d(A_1), d(A_2) \dots d(A_m)]$ is extracted where W is a nonfuzzy number.

Definition 6 As stated previously, a fuzzy number representing a fuzzy judgment is defined as (l_{ij}, m_{ij}, u_{ij}). If we consider Zhu et al. (1999) δ (degree of fuzziness or the absolute distance of the modal value by the lower and upper bound) then this number can be defined as $(m_{ij} - \delta, m_{ij}, m_{ij} + \delta)$ and Zhu et al. (1999) report that $1/2 > \delta > 1$ is more suitable.

Fuzzy AHP is then applied to the number of the Indicators/Variables retained in the supplier selection model after PCA's implementation, for a hypothetical number of three suppliers. Saaty's nine point scale was used to make the pairwise comparisons and δ is set to 1 which is an acceptable value, considering simultaneously the degrees of fuzziness and confidence in various δ values (Zhu 1999). Table 2.2 provides Saaty's scale and the correspondent fuzzy numbers.

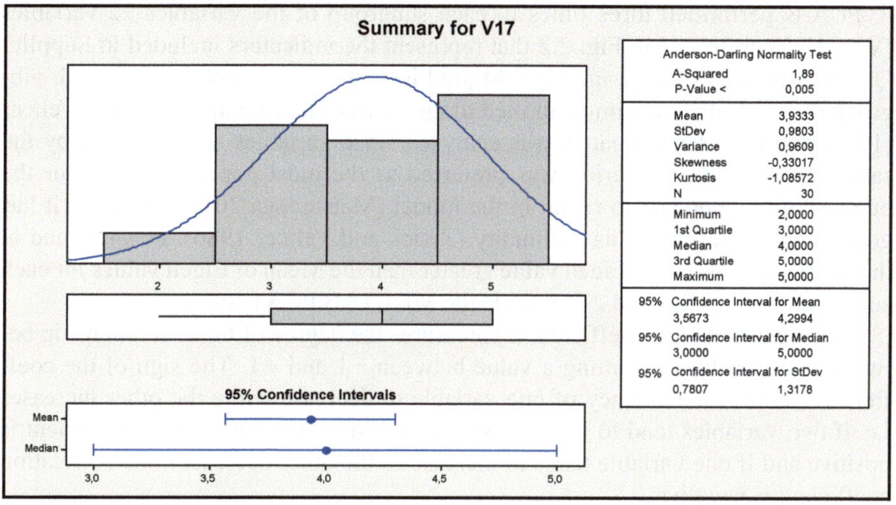

Fig. 2.3 Descriptive statistics for V17

2.3 Proposed Model of the Integrated Approach with Real Data Evaluation

2.3.1 First Step of the Integrated Approach

In Fig. 2.1 the first step, is to analyze the real data collected in order to provide a simple and clear statistical view and then to identify and reduce the Supplier Selection Criteria (SSC) to a number that will be manageable for the Decision Makers to handle, for the application of the FAHP.

Descriptive statistics describe quantitatively the main features of a collection of data. MINITAB produces such descriptive statistics that contain all the necessary parameters to check normality hypothesis and the spread of the data. An example to a randomly selected variable is provided in Fig. 2.3 where it is shown that no normality assumption can be made under the Anderson-Darling statistic test. Skewness value of −0.33, indicates that in V17 distribution, the tail on the left side of the probability density function is longer than the right side and the majority of the values lie to the right of the mean. Kyrtosis value of −1.08 indicates a platykurtic distribution. 95 % Confidence Interval (CI) for sample mean may be used for the calculation of the mean 95 % CI for the V17 population iaw Kotrouvelis (2000). Central Limit Theorem (CLT) synoptically, denotes that the sample mean of a large random sample of random variables with mean μ and finite variance σ^2 has approximately the normal distribution with mean μ and variance σ^2/n (De Groot and Schervish 2012). A sample may be considered large if $n \geq 30$ (Koutrouvelis 2000) and consequently the sample size in this study covers the basic prerequisites for CLT to apply and ease statistical analysis.

PCA is performed three times to each subgroup of the variables 22 variables (V1…V22) presented in Fig. 2.2 that represent the indicators included in Supplier Quality, Service/Delivery and Stgic/Mgmt Fit subgroups. Sample size for each subgroup ($N=30$) fits to common applied usage in accordance with Zwick and Velicer (1986) and Covariance matrix was analyzed since variables are measured by the same scales. Kaiser Criterion was preferred as the most popular method for the number of components to retain in the model (Matsumaga 2010), although it has gone under criticism for its optimality (Zwick and Velicer 1986). PCs retained in the model are those with Eigen value greater than the Mean of Eigen values for each subgroup. Figures 2.4 and 2.5 provide the MINITAB PCA results.

Pearson correlation coefficient (r) measures the degree of linear relationship between two variables assuming a value between -1 and $+1$. The sign of the coefficient denotes the tendency of one variable to decrease while the other increases i.e. if two variables tend to increase simulataneously, the correlation coefficient is positive and if one variable tends to increase as the other decreases, the correlation coefficient is negative.

Minitab calculates the correlation coefficient for every possible pair and displays *p*-values for the hypothesis test of the correlation coefficient being zero. Figure 2.6 provides the MINITAB Pearson Correlation results at a significance level of 0.001, of the three subgroups for the PCs retained in the model iaw Kaiser Criterion. Kioxos (1993) mentioned that although r values depend on the number of observations, indicative value intervals of r that denote the strength of a relationship between two variables may be provided, and values greater than 0.5 show a notable relationship.

The interpretation of PCA is not often easy to make and it involves subjectivity of the interpreters (Korhonen 1984; Krzanowski 1988; Karlis 2005). The Evaluation Team and a very austere level of confidence (*p*-value of 0,001) are selected as countermeasures to overcome safely this obstacle and provide efficient conclusions. Conclusions derived from Figs. 2.4–2.6 are summarized at the following points extracted by the Evaluation Team, that besides its experience also considered selection criteria of five seminal reviews in supplier selection area (Weber et al. 1991; Degraeve et al. 2000; DeBoer et al. 2001; Ho et al. 2010; Ware et al. 2012):

a. Miller's (1956) maximum number of factors (7–9 factors) that most decision makers can handle at the same time is reached, out of a number of 22 initial variables using the Kaiser Criterion in PCA.
b. There are notable relationships of the initial variables and the PCs in every subgroup at a very high level of confidence and these initial variables may the basis for PC's interpretation.

Figure 2.7 provides the results of the interpretation conducted by the Evaluation Team and the hierarchical structure of the remaining variables in the supplier selection fuzzy model.

PCA FOR SUPPLIER QUALITY SUBGROUP

- **Principal Component Analysis: V1; V2; V3; V4; V5; V6; V7; V8; V9**
- Eigenanalysis of the Covariance Matrix

Eigenvalue	**2,9199**	**1,8127**	**1,1718**	0,8112	0,7283	0,6138	0,4310	0,3124	**MEAN EIGEN VALUE=1,00026**
Proportion	0,324	0,201	0,130	0,090	0,081	0,068	0,048	0,035	
Cumulative	0,324	0,526	0,656	0,746	0,827	0,895	0,943	0,978	

Eigenvalue	0,2012
Proportion	0,022
Cumulative	1,000

Variable	**PC1**	**PC2**	**PC3**	PC4	PC5	PC6	PC7	PC8
V1	0,186	-0,195	0,325	0,102	-0,608	0,615	-0,050	0,235
V2	-0,092	0,104	0,480	-0,405	0,334	0,268	-0,018	0,041
V3	0,286	-0,434	-0,317	-0,439	0,092	0,316	0,221	-0,524
V4	0,309	-0,434	-0,157	0,133	0,272	-0,024	-0,727	0,218
V5	0,180	-0,024	0,007	-0,702	-0,124	-0,309	0,032	0,542
V6	0,242	0,189	0,577	-0,093	0,070	-0,144	-0,353	-0,461
V7	0,439	-0,102	0,109	0,079	-0,437	-0,514	0,139	-0,203
V8	0,612	0,094	0,131	0,304	0,455	0,094	0,454	0,267
V9	0,347	0,720	-0,420	-0,126	-0,137	0,246	-0,261	-0,051

Variable	PC9
V1	0,078
V2	-0,633
V3	0,070
V4	-0,152
V5	0,262
V6	0,449
V7	-0,513
V8	0,116
V9	-0,135

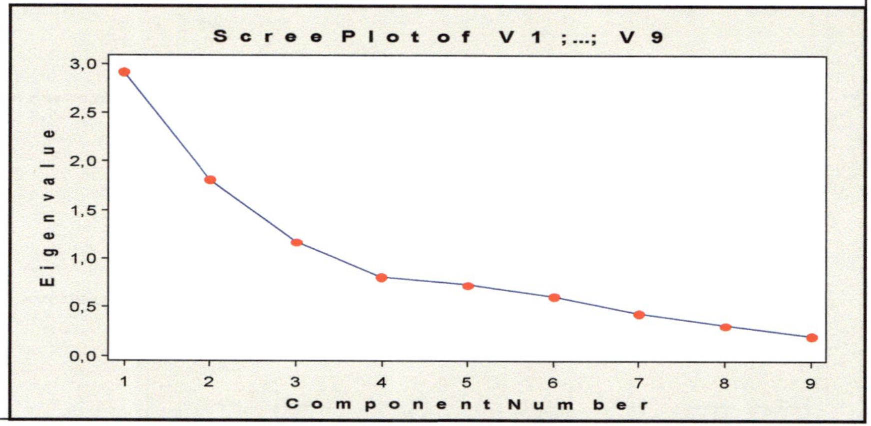

Fig. 2.4 PCA for supplier quality subgroup

PCA FOR SUPPLIER SERVICE AND STGIC MGMT FIT SUBGROUPS

Principal Component Analysis: V10; V11; V12; V13; V14 (SUPPLIER QUALITY)

Eigenanalysis of the Covariance Matrix

Eigenvalue	**2,1773**	**1,3545**	0,8865	0,5720	0,3833	**MEAN EIGEN VALUE=1,074**
Proportion	0,405	0,252	0,165	0,106	0,071	
Cumulative	0,405	0,657	0,822	0,929	1,000	

Variable	**PC1**	**PC2**	PC3	PC4	PC5
V10	0,150	-0,262	0,388	0,417	0,765
V11	0,067	0,109	0,825	0,209	-0,509
V12	0,188	0,083	-0,405	0,850	-0,266
V13	0,844	-0,453	-0,057	-0,223	-0,170
V14	0,474	0,841	0,023	-0,101	0,239

Principal Component Analysis: V15; V16; V17; V18; V19; V20; V21; V22 (STGIC/MGMT FIT)

Eigenanalysis of the Covariance Matrix

MEAN EIGEN VALUE=1,025

Eigenvalue	**2,4306**	**1,4847**	**1,2079**	**1,0264**	0,8461	0,5128	0,4303	0,2612,
Proportion	0,296	0,181	0,147	0,125	0,103	0,063	0,052	0,032
Cumulative	0,296	0,477	0,625	0,750	0,853	0,916	0,968	1,000

Variable	**PC1**	**PC2**	**PC3**	**PC4**	PC5	PC6	PC7	PC8
V15	-0,225	-0,231	-0,444	0,291	-0,370	-0,463	-0,085	-0,505
V16	-0,323	-0,090	0,813	0,228	0,062	-0,348	0,165	-0,152
V17	0,029	-0,683	0,073	0,057	0,295	0,511	-0,148	-0,393
V18	-0,337	-0,333	-0,044	-0,672	-0,279	0,009	0,491	0,066
V19	-0,372	-0,255	0,092	0,115	-0,397	0,131	-0,562	0,533
V20	-0,104	-0,114	-0,085	-0,449	0,555	-0,502	-0,453	0,044
V21	-0,646	0,517	-0,050	-0,122	0,103	0,366	-0,165	-0,357
V22	-0,405	-0,132	-0,342	0,423	0,467	-0,011	0,393	0,387

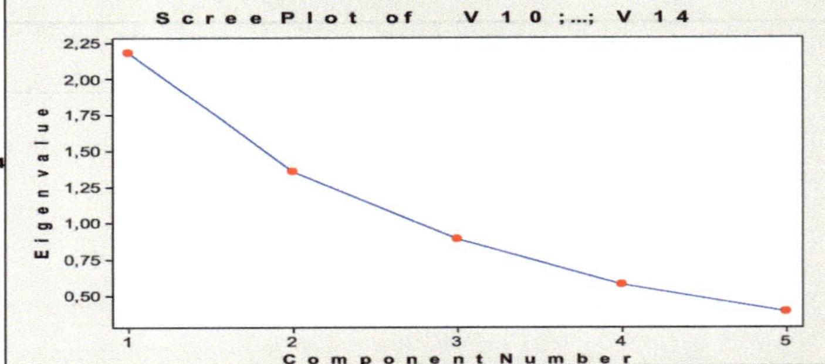

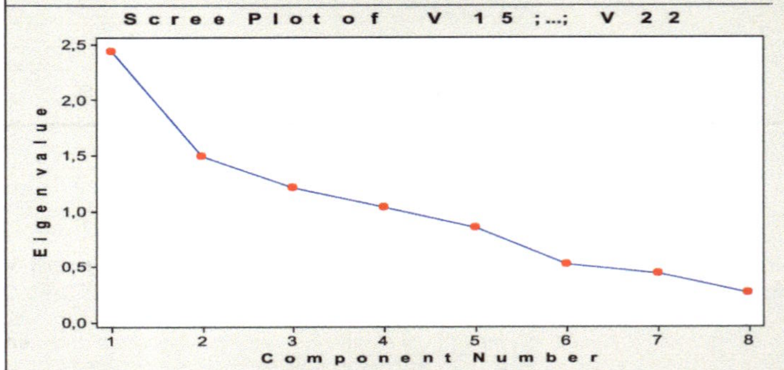

Fig. 2.5 PCA for supplier service and stgic/mgmt fit subgroups

VARIABLES CORRELATIONS WITH PCs RETAINED IN THE MODEL
Cell Contents: Pearson correlation (above number) P-Value (below number)

SUPPLIER QUALITY INDICATORS

	V1	V2	**V3**	**V4**	V5	V6	**V7**	**V8**	**V9**
SPC1	0,351	-0,195	0,482	0,538	0,376	0,459	0,759	0,861	0,469
	0,057	0,302	0,007	0,002	0,041	0,011	**0,000**	**0,000**	0,009
SCP2	-0,289	0,172	-0,575	-0,595	-0,040	0,283	-0,140	0,105	0,767
	0,121	0,362	**0,001**	**0,001**	0,834	0,129	0,462	0,582	**0,000**
SPC3	0,388	0,643	-0,338	-0,173	0,009	0,694	0,119	0,117	-0,360
	0,034	0,000	0,068	0,360	0,962	0,000	0,530	0,539	0,051

SUPPLIER SERVICE INDICATORS

	V10	V11	V12	**V13**	**V14**
SPC10	0,286	0,114	0,338	0,910	0,576
	0,125	0,550	0,067	**0,000**	**0,001**
SPC11	-0,394	0,147	0,118	-0,385	0,806
	0,031	0,439	0,535	0,036	**0,000**

STGIC/MGMT FIT INDICATORS

	V15	**V16**	**V17**	**V18**	V19	V20	**V21**	**V22**
SPC15	-0,387	-0,460	0,046	-0,506	-0,645	-0,188	-0,809	-0,620
	0,035	0,011	0,811	0,004	0,000	0,319	**0,000**	**0,000**
SPC16	-0,310	-0,100	-0,848	-0,391	-0,345	-0,161	0,506	-0,158
	0,096	0,600	**0,000**	0,033	0,062	0,395	0,004	0,404
SPC17	-0,538	0,815	0,082	-0,047	0,112	-0,108	-0,044	-0,369
	0,002	**0,000**	0,667	0,806	0,556	0,569	0,817	0,045
SPC18	0,325	0,211	0,059	-0,656	0,130	-0,529	-0,099	0,420
	0,079	0,263	0,757	**0,000**	0,495	0,003	0,601	0,021

PS: Numbers and Letters in Bold denote a sufficient linear relationship at a significance level of 0,001

Fig. 2.6 Pearson correlation coefficient and *P*-value at 0.001 significance level

2.3.2 Second Step of the Integrated Approach

The variables retained in the model (Fig. 2.7) comprise the group of criteria for the application of FAHP by the Evaluation Team (the Decision Makers) that judges the relative importance of each criterion against all others, at the same level of hierarchy on a fuzzy scale. It is more confident to give interval judgments than fixed value judgments (Kahraman et al. 2003). In this numerical example, only the FAHP judgment matrices and calculations of the first subgroup (Supplier Quality Indicators) for three hypothetical suppliers are provided. In any case, the suppliers should be selected from official lists of approved economic operators under the provisions of the European Directive 2009/81/EC or by a transnational agreement (article 12 and 13 of the Directive). Subsequently, the judgments and calculations for the rest subgroups are dealt in an identical manner. The fuzzy comparison matrix over the Supplier Quality Indicators Criteria (MPQ, LDA, QMP) is provided in Table 2.3.

Using Equations (2) to (7) and the comparisons of Table 2.3, fuzzy synthetic extents of the criteria MPQ, LDA and QMP were obtained as follows:

$$S_{mpq} = (4,\ 6,\ 8) \otimes (0.064,\ 0.088, 0.126) = \mathit{(0.256, 0.528, 1.008)}$$ [1]

[1] Smpq $_{\text{under fuzzy arithmetic}}$=4*0.064=0.256, 6*0.088=0.582, 8*0.126=1.008 → Smpq=(0.256, 0.528, 1.008)

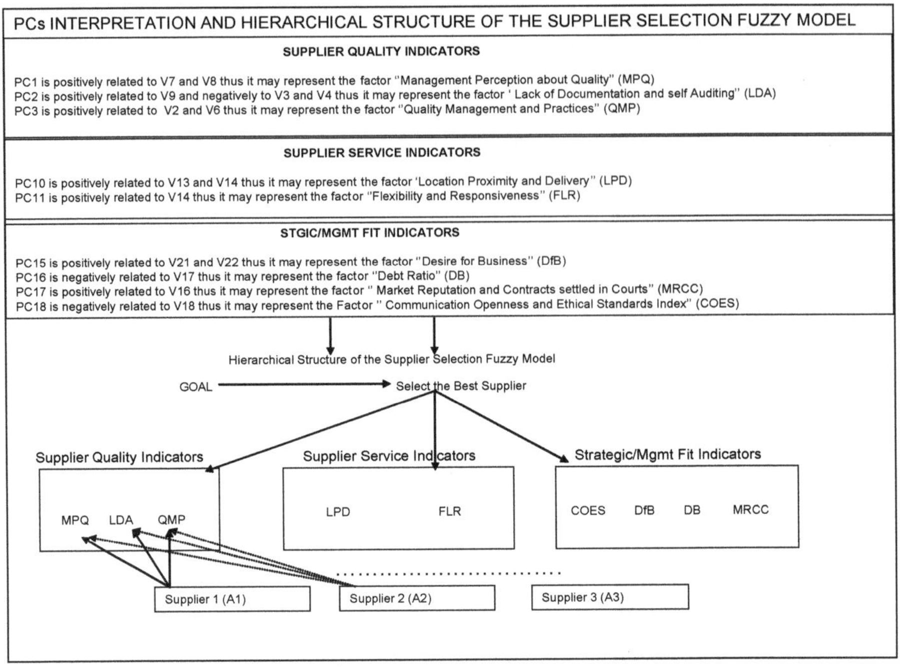

Fig. 2.7 PCs interpretation and hierarchical structure of the fuzzy model

$$S_{lda} = (2.33,\ 3.5,\ 5) \otimes (0.064,\ 0.088, 0.126) = (0.149, 0.308, 0.63)$$

$$S_{qmp} = (1.58,\ 1.83,\ 2.5) \otimes (0.064,\ 0.088,\ 0.126) = (0.101, 0.161, 0.315)$$

By these Vectors, we calculate the degrees of possibilities $V(S_{mpq} \geq S_{lda}) = 1$, $V(S_{mpq} \geq S_{qmp}) = 1$, $V(S_{lda} \geq S_{qmp}) = 1$, $V(S_{lda} \geq S_{mpq}) = 0.629$, $V(S_{qmp} \geq S_{mpq}) = 0.138$, $V(S_{qmp} \geq S_{lda}) = 0.53$. By Formula (8) the minimum degrees of possibilities are obtained and by formula (9) we have $W' = (1,\ 0.629,\ 0.138)$. Via normalization, weight vectors are obtained for criteria MPQ, LDA, QMP $W = (0.56,\ 0.36,\ 0.08)^T$ where W a non fuzzy number. Then by the same procedure the Evaluation Team compares potential Suppliers ($A_1 \ldots A_3$) under each of the criteria separately. The results are shown in Tables 2.4a, b, c. It should be noted that when the results from equation (7) are negative numbers, they are replaced by zero (Tang and Beynon 2005) and this is the case in Table 2.4b.

The final score for the first subgroup (Supplier Quality Indicators) is calculated by adding the weights per supplier multiplied by the weights of the corresponding criteria. Table 2.5 shows theses scores and concludes Step 2 of Fig. 2.1. It is clear that Supplier A1 is the preferred candidate.

Table 2.3 The fuzzy comparison matrix for the criteria of the first subgroup

Fuzzy comparison matrix	MPQ	LDA	QMP	Importance weight
MPQ	1, 1, 1	1, 2, 3	2, 3, 4	0.56
LDA	0.33, 0.5, 1	1, 1, 1	1, 2, 3	0.36
QMP	0.25, 0.33, 0.5	0.33, 0.5, 1	1, 1, 1	0.08

Table 2.4a, b, c **a** The comparison of suppliers under MPQ criterion **b** The comparison of suppliers under LDA criterion **c** The comparison of suppliers under QMP criterion

	A_1	A_2	A_3	Importance weights
MPQ criterion				
A_1	1, 1, 1	1, 2, 3	1, 2, 3	0.46
A_2	0.33, 0.5, 1	1, 1, 1	1, 2, 3	0.35
A_3	0.33, 0.5, 1	0.33, 0.5, 1	1, 1, 1	0.19
LDA criterion				
A_1	1, 1, 1	2, 3, 4	2, 3, 4	0.64
A_2	0.25, 0.33, 0.5	1, 1, 1	2, 3, 4	0.36
A_3	0.25, 0.33, 0.5	0.25, 0.33, 0.5	1, 1, 1	0
QMP criterion				
A_1	1, 1, 1	2, 3, 4	1, 2, 3	0.55
A_2	0.25, 0.33, 0.5	1, 1, 1	2, 3, 4	0.4
A_3	0.33, 0.5, 1	0.25, 0.33, 0.5	1, 1, 1	0.04

Table 2.5 Final score of suppliers in step 2

STEP 2	A_1	A_2	A_3
Final scores	0.532	0.357	0.109

2.3.3 *Third Step of the Integrated Approach*

The previous step focused mainly on quality and delivery/service issues for the specific procurement case, but it is not able to provide information to the Decision Makers about factors such as candidate supplier's financial health. In this Step, the introduction of a CI system is a way to use information about the past performance of potential suppliers which is a necessity for public sector procurement issues (Kelman 1990), and aims at minimizing the risk of a specific procurement case. It could be seen as part of the today's business management (Ding 2009) which enhances the objectivity of decision making process by reducing the risks in that process (West 2001). Its structure consists of the following three phases that do not necessarily apply simultaneously due to the expensive nature of a CI system (Miller 2001; Negash et al. 2004).

a. First phase: Information on key points of the MCI CI system (see p. 6).
b. Second phase: Information retrieved by financial statements of balance sheet and the profit and loss statement of potential suppliers (see p. 6).
c. Third phase: This part mainly applies to highly budgeted procurement cases where long term contracts are likely to be signed. It concerns expletory information on factors like supplier loyalty, political stability, economy and terrorism. These factors are hard to be quantified and may jeopardize the interests of a company at a serious point (see pp. 6–7).

A necessary condition of this step is that in the evaluation procedure, suppliers must be evaluated in the same parts of the CI system i.e. if it decided not to have information on the third part that should be a rule for all the candidate suppliers regardless of their financial size. Ranking scale is set from 0–1 and Evaluation Team is the executing team for this Step. Nevertheless, since time is a crucial element in decision making as data rapidly change, CI may be outsourced if the Evaluation Team is not able/trained to perform it timely. Outsourcing CI is a viable and increasingly interesting solution (Porfirio and Dos Santos 2011; www.scip.org). A hypothetical example of crisp values for the CI scoring procedure is provided in Table 2.6.

The final score for each supplier is obtained by adding the scores of Steps 2 and 3 of the Integrated Approach and determines that Suppliers' scores are A1: 2.112, A2: 1.917 and A3: 1.709. The small differences of the second step in the ranking of the suppliers seem incapable of changing final ranking. Supplier A1 is the most suitable followed by A2. Nevertheless it should be noted that it is possible for ranking to change in Step 3, if CI outcomes present large deviations among them. For example if CI outcome for A3 was bigger than 1.808, then the second most suitable supplier would be supplier A3. Managers of the military procurement area to whom this approach was presented, appeared to be satisfied from its flexibility due to the fuzzy environment applied, the ability to change ranking from one step of the approach to another and by the importance provided in financial and anticorruption data for the reason that these characteristics of the approach are in accordance with Greek Law 3871/2010 which provides the financial frame and transparency guidelines for public procurement.

Table 2.6 CI outcome

Competitive intelligence phases	Suppliers' Scores			
	A1	A2	A3	Remarks
First phase: Information on key points of the MCI CI system	0.5	0.6	0.7	The phases applied, are reported in this cell
Second phase: Information retrieved by financial statements	0.45	0.42	0.52	
Third phase: expletory information	0.63	0.54	0.38	
Final score	1.58	1.56	1.6	

2.4 Conclusions and Future Research Implications

Porfirio and Dos Santos (2011) pinpoint three key factors for effective decisions: The existence of a set of goals to work towards, of a way to measure whether a chosen course moves away from these goals, and third the provision of those measures to the decision makers in a timely manner. In this paper, an effort has been made to apply these key factors in an MCI supplier selection procedure. The goal is to select the best supplier, but as decision-making becomes increasingly complex, fuzzy logic is selected to cope with a level of uncertainty that may appear on the decision makers. Fuzzy logic has been proven capable to overcome the difficulty of assigning crisp evaluation scores (Kahraman et al. 2003). Fuzzy Logic provides an efficient and realistic way of measurement and in combination with the CI system, it brings us closer to the third key factor. Supplier Selection can be performed timely with crucial information for quality, service and financial factors as supplier selection decisions are often made under time pressure (Buyukozkan and Çifçi 2011). This paper combines real data with conceptual framework (Integrated Approach) and focuses to the final selection phase of the supplier selection process. It may be used for tangible and intangibles factors with imprecise information about them, regardless of how big the volume of data is, as they may be reduced efficiently by PCA. In order to exemplify this approach, an application with real data has been made, by the assistance of two senior managers in the military procurement area. Additionally it has been presented to other managers of the relevant area with good results on its realistic nature. While this study has provided the frame for the identification of an effective supplier, by no means it has answered all questions concerning this issue. Possible future inquires would be to perform a sensitivity analysis of the resultant weight values, to develop a multivariate monitoring approach for fuzzy profiles of the Supplier Quality, Service/Delivery and Stgic/Mgmt Fit Indicators and to introduce Fuzzy Logic to CI issues. Finally, limitations of Greek National Safety Regulations and Statistical confidentiality (Principle No five of the European Statistics Code of Practice) were taken into account, thus all our sources/references are available unrestricted.

2.5 Acknowledgements

Opinions and results in this paper do not reflect the official position of the Hellenic Armed Forces. The authors would like to thank the experts of the military procurement area for their support. Sincere gratitude is hereby extended to the reviewers for their helpful comments.

References

Aggarwal, R., Singh, S.: AHP and extent fuzzy ahp approach for prioritzaition of performance measurement atributes. World. Acad. Sci. Eng. Technol. **73**, 160–165 (2013)

Ahn, B.S.: The analytic hierarchy process in an uncertain environment: a simulation approach by hauser and tadikamalla (1996). Eur. J. Oper. Res. **124**, 217–218 (2000)

Amin, S.H., Razmi, J.: An integrated fuzzy model for supplier management: a case study of ISP selection and evaluation. Expert. Syst. Appl. **36**, 8639–8648 (2011)

Apte, A.U., Rendon, R.G., Salmeron, J.: An optimization approach to strategic sourcing: a case study of the United States air force. J. Purch. Supply. Manage. **17**, 222–230 (2011)

Beil, D.: encyclopedia of operations research and management science. http://www-personal.umich.edu/~dbeil/ (Invited Articles and Chapters) (2010). Accessed 1 Nov 2013

Bernhardt, D.C.: I want it fast, factual, actionable-tailoring competitive intelligence to executives needs. Long. Range. Plann. **27**, 12–24 (1994)

Bilsel, R.U., Buyukozkan, G., Ruan, D.: A fuzzy preference-ranking model for a quality evaluation of hospital web sites. Int. J. Intell. Syst. **21**, 1181–1197 (2006)

Blenkhorn, D.L., Fleischer, S.F.: Competitive Intelligence and Global Business. Greenwood Publishing Group, USA (2005)

Bottani, E., Rizzi, A.: An adapted multi-criteria approach to suppliers and product selection-An application oriented to lead-time reduction. Int. J. Prod. Econ. **111**, 763–781 (2008)

Buyukozkan, G., Cifci, G.: A novel fuzzy multi-criteria decision framework for sustainable supplier selection with incomplete information. Comput. Ind. **62**, 164–174 (2011)

Cancro, J., Mc Ginnis, M.: Financial accounting basics for purchasing and supply professionals. 88th annual international supply management conference. (2003)

Cancro, J., Mc Ginnis, M.: Evaluating the financial condition of suppliers. 89th annual international supply management conference. (2004)

Chan, F., Kumar, N.: Global supplier development considering risk factors using fuzzy extended AHP-based approach. Omega. **35**, 417–431 (2007)

Chang, D.Y.: Extent analysis and synthetic decision, optimization techniques and applications. World. Scientific. **1**, 352 (1992)

Chang, D.Y.: Application of the extent analysis method on fuzzy AHP. Eur. J. Oper. Res. **95**, 649–655 (1996)

Cheragi, S.H., Dadashzadeh, M., Subramanian, M.: Critical success factors for supplier selection: an update. J. App. Bus. Res. **20**(2), 91–108 (2004)

Choi, J.W.: A study of the role of public procurement—Can public procurement make society better?. Paper presented at the 4th international public procurement conference in south korea. http://www.ippa.org/IPPC4/.Proceedings/13ProcurementPreferences/Paper13.4.pdf (2010). Accessed 13 Oct 2013

De Boer, L., Lambro, E., Morlacchi, P.: A review of methods supporting supplier selection. Eur. J. Purch. Supply. Manage. **7**, 75–89 (2001)

Defense Acquisition University: Defense acquisition guidebook. http://www.dau.mil. (2010). Accessed 10 Oct 2013

Degraeve, Z., Lambro, E., RoodHoft, F.: An evaluation of vendor selection models from a total cost of ownership perspective. Eur. J. Oper. Res. **125**, 34–58 (2000)

DeGroot, M.H., Schervish, M.J.: Probability and Statistics, 4th edn. Pearson Education, Inc., New York (2012)

Ding, L.: Analysis on the Competitive Intelligence in Business Management. Second International Symposium on Information Science and Engineering (ISISE) (2009)

European Committee: European directive 81 for defence procurement. http://ec.europa.eu/internal_market/publicprocurement/rules/defence_(2009) Accessed 5 Oct 2013

European Anti Fraud Office: Identifying and reducing corruption in public procurement in the EU. A research study conducted by PwC EU Services and Ecorys. http://ec.europa.eu/anti_fraud/documents/anti-fraud-policy/research-and-studies (2013). Accessed 29 Oct 13

Greek MoD: Greek Intelligence Doctrine-GID. Hellenic Army General Staff publications. http://www.army.gr (2005). Accessed 1 Oct 13

Greek, Law 3871/10: http://www.et.gr (2010). Accessed 13 Oct 2013
Greek, Law 3978/11: http://www.et.gr (2011). Accessed 13 Oct 2013
Greek.MoD: Public.Greek.DocumentPGD.F.812/91/135598/S.2361. http://et.diavgeia.gov.gr/f/ypetha.with.search.criterion:ADA:B45N6-P0T (2012). Accessed 13 Sept 2013
GreekMinFin: Public.Greek.Document-PGD.2/58986/DPDSM. http://et.diavgeia.gov.gr with search criterion:ADA: BL4CH-TCZ. (2013). Accessed 13 Sept 2013
Ho, W., Xiaowei, X., Prasanta, D.: Multi-criteria decision making approaches for supplier evaluation and selection: a literature review. Eur. J. Oper. Res. **202**, 16–24 (2010)
Hopple, G.W.: Intelligence and Warning Lessons. In: Military Lessons of the Falkland Islands War by BW Watson and PM Dunn. Arms and Armour, London (1984)
Hsu, C., kannan, V.R., Leong, G. K., et al.: Supplier selection construct: instrument development and validation. Int. J. logist. Manage. **17**(2), 213–239 (2006)
Jiang, L., Barone, D., Amyot, D., et al.: Strategic models for business intelligence. In: Jeusfeld, M., Delcambre, L., Ling, T.W. (eds.): ER 2011, LNCS 6998, pp. 429–439. Springer, Heidelberg (2011)
Johnson, R., Wichern, D.: Applied Multivariate Statistical Analysis. Pearson Prentice Hall, New Jersey (2007)
Joint Logistics Commanders-JLC/Department of the US Navy: ACSIMH-Aviation Critical Safety Item Management Handbook. Patuxent River, USA (2005)
Inman, M.: Z-scores and recent events: do they shed any light? Manage. Account., CIMA, **69**, 44–48 (1991)
Kahaner, L.: Competitive Intelligence: How to Gather, Analyze, and Use Information to Move Your Business to the Top. Simon & Schuster, New York (1996)
Kahraman, C., Cebeci, U., Ulukan, Z.: Multi criteria supplier selection using fuzzy AHP. Logist. Inf. Manage. (2003). doi:10.1108/09576050310503367
Kannan, V.R., Tan, K.C.: Supplier selection and assessment: their impact on business performance. J. Supply. Chain. Manage. **38**, 11–22 (2002)
Karlis, D.: Multivariate Statistical Analysis. Stamoulis, Athens (2005)
Kelman, S.: Procurement and Public management: The Fear of Discretion and the Quality of Government Performance. The AEI, Washington (1990)
Kioxos, P.: Statistics. Interbook, Athens (1993)
Korhonen, P.J.: Subjective principal component analysis. Comput. Stat. Data. Anal. **2**, 243–255 (1984)
Koutrouvelis, J.: Probabilities and Statistics I. Hellenic Open University press, Patras (2000)
Koutrouvelis J.: Probabilities and Statistics II. Hellenic Open University press, Patras (2000)
Krzanowski, W.J.: Principles of Multivariate Analysis: A user's perspective. Oxford University Press, UK (1988)
Laios, L.: Supply Management. Humantec, Piraeus (2010)
Lam, K.C., Tao, R., Lam, M.C.K.: A material supplier selection model for property developers using fuzzy principal component analysis. Autom. Construction **19**, 608–618 (2010)
Lee, C.K.M., Lau, H.C.W., Ho, G.T.S., et al.: Design and development of agent-based procurement system to enhance business intelligence. Expert Syst. Appl. **36**, 877–884 (2009)
Liu, F., Hai, H.L.: The voting analytic hierarchy process method for selecting supplier. Int. J. Prod. Econ. **97**, 308–317 (2005)
Lysons, K., Farrinton, B.: Purchasing and Supply Chain Management, 7th edn. Pearson Education Limited, Essex (2006)
Matsunaga, M.: How to factor-analyze your data right. Do's, don'ts, and how-To's. Int. J. Psycol. Res. **3**, 97–110 (2010)
Miller, G.A.: The magical number seven plus or minus two: some limitations on our capacity for processing information. Psychol. Rev. **63**, 81–97 (1956)
Miller, S.H.: Competitive Intelligence-an overview. Competitive Intelligence magazine. http://www.ventesmarketing.com/References/Intelligence%20concurrentielle/Articles/CI%20Overview.pdf (2001). Accessed 29 Oct 2013
NATO Support Agency: FD 251-01-NAMSA Procurement Regulations Functional Directive 251-01 Amendment 6. Capellen G.D. of Luxembourg (2012)

Negash, S.: Business Intelligence. Communications of the Association for Information Systems 13 Article 15 (2004)
Omurca, S.I.: An intelligent supplier evaluation, selection and development system. Appl. Soft. Comput. **13**, 690–697 (2013)
Porfirio, J.A., Correia, S.: Business Intelligence as a service-strategic tool for competitiveness. In: Cruz-Cunha, M.M., et al. (eds.): CENTERIS 2011, Part I, CCIS 219, pp. 106–117. Springer, Heidelberg (2011)
Porteous, S.D.: Economic espionage: Issues arising from increased government involvement with the private sector. Intell. Natl. Secur. **9**(4), 735–752 (1994). dOI:10.1080/02684529408432279
Rouach, D., Santi, P.: Competitive intelligence adds value: five intelligence attitudes. Eur. Manage. J. **19**, 552–559 (2001)
Saaty, T.L.: The Analytic Hierarchy Process. McGraw-Hill, New York (1980)
Sen, C.G., Selcuk, Sen., Basligil, H.: Pre selection of suppliers through an integrated fuzzy analytic hierarchy process and max-min methodology. Int. J. Prod. Res. **48**, 1603–1625 (2010)
Shen, L., Olfat, L., Govindan, K., et al.: A fuzzy multi criteria approach for evaluating green supplier's performance in green supply chain with linguistic preferences. Resour. Conserv. Recycl. **74**, 170–179 (2013)
Strategic and competitive intelligence professional website. http://www.scip.org/Publications/CIMArticleDetail.cfm?ItemNumber=681. Accessed on 21 Oct 2013.
Tang, Y.U., Beynon, M.J.: Application and development of a fuzzy analytic hierarchy process within a capital investment study. J. Econ. Manage. **1**, 207–230. (2005)
Thai, K.V. Symposium introduction. J. Public. Manage. **4**, 312–318 (2004)
Theodorou, J.: Introduction in Fuzzy Logic. Tziolas, Athens (2012)
UK Transparency International: UK 2010 Bribery Act Adequate Procedures. http://www.transparency.org.uk/our-work/bribery-act/adequate-procedures. (2010) Accessed 20 Oct 2013
UK MoD Development Concepts and Doctrine Centre-DCDC: Logistics for Joint Operations. Joint Doctrine Publication 4/00, 3rd Edn. (2007)
UK MoD JSP 886: The management of equipment procured under urgent operational requirement arrangements. Vol. 3 Part 10 (2010)
USA Government Accountability Office-GAO: Best Practices-DoD can Help Suppliers Contribute More to Weapon System Programs. GAO/NSIAD-98–87, Washington (1998)
USA DoD: Doctrine for logistic support of joint operations. Jt. Publ. 4–00 (2000)
USA DoD: DoD 4140.1-R-Supply Chain Materiel Management Regulation. Washington (2003)
US army training and doctrine command, combat studies institute of US army command and general staff college: The Proceedings of the Combat Studies Institute. Military History Symposium. http://usacac.army.mil/cac2/cgsc/carl/download/csipubs/Symposium.pdf (2006)
USA Federal Procurement Report FPR: https://www.fpds.gov/downloads/FPR_Reports/Fiscal%20Year%202007/Total%20Federal%20View.pdf (2007). Accessed 10 Oct 2013.
USA Government Accountability Office-GAO: DoD Needs to take Additional Actions to Address Challenges in Supply Chain Management. GAO-11-569, Washington (2011)
Ware, N., Singh, Banwet, D.K.: Supplier selection problem: a state-of-the-art review. Manage. Sci. Lett. **2**, 1465–1490 (2012)
Weber, C.A., Current, J., Benton, W.C.: Vendor selection criteria and methods. Eur. J. Oper. Res. **50**(1), 2–18 (1991)
West, C.: Competitive Intelligence. Palgrave Macmillan, Basingstoke (2001)
Xia, W., Wu, Z.: Supplier selection with multiple criteria in volume discount environments. Omega. **35**, 494–504 (2007)
Zadeh, L.A.: Fuzz sets. Inf. Control. 8, 338–353 (1965)
Zanakis, S.H., Solomon, A., Wishart, N., et al.: Multi-attribute decision making: a simulation comparison of selected methods. Eur. J. Oper. Res. **107**, 507–529 (1998)
Zhu, K.J., Jing, Y., Chang, D.Y.: A discussion on extent analysis method and applications of fuzzy AHP. Eur. J. Oper. Res. **116**, 450–456 (1999)
Zwick, W.R., Velicer, W.F.: Comparison of five rules for determining the number of components to retain. Psychol. Bull. **99**, 432–442 (1986)

Chapter 3
The Proposal of Demand Estimation of Repairable Items for the Weapon Systems During the Initial Provisioning Period: F-16 Case Study

Bahtiyar Eren and Serpil Erol

Abbrevations

A/C	Aircraft
APPL PCT	Application Percentage
DDR	Daily Demand Rate
DOTMPLF	Doctrine, Organization, Training, Material, Personnel, Leadership and Facilities
EF	Expected Failures
FPS	Failures per sortie
IBA	Item Based Approach
METRIC	Multi-Echelon Technique for Recoverable Item Control
NRTS	Not Repairable at This Station
NSG	NATO Supply Group
NSN	NATO Stock Number
OIM ANN DEM	OIM Annual Demand
OIM	Organizational or Intermediate Maintenance
PFP	Program Forecast Period
QPEI	Quantity Per End Item
RDS	Requirement Distribution System
RTS	Repairable at This Station
TOIMDR	Total Organizational or Intermediate Maintenance Demand Rate
TURAF	Turkish Air Force
USAF	United States of Air Force

B. Eren (✉)
Hv.K.K.ligi Karargahi Harekat Baskanligi, 06100 Bakanliklar-Ankara, Turkey
e-mail: erenbahtiyar@yahoo.com

S. Erol
Gazi Universitesi Endustri Muhendisligi Bolumu, Ankara, Turkey
e-mail: serpiler@gazi.edu.tr

V. Zeimpekis et al. (eds.), *Military Logistics,* Operations Research/Computer Science Interfaces Series 56, DOI 10.1007/978-3-319-12075-1_3

3.1 Problem Statement

Nowadays the uncertainties in security environment and changes based on those uncertainties compel the armed forces to be operational ready for all time. For being 'an operational ready' force, a lot of activities such as keeping the weapon systems operational, training the personnel, making military exercises, inspecting and evaluating the military units and headquarters are carried out in a systematic approach at the same time. As a result of these activities, several needs are determined in the DOTMPLF[1] areas such as acquisition of new weapon systems, updates in training programs, new personnel skills, changes to the current doctrines and regulations, reorganization of current processes and organization structures. We focus on determining the material (acquisition and procurement) needs of DOTMLPF in this study while keeping the other elements of DOTMLPF out of scope. Operational needs are basically fulfilled in three ways (MIL-HDBK 502 1997) as given below by:

- Changing the current DOTMLPLF aspects without acquisition of any weapons systems,
- Using the current weapon systems in different tactics, techniques and procedures, or by modernizing (upgrading) the current weapon systems,
- Acquiring the new weapon system.

It is understood that the weapon system is at hand in the first two ways but not in the third way. Logistics approach has been determined based on whether the weapon system is at hand or not. Consumer logistics is in question if the weapon system is at hand, otherwise acquisition logistics (NATO Logistics Handbook 2007). The term 'Follow-on support' is used for the consumer logistics needs while the term 'initial provisioning' is used for the acquisition logistics needs. The duration and the number of suppliers are different in these logistics approaches. The time scope for the initial provisioning is limited to the 1–3 years and there is only one main supplier which is generally main contractor of weapon system while the time scope for the follow-on support is limited to the life cycle of weapon system which is usually more than 20 years and there are many suppliers including main contractor and its sub-contractors.

3.2 Literature Review

There are two international standards regarding to the material management in either military or civilian environment: ATA SPEC2000 (2002) and AECMA SPEC2000 (2000) which is extension of ATA SPEC2000 customized for material managing of military equipment and systems. In addition to these, USA Department of Defense

[1] The term 'DOTMPLF', used in force planning procedures in NATO, stands for Doctrine, Organization, Training, Material, Personnel, Leadership and Facilities.

recommends using the MIL STD-1388 1A (1983) and MIL STD-1388 2B (1991) for managing the life-cycle requirements (including material aspect) of new military and equipment systems in order to keep the logistics support data records in discipline. These standards include what data elements are needed for calculating an initial provisioning in detail, but not include an initial provisioning algorithm. The literature reviews of Gümüs and Güneri (2007) which examine 62 papers, Wong et al. (2006) which examine 26 papers, and Paterson et al. (2011) which examine 118 papers are studied. Out of 206 papers that are examined by Gümüs, Wong and Paterson, stock problems are supposedly taken from the follow-on support phase due to the fact that it is not witnessed any comment whether the initial provisioning phase is included or not. During the literature review, Fortuin's study (1984) is only paper whose title includes both "initial provisioning" and "repairable items". Fortuin mentions that there are not many studies in his paper such that he referenced only five papers. Fortuin forecasts the failure rate[2] of the repairable items of home appliances such as TV, refrigerator and washing machine and determines the required quantity of repairable items to buy to meet the failures in the future. Guide and Srivastava (1997) group the almost 70 papers related to the inventory problems that deal with only repairable items as regards to the three aspects: solution techniques (exact, approximate and simulation), echelon levels (single and multi), and inventory models (deterministic and stochastic). They note that Sherbrooke's METRIC (Multi-Echelon Technique for Recoverable Item Control) model (1968) and Muchkstadt's MOD-METRIC model (1973) can be used for both initial provisioning and follow-on support phase in the US Air Forces (USAF). Anderson (2009) categorize the inventory models related to repairable items into the four groups: (1) independent or dependent demand, (2) stationary or dynamic demand, (3) single or multi-echelon inventory systems, and (4) single or multi-commodity. Based on Daniel and Anderson papers, we can conclude that USAF is able to use system-based models such as METRIC, Vari-METRIC (Sherbrooke 1986) which is advanced extension of METRIC, Dynamic METRIC (Hillstad 1982), Aircraft Sustainability Model (ASM) (Slay et al. 1996) for repairable items. US Air Force Material Command Instruction (AFMCI) 23–106 Initial Requirement Determination (1997) presents the material-based algorithm called Total Organizational or Intermediate Maintenance Demand Rate (TOIMDR) for the initial provisioning of military equipment and systems. It is concluded that USAF can use either system-based model such as Vari-METRIC, ASM or material based model like TOIMDR for the demand estimation during the initial provisioning. Turkey, on the other hand, has used material based algorithm called Requirement Distribution System (RDS) for almost 25 years in calculating the initial provisioning and follow-on support. Since RDS runs a material based algorithm, it is decided to compare RDS with TOIMDR algorithm in this study.

[2] Failure rate is the frequency with which weapon system or components fail per unit time.

Table 3.1 The information about the acquisition of the weapon systems used in Turkey

A/C type	Manufacturer/ country	Production year	Turkey's acquisition year	Number of user countries	Country/recent acquisition year
F-16	Lockheed Martin/USA[a]	1979[3]	1987[b]	25[3]	Egypt, 2010[c]
KC-135R	Boeing/USA[d]	1957[4]	1994[4]	5[4]	Chile, 2010[4]
COUGAR	Eurocopter/ France, TAI/ Turkey[e]	1977[5]	1997[f]	39[5]	Bulgaria, 2010[g]
CN-235	EADS CASA/ Spain, IPTN/ Indonesia[h]	1988[8]	1991[i]	30[8]	Mexico, 2010[j]
SF-260D	Aermacchi/Italy[k]	1964[11]	1992[11]	25[11]	Italy, 2007[l]

[a] Lockheed Martin. 01 Mart 2012. <http://www.f-16.net/timeline_1979.html/>
[b] F-16. 01 Mart 2012. <http://www.f-16.net/f-16_users_article21.html/>
[c] F-16. 01 Mart 2012. <http://www.lockheedmartin.com/us/news/press-releases/2010/march/LockheedMartinReceives213.html/>
[d] KC-135R Stratotanker. 01 Mart 2012. <http://en.wikipedia.org/wiki/Boeing_KC-135_Stratotanker/>
[e] Eurocopter Cougar. 01 Mart 2012. <http://en.wikipedia.org/wiki/Eurocopter_Cougar/>
[f] Europter Cougar. 01 Mart 2012. <http://www.tai.com.tr/prog.aspx?contentDefID=29/>
[g] Bulgaristan Hava Kuvvetleri. 01 Mart 2012. <http://en.wikipedia.org/wiki/Bulgarian_Air_Force/>
[h] CN-235. 01 Mart 2012. <http://en.wikipedia.org/wiki/CASA_CN-235/>
[i] CN-235. 01 Mart 2012. <http://www.tai.com.tr/arama.aspx?keyword=casa cn235/>
[j] CN-235. 01 Mart 2012. <http://www.janes.com/news/defence/jni/jni081203_1_n.shtml/>
[k] SF-260D. 01 Mart 2012 <http://www.siai-marchetti.nl/sf260mil.html/>
[l] SF-260D. 01 Mart 2012 <http://www.janes.com/articles/Janes-All-the-Worlds-Aircraft/Aermacchi-SF-260-Italy.html/>

3.3 Scope and Limitations

As shown in Table 3.1, the same type of aircraft can be in either acquisition or consumer logistics for different user countries. Table 3.1 presents a variety of classes of aircraft (A/C) such as fighter, air refuelling, helicopter, transportation and training that Turkey and other user countries have. The acquisition costs of weapon systems that Turkey has are in Table 3.2. It is generally assumed that the cost of spare parts is almost 15 % of acquisition cost (JSF COPT 2000).

Due to the fact that Turkey is considering adding new weapons systems into her inventory, the paper is focused only on the determining the right quantity of initial provisioning of new weapon systems.

The limitation of this study can be summarized as follows: (1) In order to calculate demand quantities based on flight hours, sortie number of usage data, the weapon system should be in use or available at the time of computing. (2) If the weapon system is not available, or not in the countries inventory, demand quantities associated with the flight hours, sortie number and usage data should be obtained

Table 3.2 Initial acquisition cost and estimated initial provisioning cost

Project name	Country	Approach	Cost (Million US $)	Estimated spare cost (Million US $)
24 x F-16[a]	Egypt	New acquisition	3200	160
8 x CN-235[b]	France	New acquisition	305	15.25
27 x Cougar[c]	France	New acquisition	314	15.7
18 x SF-260D[d]	Philippines	New acquisition	13.8	0.65
F-16 modernization[e]	Pakistan	Modernization	226	11.3

[a] F-16. 01 Mart 2012. <http://www.defensenews.com/story.php?i=4437627&c=AIR&s=TOP>
[b] C N-235. 01 Mart 2012. <http://www.defensenews.com/story.php?i=4564377&c=AIR&s=TOP>
[c] Cougar. 01 Mart 2012. <http://www.defensenews.com/story.php?i=4430245&c=AIR&s=TOP>
[d] SF-260D. 01 Mart 2012. <http://www.defensenews.com/story.php?i=3524221>
[e] F-16. 01 Mart 2012. <http://www.janes.com/news/defence/jdw/jdw080729_1_n.shtml>

Table 3.3 The importance of repairable items in spare parts

Material type	Usage quantity (%)	Demand quantity percentage (%)	Procurement percentage (%)
Consumables	73	96	7
Repairable	27	4	93

from the user countries. (3) The data taken from user countries should be used cautiously due to the fact that it may not reflect the real condition. (4) The engineering data can be used if the weapon system in the development phase to get a rough idea on the demand quantities while keeping the fact in mind that engineering data generally does not match with the real condition.

3.3.1 The Importance of Repairable Items

Any weapon system is generally composed of repairable and consumables. If any failed item can be repaired, it is called repairable, otherwise called consumables (Muckstadt 2005). In order to understand the importance of repairable items in any weapon system, we take an example of F-16 as a case study. F-16 has almost 21,000 items whose usage and demand quantities and procurement percentages over total cost is given in Table 3.3.

It is clear that 73 % of items and 96 % of demand is all about consumables in Table 3.3. But only 7 % of budget allocated to the procurement of initial provisioning is for consumables, remaining of budget is for repairable. That's the reason why the repairable items called "slow moving with low demand but expensive items" (Sherbrooke 2004). As stated before, this paper is only focused on the repairable items that constitute 93 % of total procurement budget.

3.4 The Aim and Contribution of the Study

The main aim of this chapter is developing an algorithm that forecasts the yearly demand of repairable items better than RDS and TOIMDR for the initial provisioning period by using a new approach.

The contribution of the new approach can be stated in a short as follows: (1) Analyze the data set based on NATO Federal Supply Group as explained in Sect. 8 below, and try to compute the best scenario for each group instead of analyzing all data all at once as it is done in the literature and compute one scenario for all in calculating the demand quantities. (2) Use new parameters such as sortie numbers in addition to the flight hours and usage quantities. (3) In contrast to the previous comparisons made in the literature by just evaluating the mean absolute error values, The Friedman Test is run to determine whether there is a significant difference among scenarios at the confidence level of 95 %. If there is a difference, and Wilcoxon Sign Test is run by pairwise comparison to determine the scenarios that make the difference.

3.5 Algorithms Used in Turkey and USAF

3.5.1 RDS Algorithm

RDS algorithm is used for determining the annual demand for repairable items in Turkey. RDS calculates the annual demand on a daily basis at most taking care of last 3 years[3] (RDS 1997). Daily Demand Rate (DDR) given in Eq. 3.1 below calculates the annual demand.

$$\text{DDR} = \text{Usage (RTS + NRTS)/Days in System} \tag{3.1}$$

Usage	Is the number of total failures
RTS	Acronym of "Repairable At This Station". It is used for the failures repaired in the unit where the system is stationed
NRTS	Acronym of "Not Repairable At This Station". It is used for failures that need to be evacuated to a depot repair facility
Days in system	It can be any number of quarters between 2 and 12. It is generally assumed that it is equivalent to 12 quarters (1092 days)

The RDS algorithm for annual demand has two steps.

Step 1. Calculate DDR: Count the total failures during the last 3 years for the particular repairable item and divide it into the days in system.

[3] 1 year = 4 quarters, 1 quarter = 3 months = 91 days.

Step 2. Calculate EF: Expected Failures (EF) given in Eq. 3.2 below calculates the number of expected failures during the planning horizon in days.

$$\text{EF} = \text{DDR} \times \text{Planning horizon in days} \tag{3.2}$$

Planning horizon in days It can be any number of quarters in days between 4 and 40. It is generally assumed as 40 quarters

3.5.2 TOIMDR Algorithm

TOIMDR algorithm is used for determining the annual demand for repairable items in USAF during the initial provisioning. It takes care of the failure data based on flying hours as far as possible. The TOIMDR algorithm for annual demand has four steps.

Step 1. Calculate TOIMDR[4]: It is called maintenance factor that gives the projected number of failures per one hundred flying hours, or per unit installed in the end item population. It will be calculated for every repairable item.

Step 2. Determine the number of PFP: It is equivalent to the planning horizon in quarter terms. It can be a minimum of 4 quarters and above. There is no upper limit as in RDS.

Step 3. Determine OIM PROG at PFP[5]: It is equivalent to the expected flying hours per A/C in which the particular repairable item is applied during the PFP. The decision maker makes an assumption about the average flying hour per month per A/C.

$$\text{OIM PROG at PFP} = \text{Step 2 in months} \times \text{Flying Hour Per Month Per A/C} \times \#\text{of A/C} \tag{3.3}$$

Step 4. Determine OIM ANN DEM[6]: It is equivalent to the projected number of failures during the PFP.[7, 8]

$$\text{OIM ANN DEM} = \text{TOIMDR} \times \text{APPL PCT} \times \text{QPEI} \times (\text{OIM PROG at PFP}) \tag{3.4}$$

[4] TOIMDR algorithm, unlike the RDS does, takes the history date as back as possible. The maintenance factor data is calculated based on 8 year at most in this study.

[5] OIM PROG at PFP: Abbreviation of "Organizational or Intermediate Maintenance Program at Program Forecast Period". It shows the number of flying hours expected per month per A/C during the planning horizon. It is quarterly basis as in RDS.

[6] OIM ANN DEM: Abbreviation of "Organizational or Intermediate Maintenance Annual Demand".

[7] APPL PCT: Abbreviation of "Application Percent". It show the percentage of the particular item apply to the fleet of weapon systems.

[8] QPEI: Acronym of "Quantity Per End Item".

Table 3.4 Examples of naming scenarios

Scenario name	Scenario's explanation
RDS (1)	RDS algorithm takes the last year of usage data as an input
TOIMDR (5)	TOIMDR algorithm takes the last 5 years of flight hour data as an input
SORTIE (3)	SORTIE algorithm takes the last 3 years of SORTIE s flown data as an input

3.5.3 Developed SORTIE[9] Algorithm

Taking into consideration the RDS and TOIMDR algorithm approaches together, a new algorithm is developed in this paper, which is called SORTIE algorithm. It calculates the annual demand for repairable items based on past SORTIE data.

The SORTIE algorithm for annual demand has four steps.

Step 1. Calculate FPS[10]: The projected number of failures per sortie will be calculated as given in Eq. 3.5 below. It will be calculated for every repairable item.

$$\text{FPS} = \text{Total \# of failures} / \text{Total sorties flown in which the repairable item is applied.} \tag{3.5}$$

Step 2. Determine the number of PFP: As explained in the step 2 of TOIMDR algorithm.

Step 3. Determine OIM PROG at PFP: It is very similar to the step 3 of TOIMDR algorithm but requires replacing the flying hour data with sortie data in Eq. 3.3

Step 4. Determine OIM ANN DEM: It is equivalent to the projected number of failures during the PFP. It is almost the same as explained in the step 4 of TOIMDR algorithm except TOIMDR term.

$$\text{OIM ANN DEM} = \text{FPS} \times \text{APPL PCT} \times \text{QPEI} \times (\text{OIM PROG at PFP}) \tag{3.6}$$

3.6 Generating Scenarios from Algorithms

Taking into consideration the flight hour, usage and sortie parameters, 24 scenarios (8 for each parameter) have been created by using real data set of F-16 with a quantity of 894 repairable items. Each scenario is named according to the usage of past data in years as shown in Table 3.4.

The data set which covers 11 years from 1999 to 2010 (44 quarters) is divided into two: the first 8 years data is used for running the scenarios, and the last 3

[9] SORTIE is the one cycle of take-off and landing of an A/C. It can be short such as 10–30 min, or long such as 2 h or even much more. Sortie duration can changes according to the several constraints such as mission type, capacity of A/C etc.

[10] FPS: Acronym of "Failures per sortie".

Table 3.5 An example of data set

			Usage data					Disposal data		
NSN	Acquisition cost (TL)[a]	Repair Cost (TL)	1999/4[b]	2000/1[c]	2000/2[d]	…	2010/3[e]	1999/4	…	2010/3
NSN-1	51	9.3	7	6	4	…	0	2	…	0
NSN-2	75	11	0	0	0	…	0	0	…	0
…	…	…	…	…	…	…	…	…	…	…
NSN-894	39	55	0	0	0	…	0	0	…	0

[a] The acquisition and repair cost in Turkish Liras (TL). 1 US $ is equivalent to approximately 2 TL

[b] 1999/4 corresponds to the 4th quarter of the year 1999. It spans the days between 1st of October and 31st of December

[c] 2000/1 corresponds to the 1st quarter of the year 2000. It spans the days between 1st of January and 31st of March

[d] 2000/2 corresponds to the 2nd quarter of the year 2000. It spans the days between 1st of April and 30th of June

[e] 2000/3 corresponds to the 3rd quarter of the year 2000. It spans the days between 1st of July and 30th of September

years data is used for comparing the results of scenarios with the actual values. While evaluating the demand prediction techniques, there are three widely used parameters such as average absolute error, mean-squared error and percentage error (Sherbrooke 2004). The first two evaluation parameters are used in assessing the performance of scenarios.

3.7 Data Set and Methodology

The real F-16 data set as shown in the Table 3.5 below, includes usage and disposal quantities per quarter for 10 years. In addition to table, the total of flight hours and the number or sortie per quarter are used for computing. NATO Stock Number (NSN) is composed of 13 numeric digits whose first two digits determine NATO Supply Group (NSG). Each NSG is formed by items of supply of the same physical or performance characteristics or utilization in the same application (NSN web). The same data set is analyzed in four different ways.

- Approach-I takes the all data set and try to determine the best scenario for all.
- Approach-II takes the data set according to the NSG and determines the best scenario for each NSG.
- Approach III uses the result of previous approach and forecasts the projected failures by using the best scenario for each NSG.
- Approach-IV takes the each item in the list and determines the best scenario for each item.

Table 3.6 Friedman test results

Forecast period	*N*	X^2	Degrees of freedom	*p*-value
1-year forecast (2007/4–2008/3)	894	35.1	23	0.050*
2-year forecast (2007/4–2009/3)	894	164.8	23	0.000*
3-year forecast (2007/4–2010/3)	894	266.9	23	0.000*

* p-value=0.05

Each scenario is run under the four approaches and results are recorded. The Friedman Test[11] is run to determine whether there is significant difference among scenarios at the confidence level of 95 %. In other words, null hypothesis is that all scenarios come from the same population. The alternative hypothesis is that there is at least one scenario comes from different population. If there is enough evidence to reject the null hypothesis, it means that there is at least one scenario comes from different population. In order determine which scenario or scenarios make that difference, Wilcoxon Sign Test[12] is applied. The null hypothesis in Wilcoxon Sign Test is that pairwise scenarios come from the same population. The alternative hypothesis is that the scenarios come from different population.

The motivation of using Friedman and Wilcoxon Sign Test is to determine the effectiveness of results statistically rather than just comparing the magnitude of results. As seen from results, the lesser mean absolute deviation may not guarantee statistically different results.

3.8 Application

3.8.1 Approach-I: (Classic Approach)

Approach-I takes the all the data set and tries to determine the best scenario for all. In order to test whether there is a difference among 24 scenarios within each forecast period in projecting the number of failures, the Friedman test is conducted. Based on the test result shown in Table 3.6 below, it is concluded that there is a significant

[11] The Friedman test is the nonparametric equivalent of a one-sample repeated measures design or a two-way analysis of variance with one observation per cell. Friedman tests the null hypothesis that k related variables come from the same population. For each case, the k variables are ranked from 1 to k. The test statistic is based on these ranks (IBM-SPSS Statistics Base 17.0 User Guide)

[12] The Wilcoxon signed-rank test is a nonparametric statistical hypothesis test used when comparing two related samples, matched samples, or repeated measurements on a single sample to assess whether their population mean ranks differ (i.e. it is a paired difference test). It can be used as an alternative to the paired Student's t-test, t-test for matched pairs, or the t-test for dependent samples when the population cannot be assumed to be normally distributed. (http://en.wikipedia.org/wiki/Wilcoxon_signed-rank_test)

Table 3.7 Comparison of algorithms' results-1

Forecast period	RDS (3)	TOIMDR (8)	RDS (1)
1-year forecast (2007/4–2008/3)	4.21	4.6	3.9
2-year forecast (2007/4–2009/3)	8.06	8.98	7.45
3-year forecast (2007/4–2010/3)	12.05	12.95	11.61

difference among the scenarios within each forecast period in projecting the number of failures at the $\alpha = 5\%$ such that for 1-year forecast period; (Friedman Test: χ^2 (23) = 35.1, $p = 0.050$), for 2-year forecast period; (Friedman Test: χ^2 (23) = 164.8 and $p = 0.000$), and for 3-year forecast period; (Friedman Test: χ^2 (23) = 266.9 and $p = 0.000$).

The mean and variances of scenarios along with the results of Friedman Test are presented in Appendix-I. As seen in Appendix-I, Scenario RDS (1) came out to be the best scenario in considering the forecast period of 1, 2 or 3-year. Scenario RDS (1) is compared with the Scenario RDS (3) and TOIMDR (8) in terms of mean and presented in Table 3.7 below.

To determine which scenarios are statistically different in projecting the number of failures at the $\alpha = 5\%$, Wilcoxon Sign Test is run and significantly different ones are listed in Appendix-II. The first comparison in Appendix-II is given as example. Scenario SORTIE (7) is significantly different from Scenario TOIMDR (7) in projecting the number of failures at the $\alpha = 5\%$, (z-value: −3.59, positive rank, and *p*-value: 0.000). The other results can be interpreted likewise.

3.8.2 Approach-II: (New Approach-I/NSG Based Approach)

Approach-II takes the data based on NSG and determines the best scenario for each NSG. The research question in this approach is the following: "Is Scenario RDS (1) the best in projecting the number of failures for all NSGs at the $\alpha = 5\%$?" So, the data set of 894 is divided into the 16 NSGs and Friedman test for each NSG are run in order to test whether there is a difference among 24 scenarios within each forecast period in projecting the number of failures. The best four or five scenarios at most are determined based on mean, standard deviation, χ^2 and p-value at the $\alpha = 5\%$. The scenarios that are recommended for projecting the failures are listed in Appendix-III. In answering the research question for 1-year forecast period, Scenario RDS (8) for NSG-10 and scenario SORTIE (1) for NSG-15 are the only ones that are significantly different from the RDS (1) in projecting the failures at the $\alpha = 5\%$ (Freidman Test: χ^2 (23) = 49.80, $p = 0.001$ and χ^2 (23) = 70.54, $p = 0.000$, respectively). Scenario RDS (1) seems to be the best for the other NSGs for 1-year forecast period. The other results can be interpreted likewise.

Table 3.8 Comparison of algorithms' results-2

Forecast period	RDS (3)	TOIMDR (8)	RDS (1)	New Aproach-I
1-year forecast (2007/4–2008/3)	4.21	4.60	3.90	3.85
2-year forecast (2007/4–2009/3)	8.06	8.98	7.45	7.39
3-year forecast (2007/4–2010/3)	12.05	12.95	11.61	11.47

The Wilcoxon Sign Test is conducted for those scenarios that are determined as a significantly different during the Friedman Test and the results of Wilcoxon Sign Test are listed in Appendix-IV. Based on test results, the one that is significantly different from the other one is marked with "**" in Appendix-IV. The NSG-10 data is given as an example for the 1-year forecast period in Appendix-IV. Recall that five scenarios are recommended in Appendix-III such as RDS (8), RDS (7), SORTIE (8), RDS (5) and RDS (6). As shown in Appendix-IV, the pairwise comparisons between RDS (1) and RDS (8) [Wilcoxon Test: Z-value:-2.386, positive rank and *p*-value: 0.017], RDS (1) and RDS (6) [Wilcoxon Test: Z-value:-2.232, negative rank and *p*-value: 0.026] and RDS (6) and RDS (8) [Wilcoxon Test: Z-value:-2.043, negative rank and *p*-value: 0.041] are significantly different in projecting the number of failures at the $\alpha = 5\,\%$ for 1-year forecast period. The other pairwise comparisons in NSG-10 are not resulted in significantly different. The other results can be interpreted likewise.

3.8.3 Approach-III: (Extension of Approach-II, NSG Based Approach)

Approach III uses the result of previous approach by taking the best scenarios for each NSG and forecasts the projected failures. This approach requires the using the RDS (8) for NSG-10, SORTIE (1) for NSG-15 and RDS (5) for NSG-49 and RDS (1) for the rest as indicated in Appendix-III at the 1-year forecast period. It can be interpreted likewise for 2 and 3-year forecast period. As seen in Table 3.8 below, the progress is almost 1 % when compared to the scenario RDS (1) based on average absolute error.

3.8.4 Approach-IV: (New Approach-II/Item Based Approach)

Approach-IV takes the each item in the data and determines the best scenario for each item. In order to display the difference of this approach from the previous ones, the first 5 NSN of NSG-10 are taken as an example and shown in the Table 3.9 below.

Table 3.9 Best Scenarios for NSG-10

NSN	Classic	NSG Based	IBA (1)	IBA (2)
NSN-1	RDS (1)	RDS (8), RDS (6)	TOIMDR (5)	TOIMDR (4)
NSN-2			TOIMDR (8)	SORTIE (8)
NSN-3			RDS (7)	RDS (8)
NSN-4			RDS (7)	RDS (6)
NSN-5			SORTIE (7)	TOIMDR (8)

IBA item based approach The scenarios that have the smallest average absolute errors are ordered up to five such that IBA (1) indicates the smallest, IBA (2) indicates the second smallest, IBA (3) indicates the third smallest scenario with respect to average absolute term. IBA (4) and IBA (5) should be read likewise

As seen in the Table 3.9 above, RDS (1) gives the minimum average absolute error for overall data set in classic approach. But when taking NSG specific approach, RDS (8) and RDS (6) appear to be the best scenarios that have minimum average absolute error. When taking item specific approach, the first two minimum results, IBA (1) and IBA (2), show that there are different scenarios appear to be the best in addition to RDS (8) and RDS (6).

The results of average absolute errors for IBA (1), IBA (2), IBA (3), IBA (4) and IBA (5) are given in Table 3.10 below. It is seen in the Table 3.10 that even the average absolute error of IBA (5) yields better result that that of RDS (1).

The research question in this approach is the following: “Are Scenario IBA (1) and IBA (5) significantly different from the scenario RDS (1) in projecting the number of failures at the $\alpha = 5\,\%$?” In answering the research question Wilcoxon Sign Test is conducted for just 1-year forecast period as an example. The pairwise comparisons between IBA (1) and RDS (1) [Wilcoxon Test: Z-value:-22.496, positive rank and *p*-value:0.000], IBA (5) and RDS (1) [Wilcoxon Test: Z-value:-10.312, positive rank and *p*-value: 0.000] are significantly different in projecting the number of failures at the $\alpha = 5\,\%$ for 1-year forecast period. It is concluded based on the previous pairwise comparisons that IBA (2), IBA (3) and IBA (4) are significantly different from RDS (1) in projecting the number of failures at the $\alpha = 5\,\%$ for 1-year forecast period, too.

3.8.5 Evaluation

The results for scenarios are presented in Fig. 3.1 and Fig. 3.2 based on average absolute error and average percentage error, respectively. It is seen that the sequence of the two demand prediction parameters are the same but the value of the average percentage error is relatively larger than the other parameter. Using the best scenarios that are close to the actual values let the decision maker make more effective buy decisions. In order to show the high acquisition and repair cost value of F-16 repairable items, Table 3.11 is prepared. It is clear to have the conclusion that im-

Table 3.10 Comparison of algorithms' results-3

Forecast Period	IBA (1)	IBA (2)	IBA (3)	IBA (4)	IBA (5)	RDS (1)
1-year forecast (2007/4–2008/3)	1.48	1.99	2.15	2.67	2.95	3.9
2-year forecast (2007/4–2009/3)	3.09	3.75	4.70	5.39	5.77	7.45
3-year forecast (2007/4–2010/3)	4.76	5.67	6.67	7.86	8.45	11.61

proving the average absolute error by one or two unit per repairable item yields a great impact on budget based on the high mean value of repairable items.

The sum of the difference between the actual repair cost per item and the projected repair cost based on the scenario result per item is shown in Fig. 3.3. It is clear that using scenario results found in this study saves almost 2–6 million TL.

3.9 Results and Recommendations

For the calculation of initial support requirements of repairable items, based on the flight hour parameter used in the United States of Air Force (USAF) and the usage parameter used in Turkey a new parameter called sortie is formed up in this study. Taking into consideration the flight hour, usage and sortie parameters, 24 scenarios (8 for each parameter) have been created by using real data set of F-16 with a quantity of 894 repairable items. Each scenario is named according to the usage of past data in years. The data set which covers the last 11 years (44 quarters) is divided into two: the first 8 years data is used for running the scenarios, and the last 3 years data is used for comparing the results of scenarios with the actual values. While evaluating the effectiveness of scenarios, parameters of mean absolute error and mean percentage error are used. In contrast to the previous comparisons made in the literature by just evaluating the mean absolute error values, The Friedman Test is run to determine whether there is a significant difference among scenarios at the confidence level of 95 %. If there is a difference, and Wilcoxon Sign Test is run by pairwise comparison to determine the scenarios that make the difference. Approach-I study that is based on finding a common scenario for all data reveals that the scenario RDS (1) yields better results than the ones used in USA and Turkey. Approach-II&III studies that are based on finding a common scenario for each NSG improve the performance of the scenario RDS (1) by 1 %. Approach-IV study that is based on finding the best scenario for each NSN in the list improve the performance of the scenario RDS (1) by almost 24–62 %.

In short, in projecting the number of failures of repairable items, it is concluded that item based approach yields better results than the NSG based and classical approach. When projecting the number of failures more close to the actual values, the workload and workforce will also be programmed more efficiently and effectively.

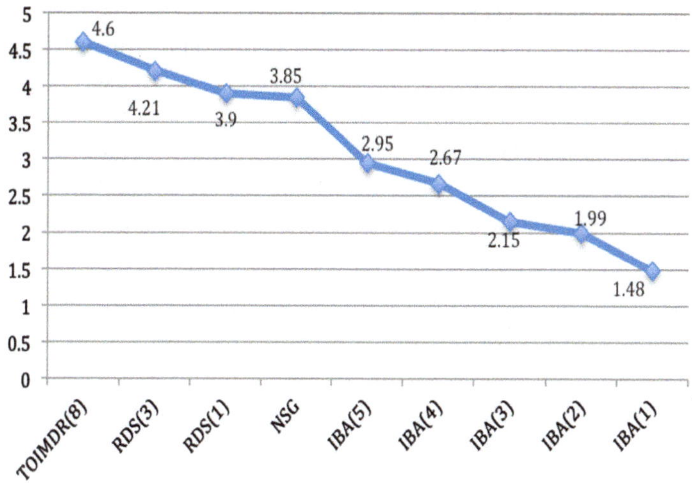

Fig. 3.1 Comparisons of scenario based on "Average Absolute Error" parameter

Fig. 3.2 Comparisons of scenario based on "Average Percentage Error" parameter

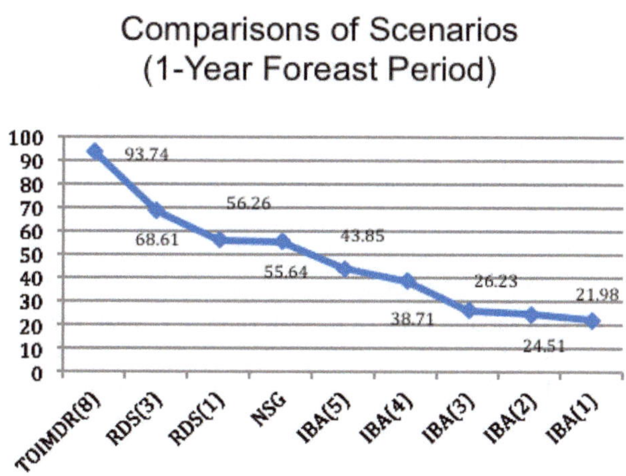

For the future studies, the scenarios that yield better results for F-16 weapon system can be used for other weapon systems. Based on the Friedman Test results, the scenarios that are insignificant should be studied from starting higher mean absolute error values. By the same token, the higher mean absolute errors in item based approach should be studied in detail. The best scenarios are found taking consideration of point estimate. The interval estimates may be defined for each approach discussed in this paper in order to assist decision makers. The scenarios that are resulted in significantly different with respect to Friedman and Wilcoxon Sign Test for projecting the number of failures at the $\alpha = 5\,\%$ can be used in operational support algorithms.

Table 3.11 The acquisition and repair cost of F-16 data set

	Acquisition cost ($)	Repair cost ($)
Mean	26,000	4800
Standard deviation	0.031	0.5
Lower confidence interval (95%)	20,000	3800
Lower confidence interval (95%)	32,500	5900

The data set includes only the 278 repairable whose source of supply and source of repair are USA due to the cost update.

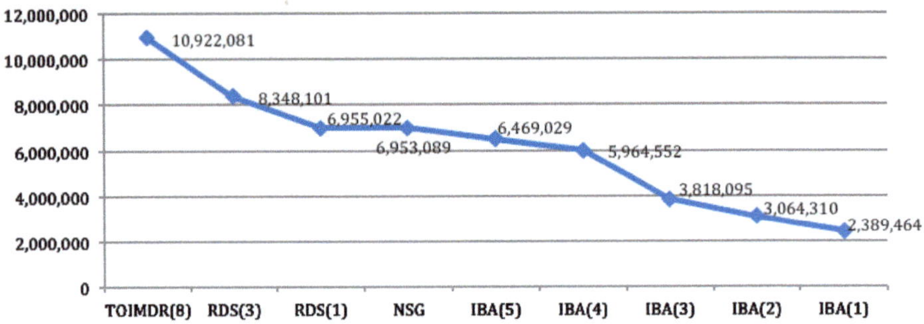

Fig. 3.3 The sum of absolute differences between actual and projected repair costs

Appendix

	1-Year forecast period[a]			2-Year forecast period			3-Year forecast period		
Nu.	Scenario name[b]	Mean	Std. dev.	Scenario name	Mean	Std. dev.	Scenario name	Mean	Std. dev.
1	TOIMDR (1)	3.90	6.40	RDS (1)	7.45	13.29	RDS (1)	11.61	20.09
2	SORTIE (1)	3.90	6.40	TIOIMDR (1)	7.51	13.32	SORTIE (1)	11.99	20.54
3	RDS (1)	3.90	6.41	SORTIE (1)	7.52	13.33	RDS (2)	11.12	20.56
4	RDS (2)	3.89	6.57	RDS (2)	7.33	13.76	TIO-IMDR (1)	12.02	20.59
5	SORTIE (2)	3.92	6.82	SORTIE (2)	7.39	14.05	SORTIE (2)	11.16	20.60
6	TIO-IMDR (2)	3.98	7.09	TIOIMDR (2)	7.55	14.62	TIO-IMDR (2)	11.27	20.94
7	RDS (3)	4.21	7.14	RDS (3)	8.06	15.25	RDS (3)	12.05	22.49
8	SORTIE (3)	4.22	7.49	SORTIE (3)	8.10	15.77	SORTIE (3)	12.04	22.65

	1-Year forecast period[a]			2-Year forecast period			3-Year forecast period		
Nu.	Scenario name[b]	Mean	Std. dev.	Scenario name	Mean	Std. dev.	Scenario name	Mean	Std. dev.
9	RDS (8)	4.33	7.59	TIOIMDR (3)	8.29	16.35	TIO-IMDR (3)	12.23	23.08
10	RDS (4)	4.38	7.59	RDS (4)	8.27	16.45	RDS (4)	12.42	24.26
11	RDS (6)	4.38	7.69	RDS (8)	8.32	16.51	SORTIE (4)	12.52	24.33
12	RDS (7)	4.34	7.72	RDS (6)	8.29	16.65	RDS (8)	12.23	24.36
13	TIO-IMDR (3)	4.29	7.79	RDS (7)	8.23	16.72	RDS (6)	12.22	24.68
14	RDS (5)	4.41	7.86	SORTI (4)	8.44	16.89	TIO-IMDR (4)	12.76	24.71
15	SORTIE (4)	4.41	7.93	RDS (5)	8.35	17.03	SORTIE (8)	12.50	24.80
16	SORTIE (6)	4.49	8.10	SORTIE (8)	8.61	17.14	RDS (7)	12.13	24.81
17	SORTIE (8)	4.46	8.11	SORTIE (6)	8.55	17.21	SORTIE (6)	12.52	24.88
18	SORTIE (7)	4.45	8.13	SORTIE (7)	8.49	17.26	SORTIE (7)	12.41	25.04
19	SORTIE (5)	4.51	8.17	TIOIMDR (4)	8.63	17.43	RDS (5)	12.47	25.16
20	TIO-IMDR (4)	4.48	8.21	SORTIE (5)	8.53	17.48	SORTIE (5)	12.67	25.19
21	TIO-IMDR (6)	4.58	8.44	TIOIMDR (6)	8.83	17.85	TIO-IMDR (6)	12.82	25.40
22	TIO-IMDR (5)	4.58	8.46	TIOIMDR (7)	8.81	17.93	TIO-IMDR (8)	12.95	25.54
23	TIO-IMDR (7)	4.56	8.49	TIOIMDR (8)	8.98	17.94	TIO-IMDR (7)	12.80	25.58
24	TIO-IMDR (8)	4.60	8.52	TIOIMDR (5)	8.77	18.00	TIO-IMDR (5)	12.80	25.59

[a] Freidman Test results for 1-Year Forecast Period χ^2 (23)=35,1, p=0.005, for 2-Year Forecast Period χ^2 (23)=164.8, p=0.000 and 3-Year Forecast Period χ^2 (23)=266.9, p=0.000

[b] The number in parenthesis shows the number of years past data are included for computing scenario projections

Approach-I (Significantly different scenarios based on Wilcoxon Sign Test)

Pairwise comparison	z-value[a]	*p*-value	Pairwise comparison	z-value	*p*-value	Pairwise comparison	z-value	*p*-value
SORTIE (7)—TOIMDR (7)	−3.590 (Positive rank)	0.000	SORTIE (6)—SORTIE (2)	−2.837 (Negative rank)	0.005	TOIMDR (8)—RDS (3)	−2.336 (Negative rank)	0.019
SORTIE (3)—TOIMDR (8)	−3.531 (Positive rank)	0.000	SORTIE (7)—TOIMDR (6)	−2.818 (Positive rank)	0.005	TOIMDR (7)—TOIMDR (3)	−2.301 (Negative rank)	0.021
SORTIE (7)—TOIMDR (8)	−4.945 (Positive rank)	0.000	TOIMDR (7)—TOIMDR (2)	−2.733 (Negative rank)	0.006	TOIMDR (2)—RDS (8)	−2.300 (Positive rank)	0.021
SORTIE (8)—TOIMDR (8)	−4.097 (Positive rank)	0.000	SORTIE (2)—TOIMDR (8)	−2.756 (Positive rank)	0.006	SORTIE 8—SOR-TIE (7)	−2.285 (Negative rank)	0.022
TOIMDR (8)—TOIMDR (3)	−3.517 (Negative rank)	0.000	SORTIE (3)—TOIMDR (7)	−2.772 (Positive rank)	0.006	TOIMDR (2)—RDS (4)	−2.259 (Positive rank)	0.024
SORTIE (3)—TOIMDR (4)	−3.529 (Positive rank)	0.000	SORTIE (6)—TOIMDR (5)	−2.699 (Positive rank)	0.007	SORTIE (5)—RDS (2)	−2.220 (Negative rank)	0.026
SORTIE (3)—TOIMDR (5)	−3.932 (Positive rank)	0.000	SORTIE (6)—TOIMDR (6)	−2.718 (Positive rank)	0.007	TOIMDR (5)—TOIMDR (4)	−2.205 (Negative rank)	0.027
TOIMDR (4)—TOIMDR (2)	−3.375 (Negative rank)	0.001	SORTIE (4)—SORTIE (2)	−2.662 (Negative rank)	0.008	SORTIE (2)—RDS (6)	−2.203 (Positive rank)	0.028
TOIMDR (5)—TOIMDR (2)	−3.267 (Negative rank)	0.001	SORTIE (2)—TOIMDR (7)	−2.596 (Positive rank)	0.009	TOIMDR (8)—TOIMDR (6)	−2.200 (Negative rank)	0.028
TOIMDR (5)—TOIMDR (3)	−3.335 (Negative rank)	0.001	SORTIE (4)—SORTIE (3)	−2.570 (Negative rank)	0.010	SORTIE 8—TOIMDR (3)	−2.156 (Negative rank)	0.031
SORTIE (2)—TOIMDR (5)	−3.315 (Positive rank)	0.001	SORTIE 8—SORTIE (3)	−2.562 (Negative rank)	0.010	TOIMDR (8)—RDS (8)	−2.137 (Negative rank)	0.033
TOIMDR (8)—TOIMDR (7)	−3.200 (Negative rank)	0.001	SORTIE (6)—TOIMDR (2)	−2.530 (Negative rank)	0.011	TOIMDR (2)—RDS (5)	−2.105 (Positive Rank)	0.035
SORTIE (6)—TOIMDR (8)	−3.032 (Positive Rank)	0.002	SORTIE 8—SORTIE (2)	−2.550 (Negative rank)	0.011	SORTIE (4)—TOIMDR (8)	−2.093 (Positive rank)	0.036

Pairwise comparison	z-value[a]	*p*-value	Pairwise comparison	z-value	*p*-value	Pairwise comparison	z-value	*p*-value
SORTIE (5)—SORTIE (2)	−3.077 (Negative rank)	0.002	TOIMDR (6)—TOIMDR (3)	−2.523 (Negative rank)	0.012	RDS (4)—RDS (2)	−2.085 (Negative rank)	0.037
SORTIE (5)—SORTIE (3)	−3.080 (Negative Rank)	0.002	SORTIE (2)—RDS (4)	−2.476 (Positive rank)	0.013	SORTIE (2)—RDS (5)	−2.080 (Positive rank)	0.037
TOIMDR (4)—TOIMDR (3)	−3.163 (Negative rank)	0.002	SORTIE (7)—SORTIE (2)	−2.469 (Negative rank)	0.014	SORTIE (7)—TOIMDR (2)	−2.079 (Negative rank)	0.038
SORTIE (2)—TOIMDR (6)	−3.041 (Positive Rank)	0.002	SORTIE (6)—SORTIE (3)	−2.465 (Negative rank)	0.014	SORTI3—RDS (4)	−2.063 (Positive rank)	0.039
TOIMDR (6)—TOIMDR (2)	−2.990 (Negative rank)	0.003	SORTIE (4)—TOIMDR (5)	−2.454 (Positive rank)	0.014	SORTIE (5)—TOIMDR (8)	−2.066 (Positive rank)	0.039
TOIMDR (8)—TOIMDR (2)	−2.997 (Negative rank)	0.003	SORTIE (5)—TOIMDR (3)	−2.422 (Negative Rank)	0.015	SORTIE (6)—TOIMDR (7)	−2.061 (Positive Rank)	0.039
SORTIE (4)—TOIMDR (2)	−2.922 (Negative Rank)	0.003	TOIMDR (5)—RDS (2)	−2.406 (Negative rank)	0.016	SORTIE 8—RDS(7)	−2.054 (Negative rank)	0.040
SORTIE (5)—TOIMDR (2)	−2.984 (Negative rank)	0.003	SORTIE (2)—RDS (8)	−2.420 (Positive Rank)	0.016	SORTIE (4)—TOIMDR (4)	−2.031 (Positive rank)	0.042
SORTIE (2)—TOIMDR (4)	−2.915 (Positive rank)	0.004	SORTIE 8—TOIMDR (2)	−2.388 (Negative rank)	0.017	TOIMDR (8)—RDS (2)	−2.002 (Negative rank)	0.045
SORTIE (3)—TOIMDR (6)	−2.908 (Positive rank)	0.004	TOIMDR (8)—RDS (7)	−2.374 (Negative Rank)	0.018	SORTIE (2)—RDS(7)	−1.957 (Positive rank)	0.050
TOIMDR (8)—RDS (7)	−2.374 (Negative rank)	0.018	TOIMDR (5)—SORTIE (5)	−2.478 (Negative rank)	0.013			

[a] "Positive Rank" means the significant difference is based on the first scenario. "Negative Rank" means the significant difference is based on the second scenario

The Friedman Test Results based on NSG for 1-Year Forecast Period

NSG No.	NSG name	n	Mean	Std. dev.	Degrees of freedom	χ^2	p-value	Recommended scenarios for decision makers (the first 5)[a]
10	Weapon	14	2.03	2.71	23	49.80	0.001	RDS (8), RDS (7), SORTIE (8), RDS (5), RDS (6)
12	Fire control equipment	46	5.83	8.66	23	36.25	0.04	RDS (1), SORTIE (1), RDS (2), SORTIE (2), TOIMDR (1)
15	A/C structural components	44	2.83	4.21	23	70.54	0.000	SORTIE (1), TOIMDR1, TOIMDR (2), SORTIE (2)
16	A/C comp.& accessories	124	5.11	8.38	23	31.40	0.113	RDS (1)
28	Engines, turbines, and components	58	9.23	9.25	23	57.61	0.000	SORTIE (3), RDS (3), TOIMDR (3), SORTIE (2), RDS (1)
29	Engines accessories	38	4.69	6.17	23	45.39	0.004	SORTIE (1), RDS (1), TOIMDR1, SORTIE (5), TOIMDR (5)
43	Pumps and compressors	5	2.80	4.21	23	9.44	0.994	RDS (1)
48	Valves	28	2.22	3.13	23	31.29	0.116	RDS (1)
49	Mainte-nance shop equip.	11	0.80	0.85	23	33.08	0.080	RDS (5), RDS (6), SORTI5, RDS (4)
58	Commu-nication equipment	45	3.19	4.02	23	32.64	0.088	TOIMDR1, SORTIE (2), RDS (2), TOIMDR (2), RDS (1)
59	Electrical, electronic equipment	286	2.18	3.91	23	17.36	0.791	RDS (1)

(continued)

NSG No.	NSG name	n	Mean	Std. dev.	Degrees of freedom	χ^2	p-value	Recommended scenarios for decision makers (the first 5)[a]
61	Electric wire, and power a equipment	71	3.30	5.17	23	73.40	0.000	RDS (2), RDS (3), SORTIE (2), RDS (4), SORTIE (3), RDS (1)
62	Lighting fixtures, lamps	16	2.74	1.94	23	7.65	0.999	RDS (1)
63	Alarm, signal and security systems	5	1.37	0.30	23	15.99	0.856	RDS (1)
66	Instruments and lab. equipment	87	3.55	5.23	23	28.34	0.203	RDS (1)
70	Auto-matic data processing	8	3.00	1.96	23	13.37	0.944	RDS (1)
	Total	886[b]						

[a] The scenarios written in bold are primarily recommended for use. The scenario RDS (1) is recommended for the NSGs that are not resulted in significantly different at the $\alpha = 5\,\%$ in the end of Friedman and Wilcoxon Sign Test

[b] 8 repairable items that belong to the five different NSGs are not included in this table due to the insufficient number of observations

The Friedman Test results based on NSG for 2-Year Forecast Period

NSG No.	NSG name	*n*	Mean	Std. dev.	Degrees of freedom	χ^2	*p*-value	Recommended scenarios for decision makers (the first 5)
10	Weapon	14	3.28	3.24	23	33.7	0.070	SORTIE (8), TOIMDR (8), SORTIE (7), RDS (8), TOIMDR (7)
12	Fire control equipment	46	11.98	16.9	23	73.5	0.000	RDS (1), SORTIE (1), RDS (2), SORTIE (2), RDS (3)
15	A/C structural components	44	3.59	3.62	23	36.2	0.040	RDS (1), SORTIE (1), RDS (2), TOIMDR (2), SORTIE (2)
16	A/C comp.& accessories	124	8.43	10.1	23	28.3	0.206	RDS (1)
28	Engines, turbines, and components	58	17.74	22.7	23	56	0.000	RDS (2), SORTIE (2), TOIMDR (2), RDS (1), RDS (3)
29	Engines accessories	38	9.24	11.5	23	48.1	0.002	SORTIE (1), RDS (1), TOIMDR (2), SORTIE (2), TOIMDR (3)
43	Pumps and compressors	5	3.00	2.55	23	8.19	0.998	RDS (1)
48	Valves	28	4.43	4.74	23	36.2	0.039	TOIMDR (2), TOIMDR (3), SORTIE (3), SORTIE (2), RDS (3), RDS (1)
49	Maintenance shop equip.	11	1.77	1.57	23	34.4	0.059	RDS (4), RDS (3), RDS (5), SORTIE (4), RDS (6), RDS (1)
58	Communication equipment	45	7.58	9.44	23	104	0.000	RDS (1), SORTIE (1), SORTIE (2), TOIMDR (2)
59	Electrical, electronic equipment	286	3.67	6.50	23	155	0.000	RDS (1), SORTIE (1), RDS (2), SORTIE (2), TOIMDR (2)
61	Electric wire, and power a equipment	71	7.17	10.4	23	121	0.000	RDS (2), SORTIE (2), TOIMDR (2), RDS (3), RDS (1)

(continued)

NSG No.	NSG name	n	Mean	Std. dev.	Degrees of freedom	χ^2	p-value	Recommended scenarios for decision makers (the first 5)
62	Lighting fixtures, lamps	16	4.89	3.84	23	33.8	0.068	SORTIE (1), RDS (2), RDS (1), SORTIE (2), RDS (4)
63	Alarm, signal and security systems	5	2.55	1.30	23	18.7	0.719	RDS (1)
66	Instruments and lab. equipment	87	9.70	20.7	23	74.2	0.000	RDS (2), RDS (8), SORTIE (1), RDS (6), RDS(7), RDS (1)
70	Automatic data processing	8	3.91	1.39	23	23.4	0.439	RDS (1)
	Total	886						

The Friedman Test Results based on NSG for 3-Year Forecast Period

NSG No.	NSG Name	*n*	Mean	Std. Dev.	Degrees of freedom	χ^2	*p*-value	Recommended scenarios for decision makers (the first 5)
10	Weapon	14	3.70	3.51	23	20.61	0.605	RDS (1)
12	Fire control equipment	46	17.65	23.22	23	30.19	0.144	RDS (1)
15	A/C structural components	44	5.98	5.02	23	46.60	0.003	TOIMDR (2), SORTIE (2), RDS (2), RDS (1)
16	A/C comp.& accessories	124	13.38	16.56	23	24.32	0.386	RDS (1)
28	Engines, turbines, and components	58	27.59	35.85	23	18.29	0.742	RDS (1)
29	Engines accessories	38	15.74	18.63	23	24.98	0.352	RDS (1)
43	Pumps and compressors	5	0.998	18.80	23	8.020	0.998	RDS (1)
48	Valves	28	5.87	5.71	23	36.15	0.040	TOIMDR (3), SORTIE (3), SORTIE (4), TOIMDR (4), RDS (5), RDS (1)
49	Maintenance shop equip.	11	1.98	1.29	23	37.64	0.028	RDS (4), SORTIE (4), RDS (1), TOIMDR (4), RDS (6)
58	Communication equipment	45	10.69	14.66	23	40.55	0.013	RDS (1), TOIMDR1, SORTIE (1), RDS (2), SORTIE (2)
59	Electrical, electronic equipment	286	5.30	10.09	23	220.7	0.000	TOIMDR1, SORTIE (3), RDS (1), TOIMDR (3), TOIMDR (2)
61	Electric wire, and power a equipment	71	12.13	18.51	23	64.94	0.000	RDS (2), SORTIE (2), TOIMDR (2), RDS (3), SORTIE (3), RDS (1)

(continued)

NSG No.	NSG Name	n	Mean	Std. Dev.	Degrees of freedom	χ^2	p-value	Recommended scenarios for decision makers (the first 5)
62	Lighting fixtures, lamps	16	8.53	6.50	23	15.90	0.860	RDS (1)
63	Alarm, signal and security systems	5	5.46	2.70	23	29.03	0.179	RDS (1)
66	Instruments and lab. equipment	87	12.53	24.90	23	73.40	0.000	RDS (2), SORTIE (1), SORTIE (2), RDS (1), RDS (8)
70	Automatic data processing	8	8.73	6.39	23	24.67	0.367	RDS (1)
	Total	886						

The Results of Wilcoxon Sign Test for the Recommended Scenarios in Appendix-III for 1-Year Forecast Period

NSG	N	Pairwise comparison	z-value	p-value
10	14	RDS (1)-RDS (8)**[a]	−2.386 (Positive rank)	0.017
		RDS (1)-RDS (6)**	−2.232 (Negative rank)	0.026
		RDS(7)-RDS (8)	−1.476 (Negative rank)	0.140
		SORTIE (8)-RDS (8)	−2.220 (Positive rank)	0.826
		RDS (5)-RDS (8)	−1.538 (Negative rank)	0.124
		RDS (6)-RDS (8)**	−2.043 (Negative rank)	0.041
12	46	SORTIE (1)-RDS(1)	−0.405 (Negative rank)	0.685
		RDS (2)—RDS (1)	−0.635 (Negative rank)	0.525
		SORTIE (2)— RDS (1)	−0.688 (Negative rank)	0.491
		TOIMDR1—RDS (1)	−0.894 (Negative rank)	0.371
15	44	SORTIE (1)-RDS (1)**	−2.048 (Negative rank)	0.041
		TOIMDR1-RDS (1)	−0.060 (Negative rank)	0.952
		TOIMDR (2)-SORTIE (1)	−1.655 (Negative rank)	0.098
		SORTIE (2)-SORTIE (1)	−1.674 (Negative rank)	0.094
28	58	RDS (3)-SORTI3	−0.230 (Negative rank)	0.818
		TOIMDR (3)-SORTI3	−0.350 (Negative rank)	0.727
		SORTIE (2)-SORTI3	−0.354 (Positive rank)	0.723
		RDS (2)-SORTI3	−0.496 (Positive rank)	0.620
		RDS (1)-SORTI3	−0.416 (Positive rank)	0.677
29	38	RDS (1)-SORTIE (1)	−1.539 (Positive rank)	0.124
		TOIMDR1-SORTIE (1)	−0.604 (Negative rank)	0.546
		SORTI5- SORTIE (1)	−1.499 (Negative rank)	0.134
		TOIMDR (5)-SORTIE (1)	−1.155 (Negative rank)	0.248
49	11	RDS (6)-RDS (5)	−1.531 (Negative rank)	0.126
		SORTI5-RDS (5)	−0.540 (Negative rank)	0.589
		RDS (3)-RDS (5)**	−2.070 (Negative rank)	0.038
		RDS (4)-RDS (5)	−0.806 (Negative rank)	0.420
		RDS (1)-RDS (5)	−1.836 (Negative rank)	0.066
58	45	SORTIE (2)-TOIMDR1	−0.780 (Positive rank)	0.436
		RDS (2)-TOIMDR1	−0.020 (Positive rank)	0.984
		TOIMDR (2)-TOIMDR1	−0.255 (Positive rank)	0.798
		RDS (1)-TOIMDR1	−1.091 (Negative rank)	0.275
61	71	RDS (3)-RDS (2)	−0.358 (Negative rank)	0.720
		SORTIE (2)-RDS (2)	−1.108 (Negative rank)	0.268
		RDS (4)-RDS (2)	−0.707 (Negative rank)	0.480
		SORTI3-RDS (2)	−0.805 (Negative rank)	0.421
		RDS (1)-RDS (2)	−1.547 (Negative rank)	0.122

[a] Based on Wilcoxon Test results, the one that is significantly different from the other one in pairwise comparison is marked with "**" in Appendix-IV

The Results of Wilcoxon Sign Test for the Recommended Scenarios in Appendix-III for 2-Year Forecast Period

NSG	*n*	Pairwise comparison	z-value	*p*-value
10	14	TOIMDR (8)-SORTIE (8)	−0.220 (Negative rank)	0.826
		SORTIE (7)-SORTIE (8)	−1.412 (Negative rank)	0.158
		TOIMDR (7)-SORTIE (8)	−1.664 (Negative rank)	0.096
		RDS (1)-SORTIE (8)**	−2.480(Negative rank)	0.013
12	46	SORTIE (1)-RDS (1)	−1.082 (Negative rank)	0.279
		RDS (2)-RDS (1)	−0.428 (Positive rank)	0.668
		RDS (3)-RDS (1)	−0.019 (Negative rank)	0.985
15	44	SORTIE (1)-RDS (1)	−1.929 (Negative rank)	0.054
		TOIMDR (2)-RDS (1)	−0.607 (Negative rank)	0.544
		RDS (2)-RDS (1)	−0.617 (Negative rank)	0.537
28	58	SORTIE (2)-RDS (2)	−0.235 (Negative rank)	0.814
		TOIMDR (2)-RDS (2)	−0.410 (Negative rank)	0.682
		RDS (1)-RDS (2)	−0.667 (Negative rank)	0.505
29	38	RDS (1)-SORTIE (1)	−0.182 (Negative rank)	0.855
		TOIMDR (2)-SORTIE (1)	−0.116 (Negative rank)	0.908
		SORTIE (2)-SORTIE (1)	−0.849 (Negative rank)	0.396
48	28	TOIMDR (3)-TOIMDR (2)	−0.586 (Positive rank)	0.558
		SORTI3-TOIMDR (2)	−0.214 (Positive rank)	0.830
		RDS (1)-TOIMDR (2)	−0.942 (Negative rank)	0.346
49	11	RDS (3)-RDS (4)	−0.206(Negative rank)	0.837
		RDS (5)-RDS (4)	−1.523 (Positive rank)	0.128
		RDS (1)-RDS (4)	−1.131 (Negative rank)	0.258
58	45	SORTIE (1)-RDS (1)	−1.108 (Negative rank)	0.268
		RDS (2)-RDS (1)**	−2.000 (Positive rank)	0.046
		SORTIE (2)-RDS (1)	−1.902 (Positive rank)	0.057
		TOIMDR (2)-RDS (1)	−1.929 (Positive rank)	0.054
59	286	SORTIE (1)-RDS (1)**	−3.713 (Negative rank)	0.000
		TOIMDR (2)-RDS (1)**	−2.060 (Positive rank)	0.039
		SORTIE (2)-RDS (1)**	−2.045 (Positive rank)	0.041
		RDS (3)-RDS (1)**	−2.281 (Positive rank)	0.023
		SORTIE (1)-RDS (1)**	−3.713 (Negative rank)	0.000
61	71	SORTIE (2)-RDS (2)	−1.284 (Negative rank)	0.199
		TOIMDR (2)-RDS (2)	−1.382 (Negative rank)	0.167
		RDS (1)-RDS (2)	−1.522 (Negative rank)	0.128
62	16	RDS (2)-SORTIE (1)	−0.336 (Negative rank)	0.737
		RDS (1)-SORTIE (1)	−1.200 (Negative rank)	0.230
		RDS (4)-SORTIE (1)	−0.440 (Negative rank)	0.660
66	87	RDS (8)-RDS (2)	−0.258 (Positive rank)	0.796
		SORTIE (1)-RDS (2)	−1.007 (Negative rank)	0.314
		RDS (1)-RDS (2)	−1.017 (Positive rank)	0.309

The Results of Wilcoxon Sign Test for the Recommended Scenarios in Appendix-III for 3-Year Forecast Period

NSG	*n*	Pairwise comparison	z-value	*p*-value
15	44	SORTIE (2)-TOIMDR (2)	−0.134 (Positive rank)	0.894
		RDS (2)-TOIMDR (2)	−0.051 (Negative rank)	0.959
		TOIMDR (3)-TOIMDR (2)**	−2.195 (Negative rank)	0.028
		RDS (1)-TOIMDR (2)	−1.256 (Negative rank)	0.206
48	28	SORTI3-TOIMDR (3)	−0.816 (Negative rank)	0.415
		SORTI4-TOIMDR (3)	−0.843 (Negative rank)	0.399
		TOIMDR (4)-TOIMDR (3)	−0.415 (Negative rank)	0.678
		RDS (1)-TOIMDR (3)	−1.172 (Negative rank)	0.241
49	11	SORTI4-RDS (4)	−1.179 (Positive rank)	0.238
		TOIMDR (4)-RDS (4)	−1.179 (Positive rank)	0.238
		RDS (5)-RDS (4)**	−2.060 (Positive rank)	0.039
		RDS (1)-RDS (4)	−0.868 (Negative rank)	0.385
58	45	TOIMDR1-RDS (1)	−1.427 (Negative rank)	0.154
		SORTIE (1)-RDS (1)	−1.329 (Negative rank)	0.184
		RDS (2)-RDS (1)	−1.393 (Positive rank)	0.164
		SORTIE (2)-RDS (1)	−1.230 (Positive rank)	0.219
59	286	SORTI3-TOIMDR1**	−2.891 (Positive rank)	0.004
		RDS (1)-TOIMDR1**	−2.393 (Negative rank)	0.017
		TOIMDR (3)-TOIMDR1**	−3.393 (Positive rank)	0.001
		TOIMDR (2)-TOIMDR1**	−2.771 (Positive rank)	0.006
61	71	SORTIE (2)-RDS (2)	−1.729 (Negative rank)	0.084
		TOIMDR (2)-RDS (2)	−1.779 (Negative rank)	0.075
		RDS (3)-RDS (2)	−1.333 (Positive rank)	0.895
		SORTI3-RDS (2)	−0.794 (Negative rank)	0.427
		RDS (1)-RDS (2)	−1.898 (Negative rank)	0.058
66	87	SORTIE (1)-RDS (2)	−1.630 (Negative rank)	0.103
		SORTIE (2)-RDS (2)	−1.513 (Negative rank)	0.130
		RDS (1)-RDS (2)	−1.947 (Negative rank)	0.051
		RDS (8)-RDS (2)	−1.236 (Positive rank)	0.216

References

AECMA Spec 2000M (Association Européenne des Constructeurs de Matériel Aérospatial) : Specification 2000M Issue 3.0 (2000)

Air Force Military Command Instruction (AFMCI): 23-106 Initial Requirement Determination (1997)

Air Transportation Association (ATA): e-Business for Material Management SPEC2000 (2002)

Anderson, B. (Lt. Col).: LOGM-570 Principles of Inventory Management Lecture Notes, Air Force Institute of Technology (AFIT) (2009)

Guide, Daniel V.R. Jr., Srivastava, R.: Repairable inventory theory: Models and applications. Eur. J. Oper. Res. **102**, 1–20 (1997)

Fortuin, L.: Initial supply and re-order level of new service parts. Eur. J. Oper. Res. **15**(3):310–319 (1984)

Gümüş, A.T., Güneri, A.F.: Multi-echelon inventory management in supply chains with uncertain demand and lead times: Literature review from an operational research perspective. J. Eng. Manuf. **221**, 1553–1570 (2007) (Part B)

Hillstad, R.J.: Dyna-METRIC: Dynamic multi-echelon technique for recoverable item control. R-2785-AF, RAND Corporation (1982)

Joint Strike Fighter Cost and Operational Performance Trade Process (JSF COPT): Concept to Baseline (2000)

MIL-HDBK-502: Military Handbook Acquisition Logistics (1997)

MIL-STD-1388-1A: Military Standard Logistics Support Analysis (LSA) (1983)

MIL-STD-1388-2B: Military standard DOD requirements for a logistic support analysis record (LSAR) (1991)

Muckstadt, J.A.: A model for a multi-item, multi-echelon, multi-indenture (MOD-METRIC) inventory system. Manage. Sci. **20**(4), 472–481 (1973)

Muckstadt, J.A.: Analysis and Algorithms for Service Parts Supply Chains. Springer, New York (2005)

NATO Logistics Handbook NSN web page http://www.nato.int/structur/ac/135/ncs_guide/english/e_1-6-1.htm (2007)

Paterson, C., Kiesmuller, G., Teunter, K.: Inventory models with lateral transshipments: A review. Eur. J. Oper. Res. **210**, 125–136 (2011)

Sherbrooke, C.: METRIC: A multi-echelon technique for recoverable item control. Oper. Res. **16**, 122–141 (1968)

Sherbrooke, C.: VARI-METRIC: Improved approximations for multi-indenture, multi-echelon availability models. Oper. Res. **34**, 311–319 (1986)

Sherbrooke, C.: Optimal Inventory Modeling of Systems. Wiley, New York (2004)

Slay, F.M., Bachman, T.C., Kline, R, C., O'Malley, T.J., Eichorn, F.L., King, R.M.: Optimizing spares support: The Aircraft Sustainability Model (ASM). AF501MR1, Logistics Management Institute, Virginia (1996)

SPSS Statistics Base 17.0 User Guide

Turkish Air Force Requirement Distribution System (RDS): User Handbook, Turkish Air Force Command Press, Ankara (1997)

Wong, H., Houtum, G.J., Oudheusden, D.Van.: Multi-item spare parts systems with lateral transshipments and waiting time constraints. Eur. J. Oper. Res. **171**, 1071–1093 (2006)

Chapter 4
A Combined Inventory and Lateral Re-Supply Model for Repairable Items—Part I: Modeling an Air Force Logistics Problem

Bahtiyar Eren and Yupo Chan

4.1 Problem Statement

In the military and especially the air force, having local repair and storage capability in site impact directly on the operational readiness of armed forces. The more operational readiness the armed forces have, the more superiority over the adversaries. Therefore "being operationally ready" is a goal toward which all activities are directed. It is clear that having local storage, repair capability and being able to resupply the neighboring sites would make the armed forces more responsive to failures.

Traditionally, logistics analysts have treated the delivery problem separately from inventory and repair problems. In other words, each of these three problems-inventory, repair and delivery-is solved individually, each of which is described by Tersine (1994), for example. While it may be expedient to solve them separately, a moment's reflection will reveal that these logistics problems are interconnected. When there is a demand for a spare part, one can either obtain a working component from inventory or to repair it. Should the inventory and repair facility be different from where the spare part is needed, the part has to be delivered. To address the interconnection, we combine the vehicle-routing, inventory-allocation, and repair problems in a single formulation. Furthermore, lateral re-supply is considered, in that supplies are not only available from the main depot, but also from other depots. Axater (2003) provided an algorithm for lateral transshipments in inventory systems. Jung et al. (2003) considered reparation in addition to tapping into the inventory. Shen et al. (2003) provided a model to analyze the relationship between the various variable demands are and where the inventory is located. In this case, the authors were considering retail merchandize instead of spare parts.

B. Eren (✉)
Hv.K.K.ligi Karargahi Harekat Baskanligi, 06100 Bakanliklar-Ankara, Turkey
e-mail: erenbahtiyar@yahoo.com

Y. Chan
Department of Systems Engineering, University of Arkansas at Little Rock,
Little Rock, AR, USA
e-mail: yxchan@ualr.edu

V. Zeimpekis et al. (eds.), *Military Logistics,* Operations Research/Computer Science Interfaces Series 56, DOI 10.1007/978-3-319-12075-1_4

Table 4.1 The comparison of two models

Topics covered	Federgruen & Zipkin (FZ) model	Extended model (research model)
Lateral resupply	Not allowed	Each base can resupply the others
Delivery type	Only delivery	Both delivery and pick-up
Local storage capability	Yes	Yes
Local repair capability	No	Yes

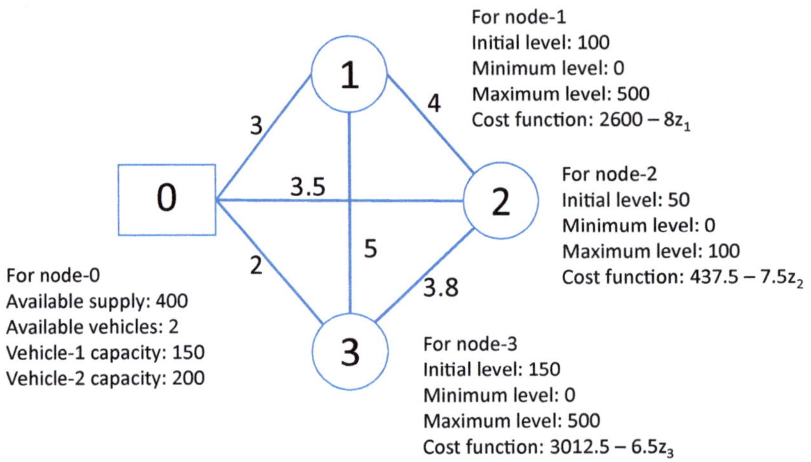

Fig. 4.1 Federgruen & Zipkin model data

Keeping the fact that the problem laid out in this paper is the extension of Federgruen & Zipkin (FZ) model (1984); the comparison of the two models in short is presented in Table 4.1 in order to make the contribution clear.

For the sake of completeness, the details of the FZ model data are shown in Fig. 4.1. The objective of the FZ model is to minimize the traveling cost and inventory cost function occurring at each demand sites. The traveling cost is related to the distance travelled between nodes. The inventory cost function is the newsvendor inventory cost function with shortage and surplus cost. The traveling cost matrix is symmetric and the "distance" is measured in terms of time. For illustration, the inventory cost function is calculated based on uniform distribution. Note that the inventory cost function is nonincreasing function. There is no inventory cost function associated with the supply depot (Node-0) because its main role is to store enough supplies to satisfy the demand occurred at each node. The main depot only supplies all nodes.

Let us refer to the example problem as shown in Fig. 4.2. While making lateral re-supply decisions between depots 1, 2, and 3, we formulate a delivery-allocation plan using the vehicle fleet of two based at the main depot 0. Lateral re-supplies

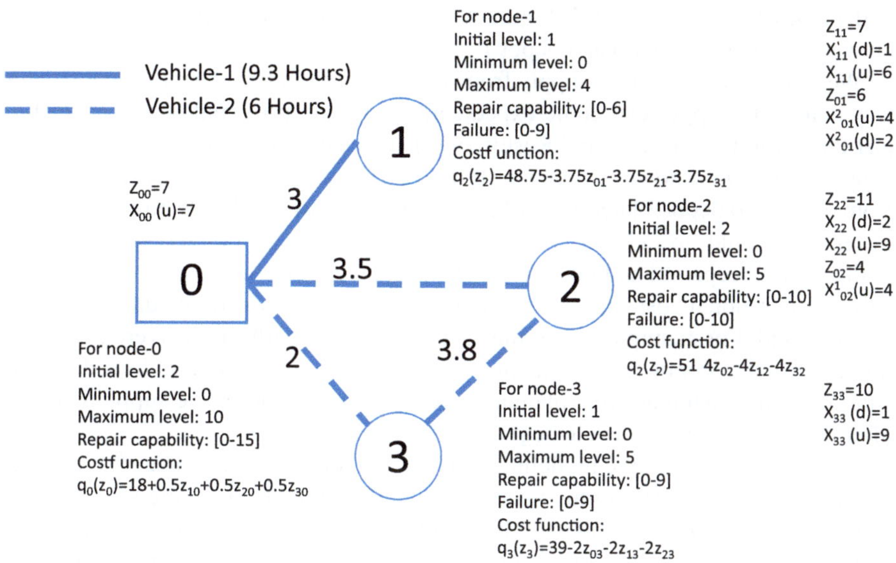

Fig. 4.2 Example problem

from all depots are then delivered via this vehicle fleet. After solving this problem, one can verify that vehicle 1 will visit depots 2 and 3 and return to the home depot 0, while vehicle 2 will make an out-and-back route to depot 1. In this paper, the repair process is not explicitly modeled, but there is a repair capability at each depot that supplements (and in fact lowers) its stored inventory (McGrath 1999). The repair capacity is expressed in terms of a range of repairable units that can be handled. For example, the repair capability at depot 1 is between 0 and 6 items. Being a mixed-integer stochastic-program with both a nonlinear objective function and constraints, we solve the model by generalized Benders' decomposition. The decomposition allows us to linearize the nonlinear constraints, solve large problems, and use general failure and repair functions familiar to logistics analysis. Analytical and computational experience via generalized Benders' cuts suggests that substantial cost efficiency is achieved by considering delivery, inventory and repair simultaneously.

In the beginning of the period, each depot has an initial inventory. For example, the initial inventory at depot 1 is one unit of spare part. There is a minimum and maximum allowable inventory level at each depot, corresponding to the threshold and the depot storage-capacity respectively. Again, for depot 1 the range is between 0 and 4. Any part can fail with a probability distribution at depots $i=0, 1, 2, 3$. Once failed, we need to replace the part from inventory or to repair the part.

At each depot, maintaining the inventory entails holding and shortage costs. We will make vehicle delivery, for example, only when a depot inventory level potentially falls below its minimum threshold—in order to lower inventory and transportation costs. There is a delivery cost for shipping serviceable parts from any depot i

to depot j, where $i, j = 0, 1, 2, 3$. Figure 4.2 shows a transportation cost of three units between the home depot 0 and depot 1.

We can provide lateral re-supply from any depot (including the main depot). This way, lateral re-supply can come expediently from any proximal depot, instead of just the main depot (Herer and Rashit 1999). The shipping cost from depot i to its adjacent depot j is known (where $i, j = 0, 1, 2, 3$). Figure 4.2 shows that re-supplying from depot 2 to depot 3 laterally will cost 3.8 units. Now we decide how many parts to repair, to hold, to deliver, and which vehicle to use for delivery—considering both available repaired and inventoried items at all depots. Supposed the problem is solved, operational cost and resource allocation are determined, including the realized demand. For example, $z_{01} = 6$ means that six spare parts are delivered from the home depot 0 to depot 1, supplementing one unit of stored inventory to address the shortage. This concludes one planning cycle. Consumption of the supplies begins after delivery, and a new cycle begins.

As will be shown in the modeling part, solving such a mixed-integer stochastic-problem even in simpler terms as in FZ model requires using some special algorithms/techniques to come up with the optimal solutions. Computational experience confirms that Benders' decomposition algorithm is very effective in solving this type of problems.

4.2 Literature Review

The inventory-routing problem (IRP) involves a set of customers, where each customer has a different demand on each day (Dror and Ball 1987). Each customer possesses a known capacity for inventory storage (Bertazzi et al. 2002). The objective is to minimize the annual delivery costs while attempting to insure that no customer runs out of the commodity at any time. A Strategic Inventory-Routing Problem estimates the delivery-vehicle fleet size for all possible tactical realization of the IRP (Webb and Larson 1995). When each customer's consumption rate is known, and a rolling horizon is considered, we have the Metered Inventory Routing Problem (Herer and Levy 1997). In the periodic Vehicle Routing Problem (VRP), one designs a set of routes for each day of a given (p-day) period (Baita et al. 1998; Christofides and Beasley 1984). Each customer may require a number of visits by a vehicle during this period. If a customer requires (say) k visits during the period, then these visits may only occur in one of a given number of allowable p-day combinations. The periodic VRP is similar to IRP in satisfying customer demand over a long-term period. However, it is different in the way the operator specifies the number of visits during the period, whereas IRPs let the model decide the number of visits and the size of delivery based on customer demands.

Coelho et al. (n.d.) classified IRPs into finite or infinite time horizon. According to this classification, the above literature review covers the infinite-horizon references. Of particular interest is the Strategic Inventory-Routing Problem, based on which we constructed our model. IRP Classification can be made based on the time at which demand becomes known. If it is fully available at the beginning of the planning horizon, the problem is then deterministic. If its probability distribution is known, it is stochastic, yielding the Stochastic Inventory-Routing Problem. Dynamic IRPs arise when demand is not fully known in advance, but is gradually revealed over time, as opposed to what happens in a static context. In this case, one can still exploit its statistical distribution in the solution process, yielding a Dynamic and Stochastic Inventory-Routing Problem. Under this classification, our model is a Stochastic Inventory-Routing Problem.

Because IRPs are typically very hard to solve, most algorithms are heuristics (Coelho et al. n.d.). These have gradually evolved from simple interchange schemes to more sophisticated meta-heuristics, sometimes combined with exact methods. In recent years, we have also witnessed the emergence of exact branch-and-cut algorithms which can be implemented within the framework of general purpose solvers. According to Federgruen and Zipkin (1984) and Federgruen et al. (1986), we can consider a combined vehicle-routing and inventory/allocation problem very similar to IRPs. While an analytic procedure was outlined, Federgruen and Zipkin (1984) used a modified interchange heuristic to solve the combined routing and inventory problem. When the demand for the resource is random, deliveries serve to replenish the customer's inventories to levels that appropriately balance inventory carrying and shortage costs. This is achieved at certain transportation cost (Berman and Larson 2001). A combined vehicle-routing and inventory/allocation model, or integrated logistics in general, will lower the total cost, including inventory and delivery cost (Bowersox and Closs 1996, Haughton and Stenger 1999). Federgruen et al. showed this important point clearly in their work. Slikker et al. (2005) considered a cooperative game between retailers in coordinating their orders, followed by transshipments after demand realization is known.

In the context of inventory/production with product recovery and remanufacturing, DeCroix et al. (2005) analyze a serial inventory system with stationary costs and stochastic demand over an infinite horizon. Clearly, inventory plays a key role in supply chain management. However, if we have high-tech equipment such as an aircraft fleet, then the repairing process (which is part of maintenance and requires time) becomes equally important (Sherbrook 1992). Remember that an aircraft is pulled out of service for every minute it is in maintenance. Here, it is critical that an aircraft part can be locally repaired or expeditiously re-supplied. Re-supply can come from both the main depot and a close-by depot. At each depot, including the main depot, a repair capability exists in our model. While the repair process is not explicitly modeled, the capability at a depot is measured by the repair-shop capacity. A demand can therefore be satisfied by a delivery, a local repair shop as well as local inventory, whichever is less costly.

In supply chain, we still know little about process orientation and advanced planning across company borders. Kaihara (2003) and Stadler (1995) provided an advanced planning system to address this issue. Meloa et al. (2005) proposed a strategic design of supply-chain networks—considering a dynamic planning horizon, multi-commodities distribution, and available inventories.

4.3 A Model with Repair and Lateral Re-supply

Success of the Federgruen-Zipkin formulation gives us encouragement that it is possible to go beyond combining inventory/allocation and VRP in a single model analytically (Yang et al. 2000). Computational experience as reported by Chan (2005) also improved on the efficiency of the Benders' decomposition as originally proposed by Federgruen & Zipkin. With this successful experience, we decided to further include repair and lateral re-supply here in our model. In other words, demands can be satisfied by either repairing locally or replacing these failed items with local inventory or inventory from a neighboring depot. Immediately following, we illustrate the extensions to the Federgruen-Zipkin-Chan (FZC) model and formulate the extended model. Then we use generalized Benders decomposition (Geoffrion 1972) to solve it.

As a first step, we will list the variables and notation used in FZ and extended model, respectively. The unique variables used in FZ model are:

z_i is a discrete variable that denotes the amount of spare-part delivery to depot i.
y^h_i is a binary assignment variable that equals 1 if vehicle h delivers from depot i, and 0 otherwise.

The other variables and notation used in FZ model such as x_{ij}^h, ξ, H, I, β_i, C_i, d_{ij}, V_h, *and* $\bar{P}_i$ are the same as in the extended model.

x_{ij}^h is a binary variable that equals 1 if vehicle h traverses the arc from i to j in making a delivery, and 0 otherwise.
$x_{ij}^h(u)$ suggests that it is a delivery of repaired items, while $x_{ij}^h(d)$ suggests that it is a delivery of stored items.

Notice the delivery can only be made if the requested repair or shipment is consistent with the repair capability $[U_i(u), L_i(u)]$ and storage capacity $[U_i(d), L_i(d)]$ respectively at depot i, as defined by the range from the lower bound L to the upper bound U.

y_j is a binary variable that equals 1 if a demand for spare parts is placed on depot j, and 0 otherwise.
y_{ij} is a binary variable that equals 1 if an order is placed to have an item delivered from depot i to depot j, and 0 otherwise.
y^h_{ij} is a binary assignment variable that equals 1 if vehicle h delivers from depot i to depot j, and 0 otherwise.
z_{ij} is a discrete variable that denotes the amount of spare-part delivery to depot j from depot i.
ξ is a random variable associated with a demand in any kind of probability distribution.
H is the set of all vehicles where $h=0, 1, \ldots, H''$; here $h=0$ is a dummy vehicle to visit depots that need no delivery.
I is the set of all nodes, where $I=0, 1, 2,$ and 3 in our example; and the main depot is node 0.

As inputs to the model, we need to know the following:

β_i is an initial inventory level of depot *i* for our single period model.
c_i is a unit carrying-cost or surplus-cost in depot i.
C_i is the unit shortage-cost in depot *i*.
d_{ij} is the unit transportation cost between depots i and j.
V_h is the *vehicle* capacity associated with vehicle *h*.
$\overline{P}_i$ is the *holding* capacity at depot *i*.

4.3.1 Extensions to the FZC Model

The FZC model really consist of the Traveling-Salesmen sub-problem and the Delivery-Allocation sub-problem. The former is manifested in terms of the VRP, while the latter is manifested in a newsvendor problem. The VRP is concerned with routing a fleet of vehicles to the depots. Because of the perishable nature of a newspaper, the newsvendor problem consists of seeking a balanced inventory that minimizes the sum of over- and under-stocking costs. First, a possible extension can be made on the newsvendor problem. The other extension is related to VRP, especially the delivery part.

To start, we should define the extra decision variables and parameters needed:

$$x_{ij}^h = \begin{cases} 1 & \text{if } L_i(u) \le x_{ij}^h(u) \le U_i(u) \text{ and/or } L_i(d) \le x_{ij}^h(d) \le U_i(d) \\ 0 & \text{otherwise} \end{cases}$$

Here, we add two components to the original FZC vehicle-routing decision-variable $x^h{}_{ij}$. They are related to the quantity repaired at depot *i* and the inventory at the depot. These repaired and inventoried items are available for both local consumption as well as re-supplies to other depots. In other words, both the repaired and inventoried items can be delivered from depot *i* to depot *j*—denoted by $x^h{}_{ij}(u)$ and $x^h{}_{ij}(d)$ respectively. Here the two new decision variables, $x^h{}_{ij}(u)$ and $x^h{}_{ij}(d)$, lie within the upper bound and lower bound as mandated respectively by the repair capability $[U_i(u), L_i(u)]$ and storage capacity $[U_i(d), L_i(d)]$ respectively at depot *i*.

Correspondingly, $x^1{}_{23}(u) = 1$ suggests vehicle 1 picks up the repaired items at depot 2 and delivers it to depot 3, where it is needed. $x^2{}_{02}(u) = 1$ suggests that vehicle 2 picks up the repaired item at the main depot (node 0) and delivers to depot 2. (Should both $x^2{}_{02}(u)$ and $x^1{}_{23}(u)$ pick up the unitary value, then vehicle 1 picked up a repaired item at location 0 and drove to depot 2 and then deliver it to depot 3—as illustrated in Fig. 4.2.) In Table 4.2, the bounds $L_2(u)$ and $U_2(u)$ for $x^1{}_{23}(u)$ reflect the repair capability at depot 2, which ranges between [0–9]—as illustrated also in Fig. 4.2. In future extensions, a probability density function can ideally be used in lieu of a uniform distribution within a range. Naturally, this would introduce another random variable into the model, aside from failure probabilities.

On the other hand, $x^1{}_{23}(d)$ denotes the amount of inventoried items vehicle 1 picks up at depot 2 and delivers to depot 3. $x^2{}_{02}(d)$ suggests that vehicle 2 picks up

Table 4.2 Inventory/Allocation for the example problem

Depot	0	1	2	3
Max. inventory ($\bar{P}_i$)	10	4	5	5
Min. inventory	0	0	0	0
Initial inventory (β_i)	2	1	2	1
Demand: uniform pdf	0.1	0.25	0.4	0.2
Shortage cost (C_i)	\$ 5	\$ 20	\$ 25	\$ 15
Surplus cost (c_i)	\$ 10	\$ 5	\$ 5	\$ 5
Inventory-cost function	$18+0.5z_{10}+0.5z_{20}+0.5z_{30}$	$48.75-3.75z_{01}-3.75z_{21}-3.75z_{31}$	$51-4z_{02}-4z_{12}-4z_{32}$	$39-2z_{03}-2z_{13}-2z_{23}$
Failure range		[0–9]	[0–10]	[0–9]
Repair capability range	[0–15]	[0–6]	[0–9]	[0–9]

stored items at main depot 0 and delivers to depot 2. Obviously, $x^1_{23}(d)$ is determined by the remaining inventory of depot 2. Similarly, $x^2_{02}(d)$ is governed by the remaining inventory at depot 0. As long as parts are available, they can be delivered. The amount of storage at depot i is determined by the manager on the basis of the newsvendor inventory-cost function, as shown in Table 4.2. Notice this cost function is computed based on Eq. (4.2) below. The unit cost of storage and repair will decide—along with transportation cost—the relative merits of re-supplying from the repair shop vis-à-vis the stored inventory.

We assume that every depot can supply the other depot and itself, as shown by the delivery decision variable z_{ij}. Thus, z_{01} is the shipment from depot 0 to depot 1. This amount is the sum of the repaired and inventoried items delivered from depot 0 to depot 1 by any vehicle. To see the significance of these new variables, let us define z_{ij} explicitly in terms of the allocation of available products from depot i to depot j (via the fleet of vehicles H):

$$z_{ij} = \sum\nolimits_{h \in H} \left[x_{ij}^h(u) + x_{ij}^h(d) \right]$$

Setting aside transportation cost, we suggest that a re-supply at j can be satisfied equally well by repaired or inventoried items available at depot i. Perhaps it is more desirable to consider the unit cost of repair and storage in the above equation for z_{ij}. Barring nonavailability, the cheaper way to re-supply is preferred. Let w_i be the unit repair-cost at depot i to supplement the delivery unit cost c_i'.

$$z_{ij} = \sum\nolimits_{h \in H} x_{ij}^h(u) \qquad \text{if } w_i < c_i'$$

$$z_{ij} = \sum\nolimits_{h \in H} x_{ij}^h(d) \qquad \text{if } c_i' \le w_i$$

We highlight the decision variable, z_{ii}, to show that each depot can re-supply itself. Thus z_{11} is the amount that depot 1 re-supplies itself, and z_{22} is the amount that depot 2 re-supplies itself. Notice that z_{11} is the sum of $x_{11}(u)$ and $x_{11}(d)$, or that local demand can be satisfied by both repaired and inventoried items:

$$\mathrm{z_{ii} = x_{ii}(u) + x_{ii}(d)}$$

Let us now examine the "placing-order" assignment-variable y_{ij}^h. Thus y^1_{01} equals unity if vehicle 1 ships supply from depot 0 to depot 1; and zero otherwise. In other words, the delivery variable z_{01} takes on a nonzero value if $y^1_{01} = 1$, in accordance with this generalization. (More will be said about this in the formal model formulation in Sect. 4.3.2).

We refer to y_i (and its allied variable y_{ij}) as a "bookkeeping" binary variable. It is equal to unity if depot i can supply other depots; we say the depot i is *sufficient*, in the sense it is fully endowed with an inventory of spare parts. It is equal to zero otherwise. In the latter case, it accepts supplies but cannot deliver to others. Thus y_i suggests that either it can send an item to the other depots or it accepts items from other depots, but not both-if we assume the triangle inequality. Remember we are covering shortage with both repaired and inventoried items, it would make little sense to supply (say) three items to the outside, while accepting one repaired item from outside. In sum, we use this variable to mark either one of these two cases: If y_1 is equal to one, then it means that depot 1 will be sufficient enough to re-supply itself and can supply the other depots. If y_1 is zero, it means that depot 1 has used up all of its available resources and has nothing to offer.

4.3.2 Research Problem Formulation

We will now set up our research problem as a model that includes *r*epair and *l*ateral re-*s*upply, or RLS model in short. The objective function of the research problem is the same as that of the FZC model. It is to minimize the traveling cost in the first term and inventory cost in the second term, shown below as sum of these two terms:

$$\sum_{i\in I}\sum_{j\in I}\sum_{h\in H\backslash 0} d_{ij}x_{ij}^h + \sum_{i\in I}\sum_{j\in I} q(z_{ij}) \tag{4.1}$$

Now that each depot can supply the other depots, we elaborate this fact in the classic inventory-cost function by way of the variable z_{ij} (Chan 2005):

$$q_i(z_{ji}) = \int_{\beta_i+z_{jij}}^{\infty} C_i(\xi-\beta_i-z_{ji})dF_i(\xi) + \int_{0}^{\beta_i+z_{ji}} c_i(\beta_i+z_{ji}-\xi)dF_i(\zeta), \quad i\in I \tag{4.2}$$

Here $F_i(\cdot)$ is the cumulative demand-distribution function at depot i (Khouja 1999). In our model, we have imbedded the newsvendor problem within this cost function. More often than not, the inventory cost function (2) is *nonlinear*. For depot 1, let us say C_1 = \$ 20 per item, which is the shortage cost; and c_1 = \$ 5 per item, which is unit carrying cost. Further, $\beta_1 = 1$ unit, which is the initial inventory level, and the depot maximum capacity is equal to 4 unit (see Table 4.2 and Fig. 4.2). By taking the integral of the inventory cost function with the given parameters, we would come up with the following result, $q_1(z_{01}) = 12.8 - 3.75z_{ij}$ for the given uniform probability-density-function and for the depot pair 0–1. Notice it is a linear demand function for this example. By considering not only one depot pair, but all depot pairs 0-1, 2-1, and 3-1, we obtain the inventory-cost function as shown in Table 4.2 and Fig. 4.2: $q_1(z_{01}) + q_1(z_{21}) + q_1(z_{31}) = 48.75 - 3.75z_{01} - 3.75z_{21} - 3.75z_{31}$.

Here, we are using the travel-time/cost matrix as shown in Table 4.3 and Fig. 4.1.

In Table 4.2, the example inventory-cost functions are the solution to Eq. (4.2) with the uniform demand functions as shown, giving rise to linear functions. They suggest that random demands can be re-supplied from any of the other three depots, 0, 1, 2, or 3. Here the three identical demand coefficients of depot 1are the same, 3.75, regardless how it is supplied. The inventory-cost functions for the remaining depots are similar. Notice that the main depot is now treated the same as any other depot. It can be a demand point theoretically, and be re-supplied from any other

Table 4.3 Travel-cost matrix

	Depot 0	Depot 1	Depot 2	Depot 3
Depot 0	–	3	3.5	2
Depot 1	3	–	4	5
Depot 2	3.5	4	–	3.8
Depot 3	2	5	3.8	–

depot. In this example, the coefficients for the demand function of depot 0, $q_0(z_0)$, are all positive, indicating its shortage cost is less than its surplus cost in Eq. (4.2). Instead of a decreasing function, it is an increasing function, suggesting it is more costly to overstock.

We will now lay down the sets of constraints found in the classical VRP. Inventory constraints are then incorporated to combine the VRP and inventory/allocation problem. These VRP equations are unchanged from the FZC model.

$$\sum_{j\in I}\sum_{h\in H} x_{ij}^h = \begin{cases} H'' & if\ i = 0 \\ 1 & if\ i = 1, 2, \cdots, |I| \end{cases} \tag{4.3}$$

$$\sum_{i\in I}\sum_{h\in H} x_{ij}^h = \begin{cases} H'' & if\ j = 0 \\ 1 & if\ j = 1,\ 2,\ \cdots, |I| \end{cases} \tag{4.4}$$

Both on the way out from and returning the main depot, constraints (3) and (4) ensure that we used all available vehicles (including the dummy vehicle) stationed at a depot to serve the demand points. At the same time, each demand node (other than the main depot where the fleet is based), is visited only once by a vehicle. In other words, delivery is made only once, whether the spare part is coming from the home depot or from another depot.

$$\sum_{i\in Mp} x_{ip}^h - \sum_{j\in \bar{M}p} x_{pj}^h = 0 \qquad \forall h \in H, \forall p \in I \tag{4.5}$$

Constraint (5) maintains the route continuity for all vehicle types, where M_p denotes the nodes incident upon node p, and $\bar{M}_p$ denotes the nodes emanating from node p.

$$\sum_{j\in \bar{M}_0} x_{0j}^h \le 1 \ \forall h \in H \ \text{ and } \sum_{i\in M_0} x_{i0}^h \le 1 \ \ \forall h \in H \tag{4.6}$$

For the fleet based at the main depot, the above two constraints in Eq. (4.6) ensure that vehicle availability (including the dummy vehicle) is not exceeded for vehicle h.

$$\sum_{i\in L}\sum_{j\in L} x_{ij}^h \le |L| - 1 \qquad L \subseteq \{1,\ \cdots,\ |I|-1\}; 1 \le |L| \le |I|-1; h \in H \tag{4.7}$$

Constraint (7) is a subtour-breaking constraint where L is the nonempty set of $I\backslash 0$. All vehicles begin their tours from the main depot and come back to it. This constraint ensures that all tours in the solution are legitimate; namely, no subtour will occur in the solution.

Here, the travel-cost matrix is symmetric: $d_{ij}=d_{ji}$—i.e., the time going from node i to node j is the same as going from node j to node i. They satisfy the triangular inequality: $d_{ij}\leq d_{ik}+d_{kj}$. Unlike a regular VRP, a depot (demand point) needs not be visited when it has no inventory shortage. This is accomplished by the use of a dummy vehicle $h=0$, which makes a visit to satisfy the VRP (or traveling-salesman problem) stipulation, but carries no delivery. Notice this mathematical property is required in a combined inventory-delivery problem when the demand at a node is a random variable.

Here, this *nonlinear* constraint set ensures that the load assigned to each vehicle h is within its capacity

$$\sum_{i\in I}\sum_{\substack{j\in I\\ i\neq j}} z_{ij}y_{ij}^{h} \leq V_h \quad h\in H \tag{4.8}$$

The FZC linking-constraint is now generalized to read

$$\sum_{j\in \bar{M}_j} x_{ij}^{h} - y_{ij}^{h} \geq 0 \quad \forall\ i\in I, h\in H,\ i\neq j \tag{4.9}$$

For the FZC allocation/inventory constraints, a fair amount of effort is required to modify them to the new settings of the RLS model.

$$\sum_{j\in I} z_{ij} \leq \bar{P}_i \quad \forall i\in I \tag{4.10}$$

$$\sum_{i\in I} z_{ij} < U_j(d) \quad \forall j\in I \tag{4.11}$$

$$\sum_{h\in H}\sum_{\substack{i\in I\\ i\neq j}} y_{ij}^{h} \leq 1 \quad \forall j\in I \tag{4.12}$$

Since we had only one main supplier in the FZC model, we had a single constraint (10) for the main depot, where $i=0$. Currently, the number of supply depots will be the same as the number of nodes, as clearly shown in Eq. (4.10) for $i=0$, 1, 2, and 3. The stored items available, together with the repair capability, define the supply quantity at each depot.

There is another constraint for each depot besides the supply constraints. Equation (4.11) ensures that the holding capacity cannot be exceeded at each demand point j. Equation (4.12) is a natural extension of the FZC model, when there are multiple sources of supply. Excluding redundant re-supply, any supply source i and any vehicle h can satisfy a demand at j.

Suppose the failures at each depot exceed replenishment available locally, counting both inventoried items and repaired items. We can secure supplies from the outside to cover the failures. In Table 4.2 and Fig. 4.2, for example, failures can be between zero and nine at depot 1. The initial level and maximum inventory level of depot 1 is one and four respectively. The repair capability is up to six units. Failures that cannot be replenished locally is two, setting aside one (at hand) and six (repaired units), resulting in two units of shortage: $9-(1+6)=2$. If it is prudent to do so cost-wise, depot 1 can demand up to six units to be delivered—which is four units of inventory stored in the spare depot capacity plus two units' shortages. The model calculates the supplies to other depots in the same fashion. It is time to talk about these additional constraints in the RLS model. In all the following four equations, M is an arbitrarily large number:

$$x_{ij}^{h}(u)+x_{ij}^{h}(d)-Mx_{ij}^{h}\leq 0 \tag{4.13}$$

$$z_{ij}=\begin{cases} x_{ii}(u)+x_{ii}(d) & i=j \\ \sum_{h\in H}\left[x_{ij}^{h}(u)+x_{ij}^{h}(d)\right] & i\neq j \end{cases} \tag{4.14}$$

$$\begin{aligned} &\Sigma_{i\in I\setminus j}z_{ij}+My_{j}\geq 0 && \text{(i)}\\ &\Sigma_{i\in I\setminus j}z_{ji}-My_{j}\leq 0 && \text{(ii)}\\ &\Sigma_{i\in I\setminus j}z_{ij}+My_{j}\leq M && \text{(iii)}\\ &\Sigma_{i\in I\setminus j}z_{ji}-My_{j}\geq -M && \text{(iv)} \end{aligned} \tag{4.15}$$

$$\begin{aligned} &z_{jj}-\left[\beta_{j}+U_{j}(u)\right]+My_{j}\geq 0 && \text{(i)}\\ &z_{jj}-My_{j}\geq -M && \text{(ii)} \end{aligned} \tag{4.16}$$

$$x_{ii}(u)+x_{ij}^{h}(u)\leq U_{i}(u) \tag{4.17}$$

$$x_{i}(d)+x_{ij}^{h}(d)\leq \beta_{i} \tag{4.18}$$

$$\sum_{i\in I}t_{i}^{h}\sum_{j\in I}x_{ij}^{h}+\sum_{i\in I}\sum_{j\in I}d_{ij}^{h}x_{ij}^{h}\leq U_{h} \qquad \forall h\in H \tag{4.19}$$

$$z_{ij}-M\sum_{h\in H}y_{ij}^{h}\leq 0 \qquad \forall\, i,j\in I; i\neq j \tag{4.20}$$

Equation (4.13) above suggests that we can deliver if the vehicle-routing arc (i, j) is open. At the same time, we put all z in one place in Eq. (4.14)–(4.16) so that we can understand the relation between them. Equation (4.14) distinguishes between local re-supply vs. re-supplying other depots. Equations (4.15) and (4.16) are connected to each other as follows. Equation (4.15) suggests that we either deliver the items to the other depots or get the items from the other depots. Equation (4.16) ensures that before obtaining the items from the other depots, we make sure that the depot has used all its available resources.

Let us give an example of Eqs. (4.15) and (4.16):

$$
\begin{aligned}
&z_{01}+z_{21}+z_{31}+50y_1 \geq 0 && \text{(i)}\\
&z_{10}+z_{12}+z_{13}-50y_1 \leq 0 && \text{(ii)}\\
&z_{01}+z_{21}+z_{31}+50y_1 \leq 50 && \text{(iii)}\\
&z_{10}+z_{12}+z_{13}-50y_1 \geq -50 && \text{(iv)}
\end{aligned} \tag{4.21}
$$

$$
\begin{aligned}
&z_{11}-7+50y_1 \geq 0 && \text{(i)}\\
&z_{11}-50y_1 \geq -50 && \text{(ii)}
\end{aligned} \tag{4.22}
$$

Here big-M is set at 50, $i=0, 2, 3$ and $j=1$. This suggests that in our four-depot example network, we are focusing on depot 1, with the other depots being the home depot 0, depot 2 and depot 3. The local resources available at depot 1 is seven units as shown in Eq. (4.22)—corresponding to the sum of the inventory at hand ($\beta_{1=}1$ unit) and the repair capability ($U_1(u)=6$ units). If $y1$ is zero, or there is no demand for spare parts placed on depot 1, then Eqs. (i) and (iii) will hold, allowing depot 1 to receive spare parts from other depots. Meanwhile, Eqs. (ii) and (iv) will reflect no delivery from depot 1 to other depots. If $y1$ equals unity, or there is demand for spare parts placed on depot 1, then Eqs. (ii) and (iv) would hold. This allows the delivery of spare parts from depot 1 to the other three depots. Meanwhile, Eqs. (i) and (iii) translate to no deliveries from the other depots to depot 1.

Equation (4.22) suggests that if $y1$ is equal to zero, or no spare-part demand is placed on depot 1, all available resources are to be "delivered" locally–a total of seven units in this case. If $y1$ is unity, or there is spare-part demand placed on depot 1, then Eq. (4.22) is relaxed, or that the resource may not be used locally.

Equation (4.17) relates to the repair capacity at the depot. This repair capacity $U_i(u)$ includes potentially what it repairs for itself and for the other depots. Equation (4.18) is the constraint related to available inventory at each depot. This constraint is similar to the repair capacity. It includes what it supplies to itself and others out of its depot inventory. We modified the VRP constraints by adding Eq. (4.19), which suggests that we operate within available crew-duty hours. Here we also add a constant loading and unloading time. Specifically, t^h_i is the given amount of time vehicle h spends at demand point i. U_h is the time that a vehicle h spends "on the road" (or the crew duty hours). Equation (4.20) is a natural statement to accompany the "placing order" variable y_{ij} when there are multiple sources of supply.

4.4 Summary, Conclusions and Recommendations

In this chapter, we put forth a real-life air force logistics problem. We consider a single repairable item, one main-depot and multiple satellite-depot supply–chain-management problem. Each depot, including the main depot, faces random demand of the item. Besides inventory, each depot or the main depot has a repair capacity and thus can re-generate a failed item. Items can be transported from one depot to another to satisfy the demand, using a fleet of vehicles stationed at the main depot. Each vehicle makes a tour to visit one or more depots before returning to the main depot. Transportation cost is charged against the total operating cost. Inventory holding and shortage costs for unsatisfied demands are charged at the depots, contributing toward the total operating cost. The objective is to decide the amount of items to repair at the depots and a distribution plan of the available items among the depots so as to minimize the total transportation and expected holding and shortage costs. We formulate the problem as a nonlinear MIP, consisting of a generally nonlinear objective-function and nonlinear constraints. Generalized Benders' decomposition is proposed to solve the resulting RLS problem.

Acknowledgements The authors like to acknowledge the valuable inputs from M. Arostegui, M. Niklas, J. Stewart, and J. Weir, for their contribution during the conduct of this study. They also benefited from the insightful comments of reviewers. The study was conducted under the sponsorship of the Air Force Materiel Command at Wright-Patterson AFB while the first author was stationed at the Base and while the second author was a faculty member of the Air Force Institute of Technology. Obviously, the authors alone are responsible for the document as presented. The views expressed here do not represent those of the organizations the authors are/were affiliated with.

References

Axater, S.: A new decision rule for lateral transshipments in inventory systems. Manage. Sci. **49**, 1168–1179 (2003)

Baita, F., Ukovich, W., Pesenti, R., Favaretto, D.: Dynamic routing-and–inventory problems: A review. Transp. Res-A. **32**, 585–598 (1998)

Berman, O., Larson, R.C.: Deliveries in an inventory/routing problem using stochastic dynamic programming. Transp. Sci. **35**, 192–213 (2001)

Bertazzi, L., Paletta, G., Speranza, M.G.: Deterministic order-up-to-level policies in an inventory routing problem. Transp. Sci. **36**, 119–132 (2002)

Bowersox, D.J., Closs, D.J.: Logistical Management: The Integrated Supply Chain Processes. McGraw-Hill, New York (1996)

Chan, Y.: Location, Transport and Land-Use: Modelling spatial-temporal information. Springer, Heidelberg (2005)

Christofides, N., Beasley, E.J.: The period routing problem. Networks. **14**, 237–256 (1984)

Coelho, L.C., Cordeau, J.-F., Laporte, G.: (n.d.): "Thirty years of inventory-routing." Working paper, Faculte des sciences de l'administration, Laval University, Quebec City

DeCroix, G., Song, J.-S., Zipkin, P.H.: A series system with returns: Stationary analysis. Op. Res. **53**, 350–362 (2005)

Dror, M., Ball, M.: Inventory/routing: Reduction from an annual to a short-period problem. Nav. Res. Logist. **34**, 891–905 (1987)

Federgruen, A., Zipkin, P.: A combined vehicle routing and inventory/allocation problem. Op. Res. **32**, 1019–1037 (1984)

Federgruen, A., Prastacos, G., Zipkin, P.H.: An allocation and distribution model for perishable products. Op Res. **31**, 75–82 (1986)

Geoffrion, A.M.: Generalized benders decomposition. J. Optim. Theory Appl. **10**, 237–260 (1972)

Haughton, M.A., Stenger, A.J.: Comparing strategies for addressing delivery shortages in stochastic demand settings. Transp. Res-E. **35**, 25–41 (1999)
Herer, Y.T, Levy, R.: The metered inventory problem, an integrative heuristic algorithm. Prod. Econ. **51**, 69–81 (1997)
Herer, Y.T., Rashit, A.: Lateral stock transshipments in a two-location inventory system with fixed and joint replenishment costs. Nav. Res. Logist. **46**, 525–547 (1999)
Hooker, J. N.: Planning and scheduling by logic-based benders decomposition. Oper. Res. **55**(3), 588–602 (2007)
Jung, B.-R., Sun, B.-G., Kim, J.-S., Ahn, S.-E.: Modeling lateral transshipments in multiechelon repairable-item inventory systems with finite repair channels. Comput. Op. Res. **30**, 1401–1417 (2003)
Kaihara, T.: Multi-agent based supply chain modelling with dynamic environments. Int. J. Prod. Econ. **85**, 263–269 (2003)
Khouja, M.: The single-period (news-vendor) problem: Literature review and suggestions for future research. Omega—Int. J. Manage. Sci. **27**, 537–553 (1999)
McGrath, R.N.: Maintenance: The missing link in supply chain management. Ind. Manage. **41**, 29–33 (1999)
Meloa, M.T., Nickel, S., Saldanha da Gama, F.: Dynamic multi-commodity capacitated facility location: a mathematical modeling framework for strategic supply chain planning. Comput. Op. Res. **33**, 181–208 (2005)
Shen, Z-.J. M., Coullard, C., Daskin, M.S.: A joint location-inventory model. Transp. Sci. **37**, 40–55 (2003)
Sherbrook, C.C.: Optimal Inventory Modeling of Systems: Multi-echelon Techniques. Wiley, New York (1992)
Slikker, M., Fransoo, J., Wouters, M.: Cooperation between multiple new-vendors with transshipments. Eur. J. Oper. Res. **167**, 370–380 (2005)
Stadler, H.: Supply chain management and advanced planning—basics, overview and challenges. Eur. J. Oper. Res. **163**, 575–588 (1995)
Tersine, R.J.: Principles of Inventory and Materials Management. PTR Prentice-Hall, Saddle River (1994)
Webb, I.R., Larson, R.C.: Period and phase of customer replenishment: A new approach to the strategic inventory/routing problem. Eur. J. Oper. Res. **85**, 132–148 (1995)
Yang, W-W; Mathur, K.; Ballou, R.H.: Stochastic vehicle routing problem with restocking. Transp. Sci. **34**, 99–112 (2000)

Chapter 5
A Combined Inventory and Lateral Resupply Model for Repairable Items—Part II: Solution by Generalized Benders' Decomposition

Bahtiyar Eren and Yupo Chan

5.1 Background

We consider a single repairable item, one main-depot and multiple satellite-depot supply–chain-management problem. Each depot, including the main depot, faces random demand of the item. Besides inventory, each depot or the main depot has a repair capacity and thus can regenerate a failed item (Wang et al. 2000). Items can be transported from one depot to another to satisfy the demand, using a fleet of vehicles stationed at the main depot. Each vehicle makes a tour to visit one or more depots before returning to the main depot. Transportation cost is charged against the total operating cost. Inventory holding and shortage costs for unsatisfied demands are charged at the depots, contributing toward the total operating cost. The objective is to decide the amount of items to repair at the depots and a distribution plan of the available items among the depots so as to minimize the total transportation and expected holding and shortage costs. We formulate the problem as a nonlinear MIP, consisting of a generally nonlinear objective-function and nonlinear constraints. Generalized Benders' decomposition is used to solve the resulting a model that includes repair and lateral resupply or the RLS problem in short.

B. Eren (✉)
Hv.K.K.ligi Karargahi Harekat Baskanligi, 06100 Bakanliklar-Ankara, Turkey
e-mail: erenbahtiyar@yahoo.com

Y. Chan
Department of Systems Engineering, University of Arkansas at Little Rock,
Little Rock, AR, USA
e-mail: yxchan@ualr.edu

V. Zeimpekis et al. (eds.), *Military Logistics*, Operations Research/Computer Science Interfaces Series 56, DOI 10.1007/978-3-319-12075-1_5

5.1.1 Generalized Benders' Decomposition

With the background and literature review provided in Chap. 5, we will dive directly into model formulation and solution. Now let describe the detailed procedure to solve the RLS model by generalized Benders' decomposition.

$$\min_{\mathbf{x},\mathbf{y}} f(\mathbf{x},\mathbf{y}) \text{ s.t. } G(\mathbf{x},\mathbf{y}) \le 0 \qquad \mathbf{x} \in X, \mathbf{y} \in Y'' \tag{5.1}$$

where $f(\mathbf{x})$ is the objective function as shown in Eq. (5.1), with the variable **y** implicitly included. Here, f and G are general differentiable functions. This means that f and G can be differentiable nonlinear functions, as they are in the RLS model. The constraints define the routing variables, and represent all assignment of demands. For a fixed binary assignment vector **y**, we have independent subproblems, each of which has their own solution vector **x**, corresponding to delivery allocations. $G(\mathbf{x}, \mathbf{y})$ represents all the other linear inequalities defining the traveling salesman problem (TSP) polytope. The LP-relaxation of this problem will be in a convex set, and we have a special structure that can be exploited.

Correspondingly, the solution to the RLS model is broken down into two subproblems: the TSP and Delivery-Allocation.

Traveling-Salesmen Subproblem: The objective of the TSP subproblem is to derive the constants κ associated with the vehicles h in Eq. (5.3) below. These κ are to be obtained by first solving the TSP for the σh multipliers. This amounts to solving a linear program (LP), with the σ showing up as the dual variables for the constraints that describe the hth TSP polytope. The TSP subproblem that must be solved consists of all the constraints of the model except the nonlinear constraints (8) and the capacity constraints (10) in the Part I chapter. We substitute the assignment vector y into the delivery-prohibition or linking constraints (9) in the Part I chapter and solve the corresponding TSP. The end result is a routing pattern characterized by x.

Delivery-Allocation Subproblem: Solution of the second subproblem, Delivery-Allocation, is represented by minimization over the vector z, or the deliveries from depot i to j. Instead of a traditional newsvendor problem, the Delivery-Allocation subproblem can be solved as the following mathematical program: $\min_{\mathbf{z}} \Sigma_{i\in I} \Sigma_{j\in I} q_i(z_{ij})$ subject to constraints (8) and (10) in the Part I chapter. Traditional solution of the newsvendor problem via Eq. (2) in the Part I chapter poses a "chicken -and-egg" dilemma where ξ and the dual variables Ω and ρ are interdependent, reflecting the competition among the three demand locations for supplies. Furthermore, there are the upper bounds on ξ as imposed by Eq. (5.10) and the maximum inventories $\bar{P}_i$ allowable at a depot. This poses additional complications, defying a traditional newsvendor solution. The problem is best solved by taking out the z components of the original objective function (1), plus constraints (8) and (9); with a given assignment vector **y**. This constitutes the Delivery-Allocation subproblem. The usual bounds on decision variables z and nonnegativity constraints apply. Solution of this mathematical program yields z as well as the dual variables Ω for constraints (8) and (10) in the Part I chapter, and ρ^h for the vehicle-capacity constraints. Notice these dual variables are exactly the ones needed in the master problem.

Having separated into subproblems, the remaining question is how to reassemble them to solve the original model. The challenging part of generalized Benders' decomposition is to define the relaxed master problem, which is equivalent to the original problem

$$\min\{z \mid z \geq z'(\mathbf{y}), \mathbf{y} \in Y''\} \tag{5.2}$$

where represents all possible assignments of y_{ij}^h. The relaxed master problem defines a set of existing cuts $z \geq z'(\mathbf{y})$ that eventually lead toward the optimal solution. The Delivery-Allocation subproblem determines the delivery-allocation **z** vector, and more importantly the associated dual variables Ω and ρ^h, corresponding to the depot and vehicle capacities.

Associated with these dual variables and those from the TSP subproblem (κ), the Benders' cut for the model is:

$$z \geq \Omega_j \overline{P}_j + \sum_{h \in H} (\rho^h V_h + \kappa^h + \kappa_0^h) + \sum_{i \in I-j} \varphi_i^0 y_i^0 + \sum_{h \in H} \sum_{i \in I-j} (\kappa_i^h + \varphi_i^h) y_i^h \qquad \forall j \in I \tag{5.3}$$

Here,

- Ω_j is the dual variables corresponding to the depot capacity constraints—a parameter to account for the given warehouse capacity;
- ρ^h is the parameter or dual variable to account for the *h*th delivery-vehicle capacity;
- κ^h is the cost of operating vehicle *h*;
- κ_i^h is the marginal cost of serving demand-node *i* using vehicle *h*;
- φ_i^h is the expected cost between stockout and storage in a newsvendor problem (for depot involving vehicle *h*);
- V_h is the vehicle capacity associated with vehicle *h*.

In our RLS model, we add this definition: $y_i^h = y_{ij}^h$. Setting aside Ω, the first two single summations in Eq. (5.3) are referring to the "intercept" of the Benders' cut, and the last double summations represent the "slope." Since the RLS model has four supply depots instead of simply from the main depot, we should write down four separate cuts. The first cut is generated for main depot 0, which is shown in Eq. (5.4). The other cuts are generated for depot 1, 2 and 3 in Eqs. (5.5), (5.6), and (5.7) respectively.

$$z \geq \Omega_0 \overline{P}_0 + \sum_{h \in H} (\rho^h V_h + \kappa^h + \kappa_0^h) + \sum_{i \in I-0} \varphi_i^0 y_i^0 + \sum_{h \in H} \sum_{i \in I-0} (\kappa_i^h + \varphi_i^h) y_i^h \tag{5.4}$$

$$z \geq \Omega_1 \overline{P}_1 + \sum_{h \in H} (\rho^h V_h + \kappa^h + \kappa_0^h) + \sum_{i \in I-1} \varphi_i^0 y_i^0 + \sum_{h \in H} \sum_{i \in I-1} (\kappa_i^h + \varphi_i^h) y_i^h \tag{5.5}$$

$$z \geq \Omega_2 \overline{P}_2 + \sum_{h \in H} (\rho^h V_h + \kappa^h + \kappa_0^h) + \sum_{i \in I-2} \varphi_i^0 y_i^0 + \sum_{h \in H} \sum_{i \in I-2} (\kappa_i^h + \varphi_i^h) y_i^h \tag{5.6}$$

$$z \geq \Omega_3 \overline{P}_3 + \sum_{h\in H} (\rho^h V_h + \kappa^h + \kappa_0^h) + \sum_{i\in I-3} \varphi_i^0 y_i^0 + \sum_{h\in H}\sum_{i\in I-3} (\kappa_i^h + \varphi_i^h) y_i^h \tag{5.7}$$

We want to explain the inventory-cost portion of the Benders' cut. The inventory-cost function is modified from the FZC cut. Here we define the inventory-cost functions associated with the "intercept" of Eq. (5.4). This is accomplished by solving the newsvendor problem parametric in terms of the dual variables Ω and ρ, associated with the constraints of the Delivery-Allocation subproblem. The φ_i^0 results for the main depot are shown as follows, where the z_{ij} are obtained by the Delivery-Allocation Subproblem as described above (Chan 2005).

$$\begin{aligned}
\varphi_1^0 &= 48.75 - 3.75\,(z_{01} + z_{21} + z_{31}) - (\Omega_0 - \rho_0) z_{01} - (\Omega_0 - \rho_0) z_{21} - (\Omega_0 - \rho_0) z_{31} \\
\varphi_2^0 &= 51 - 4\,(z_{02} + z_{12} + z_{32}) - (\Omega_0 - \rho_0) z_{02} - (\Omega_0 - \rho_0) z_{12} - (\Omega_0 - \rho_0) z_{32} \\
\varphi_3^0 &= 39 - 2\,(z_{03} + z_{13} + z_{23}) - (\Omega_0 - \rho_0) z_{03} - (\Omega_0 - \rho_0) z_{13} - (\Omega_0 - \rho_0) z_{23}
\end{aligned} \tag{5.8}$$

In Eq. (5.4), the "slope" of the equation is based upon the operating cost (κ_i^h) and inventory cost (φ_i^h). Correspondingly, the φ_i^h results for the "slope" can be defined as

$$\begin{aligned}
\varphi_1^1 &= 48.75 - 3.75\,(z_{01} + z_{21} + z_{31}) - (\Omega_0 - \rho_1) z_{01} - (\Omega_0 - \rho_1) z_{21} - (\Omega_0 - \rho_1) z_{31} \\
\varphi_2^1 &= 51 - 4\,(z_{02} + z_{12} + z_{32}) - (\Omega_0 - \rho_1) z_{02} - (\Omega_0 - \rho_1) z_{12} - (\Omega_0 - \rho_1) z_{32} \\
\varphi_3^1 &= 39 - 2\,(z_{03} + z_{13} + z_{23}) - (\Omega_0 - \rho_1) z_{03} - (\Omega_0 - \rho_1) z_{13} - (\Omega_0 - \rho_1) z_{23} \\
\varphi_1^2 &= 48.75 - 3.75\,(z_{01} + z_{21} + z_{31}) - (\Omega_0 - \rho_2) z_{01} - (\Omega_0 - \rho_2) z_{21} - (\Omega_0 - \rho_2) z_{31} \\
\varphi_2^2 &= 51 - 4\,(z_{02} + z_{12} + z_{32}) - (\Omega_0 - \rho_2) z_{02} - (\Omega_0 - \rho_2) z_{12} - (\Omega_0 - \rho_2) z_{32} \\
\varphi_3^2 &= 39 - 2\,(z_{03} + z_{13} + z_{23}) - (\Omega_0 - \rho_2) z_{03} - (\Omega_0 - \rho_2) z_{13} - (\Omega_0 - \rho_2) z_{23}
\end{aligned} \tag{5.9}$$

We can generate Benders' cut for depot 1 in the same fashion as follows. For the "intercept" of Eq. (5.5):

$$\begin{aligned}
\varphi_0^0 &= 18 + 0.5\,(z_{10} + z_{20} + z_{30}) - (\Omega_1 - \rho_0) z_{10} - (\Omega_1 - \rho_0) z_{20} - (\Omega_1 - \rho_0) z_{30} \\
\varphi_2^0 &= 51 - 4\,(z_{02} + z_{12} + z_{32}) - (\Omega_1 - \rho_0) z_{02} - (\Omega_1 - \rho_0) z_{12} - (\Omega_1 - \rho_0) z_{32} \\
\varphi_3^0 &= 39 - 2\,(z_{03} + z_{13} + z_{23}) - (\Omega_1 - \rho_0) z_{03} - (\Omega_1 - \rho_0) z_{13} - (\Omega_1 - \rho_0) z_{23}
\end{aligned} \tag{5.10}$$

and for the "slope" in Eq. (5.5):

$$\begin{aligned}
\varphi_0^1 &= 18 + 0.5\,(z_{10} + z_{20} + z_{30}) - (\Omega_1 - \rho_1) z_{10} - (\Omega_1 - \rho_1) z_{20} - (\Omega_1 - \rho_1) z_{30} \\
\varphi_2^1 &= 51 - 4\,(z_{02} + z_{12} + z_{32}) - (\Omega_1 - \rho_1) z_{02} - (\Omega_1 - \rho_1) z_{12} - (\Omega_1 - \rho_1) z_{32} \\
\varphi_3^1 &= 39 - 2\,(z_{03} + z_{13} + z_{23}) - (\Omega_1 - \rho_1) z_{03} - (\Omega_1 - \rho_1) z_{13} - (\Omega_1 - \rho_1) z_{23} \\
\varphi_0^2 &= 18 + 0.5\,(z_{10} + z_{20} + z_{30}) - (\Omega_1 - \rho_2) z_{10} - (\Omega_1 - \rho_2) z_{20} - (\Omega_1 - \rho_2) z_{30} \\
\varphi_2^2 &= 51 - 4\,(z_{02} + z_{12} + z_{32}) - (\Omega_1 - \rho_2) z_{02} - (\Omega_1 - \rho_2) z_{12} - (\Omega_1 - \rho_2) z_{32} \\
\varphi_3^2 &= 39 - 2\,(z_{03} + z_{13} + z_{23}) - (\Omega_1 - \rho_2) z_{03} - (\Omega_1 - \rho_2) z_{13} - (\Omega_1 - \rho_2) z_{23}
\end{aligned} \tag{5.11}$$

In generating a Benders' cut for depot 0, we deliver to depot 1, 2 and 3, as shown explicitly in Eqs. (5.8) and (5.9). If we generate a Benders' cut for depot 1, we deliver to depot 0, 2 and 3, as shown in Eq. (5.10) and (5.11). Similarly, cuts for the other depots can be generated. The remaining summation term in the "intercept," regardless of supply depot, is the same (Sahinidis and Grossmann 1991).

Solution of this master problem suggests the next y vector upon which the projection is to be made and a corresponding z value found. At this point, the process repeats itself from the start. When the master problem returns the same solution as in the previous cycle, we have found the optimum.

PROPOSITION 1. *Cuts for the Relaxed Master Problem converge in a finite number of steps.* □

PROOF: Cutting-plane methods produce a dual-optimal $\boldsymbol{\sigma}^h$ for each vehicle h, where $\boldsymbol{\sigma}^h$ is defined for each TSP-subproblem solution. (Although $\boldsymbol{\sigma}^h$ is a vector of very large dimension, nearly all its components will usually be zero. Only the specified nodes visited by route h will record a nonzero "odometer reading" σ.) Solution of the Delivery-Allocation Subproblem yields optimal multipliers ($\boldsymbol{\Omega}$, $\boldsymbol{\rho}$). These values generate a cut helping to approximate $z'(\mathbf{y})$. In the minimum over z (or the deliveries made), note that by constraint (8) in the Part I chapter, exactly one y_i^h is 1 for each i. Thus the minimum is obtained in the form of Eq. (3) from the Part I chapter. The relaxed master problem is thus min z, subject to cuts of the form above, as well as constraints above. In general, since Y'' is finite, only a finite number of subproblems can be generated, and the algorithm converges to the optimum in a finite number of iterations. Using the lower bound, we can terminate the procedure prior to optimality when any given error tolerance is achieved. □

The relaxed master problem generates only an assignment constraint (cut) as necessary. As mentioned, when the master problem returns the same solution as in the previous cycle, we have found the optimum. Without considering of resupplying itself before supplying the other depots, it can be shown that the final optimal solution to our example problem is as follows:

Objective function value = 127.55, $x_{01}{}^1, x_{10}{}^1, x_{02}{}^2, x_{23}{}^2, x_{30}{}^2, y_{01}{}^1, y_{12}{}^2, y_{13}{}^2, y_{30}{}^2$ are "switched on" to unity, and $z_{01}=6$, $z_{12}=4$, $z_{13}=3$.

5.2 Analysis

The FZ and extended model are coded in GAMS (Version 23.5). The results of FZ model are shown in Table 5.1 for the sake of completeness and understanding the effect of Benders' decomposition algorithm on the optimal solution. We first try to solve the stochastic mixed integer problem with all constraints active, but unfortunately no feasible solution was found. Please note that by fixing placing-order variables, y_i^h, we come up with two individual subproblems (TSP and Inventory). An initial iteration is run based on a random selection of the y_i^h. The best solution for the TSP subproblem is a part of this optimal solution, due to fact that the master problem considers total cost including inventory/allocation cost.

Table 5.1 The results of FZ model

	y^h_i			z_i			TSP cost	Inv. cost	Total cost
Initial	$y^0_1=1$	$y^2_2=1$	$y^1_3=1$	$z_1=0$	$z_2=50$	$Z_3=150$	17	4700	4717
1st iteration	$y^1_1=1$	$y^1_3=1$	$y^2_2=1$	$z_1=150$	$z_2=50$	$Z_3=0$	17	4475	4492
2nd iteration	$y^1_1=1$	$y^2_2=1$	$y^2_3=1$	$z_1=150$	$z_2=50$	$Z_3=150$	15.3	3500	3515.3
3rd iteration	$y^1_3=1$	$y^2_1=1$	$y^2_2=1$	$z_1=200$	$z_2=0$	$Z_3=150$	14.5	3475	3489.5
4th iteration	$y^1_2=1$	$y^1_3=1$	$y^2_1=1$	$z_1=200$	$z_2=50$	$Z_3=100$	15.3	3425	3440.3

Table 5.2 The traveling cost data for FZ model with 10 nodes

	0	1	2	3	4	5	6	7	8	9
0	–	3	3.5	2	5	3	2	6	5	3
1		–	4	5	2	1.5	3	2.5	5	6
2			–	3.8	4	4.5	2	1.5	4	3
3				–	3	3.5	4	2	4.5	3.5
4					–	4.5	7	8	5	4
5						–	2	6	4	8
6							–	3	5	4.5
7								–	6	9
8									–	7
9										–

While keeping number of vehicles fixed, the efficiency of Benders' decomposition was tested positively on the FZ model with a larger number of nodes. (For example, 10 nodes are enough for a moderate size Turkish Air Force problem, with supplies primarily coming from one main depot.) The traveling cost data, the inventory cost data and the results are presented in Tables 5.2, 5.3, and 5.4, respectively.

In supply chain, we still know little about process orientation and advanced planning across company borders. Kaihara (2003) and Stadler (2005) provided an advanced planning system to address this issue. Melo et al. (2005) proposed a strategic design of supply-chain networks—considering a dynamic planning horizon, multi-commodities distribution, and available inventories.

As seen in Table 5.4, with the help of Benders' cut, a decent optimal solution is found within two iterations with two alternative solutions. For the relaxed master problem, it can be shown that the final optimal solution to our example problem is as follows: Objective function value = 14,823.00 and x_{09}^{1}, x_{90}^{1}, x_{03}^{2}, x_{37}^{2}, x_{72}^{2}, x_{28}^{2}, x_{84}^{2}, x_{41}^{2}, x_{15}^{2}, x_{56}^{2}, x_{60}^{2}, y_9^{1}, y_1^{2}, y_2^{2}, y_3^{2}, y_4^{2}, y_5^{2}, y_6^{2}, y_7^{2}, y_7^{2} are "switched on" to unity, and $z_2=50$, $z_3=250$, $z_5=66.67$, $z_6=66.67$, $z_7=66.67$.

Table 5.3 The inventory cost data of FZ model with 10 nodes

Node no.	Initial inv. level	Minimum inv. level	Maximum inv. level	Inv. cost function
1	100	0	500	2600-4z1
2	50	0	100	437.5-5.75z2
3	150	0	400	2806.25-6.625z3
4	125	0	500	2500-4z4
5	40	0	150	1550-5z5
6	80	0	300	2100-5z6
7	120	0	250	1400-5z7
8	150	0	500	2400-4z8
9	75	0	375	1950-4z9

The final solution to the RLS model is given in Table 5.5, and the results of Generalized Benders' procedure are given in Table 5.6. The master problem returns the same result of 136.00 in three iterations before reaching the optimum of 133.55. The advantage of the Generalized Benders' procedure is that we can obtain a "decent" solution prior to optimality, should we wish to terminate the computation due to resource constraints. The result for such a solution is shown below, with the first of the two alternate solutions illustrated in Fig. 1 of the Part I chapter. It can be seen this solution is "decent" since it is (136.00 − 133.55)/133.55 = 0.01802 or 1.802 % from optimum.

5.2.1 *Two Alternate Solutions*

In the solution presented in Table 5.5, we send six serviceable parts to depot 1, $z_{01} = 6$. There can be at most nine failures at depot 1. Depot 1 can meet seven of them by using local resources (initial level + repair capacity = 1 + 6 = 7). Suppose depot 1 uses all of its available repair and inventory capacity to meet the failures. It still has a shortage of two serviceable parts. Since the maximum inventory capacity is four, we can replenish at most six serviceable parts before reaching capacity. Depot 1 decides to get four serviceable items out of the repair shop and two serviceable items out of the depot-0 inventory.

For depot 2, we can have at most 10 failures during that period. But we can satisfy 11 of them by using local resources. Depot 2 uses all of its repair capabilities and inventory to satisfy the failures. Since our maximum inventory level is four, we can hold at most four serviceable items from any depot in the system. Depot 2 decides to get four repaired units from depot 0 ($z_{02} = 4$).

For depot 3, we have nine failures; but it could meet all the failures by using its own local resources. Nothing is delivered to depot 3 because it has the lowest shortage cost among all depots. In fact it has a surplus of one. Here the binary variable y_3 is equal to one; suggesting it is ready to send the surplus to the other depots.

Table 5.4 The results of FZ model with 10 nodes

	$y^h{}_i$			z_i			TSP cost	Inv. cost	Total cost
First iteration (Initial)	$y^0{}_1=1$	$y^1{}_3=1$	$y^2{}_2=1$	$z_1=0$	$z_2=50$	$z_3=250$	39	14,800	14,839
	$y^0{}_4=1$	$y^1{}_5=1$	$y^2{}_6=1$	$z_4=0$	$z_5=0$	$z_6=200$			
	$y^0{}_7=1$	$y^1{}_8=1$	$y^2{}_9=1$	$z_7=0$	$z_8=0$	$z_9=0$			
Suggested routes for initial iteration	$x^0{}_{07}–x^0{}_{71}–x^0{}_{14}–x^0{}_{40}$		$x^1{}_{03}–x^1{}_{38}–x^1{}_{85}–x^1{}_{50}$		$x^2{}_{09}–x^2{}_{92}–x^2{}_{26}–x^2{}_{60}$				
Second iteration	$y^1{}_1=1$	$y^1{}_2=1$	$y^1{}_4=1$	$z_1=0$	$z_2=0$	$z_3=250$	30.5	14,800	14,830.5
	$y^1{}_6=1$	$y^1{}_7=1$	$y^1{}_9=1$	$z_4=0$	$z_5=0$	$z_6=100$			
	$y^2{}_3=1$	$y^2{}_5=1$	$y^2{}_8=1$	$Z_7=100$	$z_8=0$	$z_9=0$			
Suggested routes for second iteration	$x^1{}_{09}–x^1{}_{94}–x^1{}_{41}–x^1{}_{17}–x^1{}_{72}–x^1{}_{26}–x^1{}_{60}$				$x^2{}_{05}–x^2{}_{58}–x^2{}_{83}–x^2{}_{30}$				
Third Iteration	$y^1{}_1=1$	$y^1{}_5=1$	$y^1{}_8=1$	$z_1=0$	$z_2=50$	$z_3=250$	30.5	14,800	14,830.5
	$y^2{}_1=1$	$y^2{}_2=1$	$y^2{}_4=1$	$z_4=0$	$z_5=0$	$z_6=100$			
	$y^2{}_6=1$	$y^2{}_7=1$	$y^2{}_9=1$	$Z_7=100$	$z_8=0$	$z_9=0$			
Suggested routes for third iteration	$x^1{}_{05}–x^1{}_{58}–x^1{}_{83}–x^1{}_{30}$			$x^2{}_{09}–x^2{}_{94}–x^2{}_{41}–x^2{}_{17}–x^2{}_{72}–x^2{}_{26}–x^2{}_{60}$					

Table 5.5 The result of the research model (w/o Benders)

		First alternate solution	Second alternate solution
Objective value		$z^* = 133.55$	$z^* = 133.55$
Routes		$x^1_{02} - x^1_{23} - x^1_{30}$	$x^1_{03} - x^1_{32} - x^1_{20}$
		$x^2_{01} - x^2_{10}$	$x^2_{01} - x^2_{10}$
Depot 0	Initial level: 2	$z_{00} = 7$	$z_{00} = 11$
	Max. level: 10	$(x_{00}(u) = 7)$	$(x_{00}(d) = 2, x_{00}(u) = 9)$
	Repair Cap.: [0–15]		
Depot 1	Initial level: 1	$z_{11} = 7$	$z_{11} = 7$
	Max. level: 4	$(x_{11}(d) = 1, x_{11}(u) = 6)$	$(x_{11}(d) = 1, x_{11}(u) = 6)$
	Repair Cap.: [0–6]	$z_{01} = 6$	$z_{01} = 6$
	Failure: [0–9]	$(x^2_{01}(u) = 4, x^2_{01}(d) = 2)$	$(x^2_{01}(u) = 6)$
Depot 2	Initial level: 2	$z_{22} = 11$	$z_{22} = 11$
	Max. level: 5	$(x_{22}(d) = 2, x_{22}(u) = 9)$	$(x_{22}(d) = 2, x_{22}(u) = 9)$
	Repair Cap.: [0–9]	$z_{02} = 4$	$z_{32} = 4$
	Failure: [0–10]	$(x^1_{02}(u) = 4)$	$(x^1_{32}(u) = 3, x^1_{32}(d) = 1)$
Depot 3	Initial level: 1	$z_{33} = 10$	
	Max. level: 4	$(x_{33}(d) = 1, x_{33}(u) = 9)$	
	Repair Cap.: [0–9]		
	Failure: [0–9]		
		$y^2_{01} = y^1_{02} = y^1_{03} = 1$	$y^2_{01} = y^1_{32} = y^1_{03} = 1$
		$y_3 = y_0 = 1$	$y_3 = y_0 = 1$

The assignment variables are consistent with the result. Since we are sending out of the main depot 0, $y_{01}{}^2 = y_{02}{}^1 = y_{03}{}^1 = 1$. Besides that, we deliver to depot 1 by vehicle 2. Therefore, assignment variable $y_{01}{}^2$ and associated vehicle-routing variables such as $x_{01}{}^2$ and $x_{10}{}^2$ are all unity. $y_{02}{}^1$ is equal to one, suggesting vehicle 1 be servicing depot 2. The binary variables y_1, and y_2 equal zero. This means that depot 1 and depot 2 need serviceable items from other depots. In this case, depots 1 and 2 are supplied by depot 0. We send nothing from depot 3 to any other depots although y3 is equal to one, because we have already satisfied the demand requirements of depot 1 and 2. If depot 0 did not have enough to send, then depot 3 would be ready to satisfy the remaining demands. Note that depot 3 has only one surplus item to deliver to the other depots, as mentioned.

Vehicle 2 goes to depot 1 and comes back. The total travel time is the sum of the time from depot 0 to depot 1, 0.5 h for unloading, and the time from depot 1 back to depot 0—which is 6.5 h together. For vehicle 1, it is the travel time from depot 0 to depot 2, plus unloading time at depot 2, plus travel time from depot 2 to 3, and the time from depot 3 back to depot 0—summing up to 9 h and 8 min. Note that

Table 5.6 The result of the research model (with Benders)

	y^h_i	Routes	z_i	TSP cost	Inv. cost	Total cost
1st iteration (Initial)	$y^0_{01}=y^1_{13}=y^1_{30}=y^2_{02}=1$	$x^0_{01}-x^0_{10}$, $x^1_{03}-x^1_{30}$, $x^2_{02}-x^2_{20}$	$z_{02}=4$, $z_{13}=4$	17	132.8	143.75
2nd iteration	$y^1_{31}=y^1_{32}=y^2_{10}=y^2_{23}=1$	$x^1_{01}-$ $x^1_{12}-x^1_{20}$, $x^2_{03}-x^2_{30}$	$z_{31}=3$, $z_{23}=4$, $z_{32}=4$,	14.5	121.5	136.00
3rd iteration	$y^0_{10}=y^1_{13}=y^2_{02}=y^2_{31}=1$	$x^1_{03}-x^1_{30}$, $x^2_{01}-x^2_{12}-$ x^2_{20}	$z_{02}=4$, $z_{13}=4$, $z_{31}=3$	14.5	121.5	136.00

vehicle 2 delivers nothing to depot 3 because depot 3 is a candidate to deliver to the other depots.

There is an alternate solution to this problem. The objective function is at the same value of 133.55. But we satisfy the demands of depots 1 and 2 from depot 0 and depot 3. We are sending six repaired items out of depot 0 to depot 1 to satisfy the demand. Depot 3 delivers three repaired and one inventoried item to depot 2. Depots 1 and 2 have the same number of failures as the previous solution, and they get the same number of serviceable items. But there is a big difference in how the demands are satisfied. Here, depot 3 can send six more units to the depot 2 if there is a need. The binary variables for delivery, y_0 and y_3, are consistent with the above results. $y_0=1$ means that we can deliver out of depot 0, similarly for $y_3=1$. The assignment variables—$y_{01}^{\ 2}$, $y_{32}^{\ 1}$ and $y_{03}^{\ 1}$—are also consistent. Since vehicle 2 goes out of depot 0, $y_{01}^{\ 2}=1$. Similarly, vehicle 1 visits depots 3 and 2. The other assignment variables are consistent with the result as well.

One can interpret these two alternate results as follows. In the first run, we satisfy the demand out of depot 0. It means depot 0 is the supply source to get the optimal result. In the second run, the supply sources consist of depot 3 and depot 0. In this problem instance, we have two viable options to satisfy the demands. One can think of it as changing the supply sources. With the current newsvendor inventory-costs, we may deploy the available fleet of vehicles to deliver from depot 3 to depot 1 and/or 2, treating depot 3 as a secondary supply depot.

The results of research problem with Benders' decomposition procedure, two alternative solutions are obtained as it is shown in Table 5.6. The two alternative results consisted in terms of the quantity delivered to depot 1 by 3 units, 2 and 3 by 4 units.

5.2.2 Implications of Including Repair and Lateral Resupply

Now we document several feasible solutions to the RLS model, to illustrate the importance of considering repair and lateral resupply together with inventory and vehicle routing. The results are shown in Table 5.7. In the first feasible solution, we

Table 5.7 The result of considering repair and lateral resupply

Feasible solutions	Delivery z_{ij}	Delivery cost	Inventory cost	Total cost
1	$z_{03}=4, z_{21}=6$	14.5	126.25	140.75
2	$z_{31}=3, z_{32}=4, z_{23}=4$	14.5	121.5	136
3	$z_{02}=4, z_{13}=4, z_{31}=3$	14.5	121.5	136
4	$z_{01}=6, z_{02}=4$	17	118.25	135.25
5	$z_{01}=6, z_{32}=4$	15.3	118.25	133.55
6	$z_{01}=6, z_{12}=4, z_{13}=3$	15.3	112.25	127.55

simply follow the shortest vehicle-tour to satisfy the demands. If we just want to satisfy the demands in the quickest way, this first solution will apply. Notice that the total cost (including the high inventory cost) is the highest among the possible options. The second and third feasible solutions have the same (reduced) inventory cost, 118.25, but different delivery costs: 17 and 15.3 respectively. Notice that in the second and third solutions, the demand points get what they need—at a lower inventory but higher delivery cost. Depot 2 gets 4 units out of depot 0 in the second solution, or out of depot 3 in the third solution. The third solution result is the lowest total cost so far, in that it has a lower delivery cost than solution 2.

Although we are satisfying the customer demands a little bit slower than the first solution, we have the best results thus far considering the savings in inventory cost. In the final optimal solution, the total cost is still lower yet—127.55 as shown in Sect. 1.1. Here, the transportation cost remains at 15.3 as the third solution, but additional inventory-cost savings can be obtained by repair and lateral resupply—including through "savings for a rainy day."

Table 5.7 shows that should repair and lateral resupply be included with inventory/allocation and vehicle routing, we have provided the real option to lower cost. Here, we extend the conclusion of Bowersox/Closs, Haughton/Stenger, and Federgruen/Zipkin in their studies, when they simply combined inventory/allocation and vehicle routing. By allowing repair and lateral resupply, we broke through solution 3 to arrive at the lowest-cost solution 4. While the result is somewhat intuitive, we will verify the result quantitatively here in Proposition 2.

Proposition 2. *The RLS model will guarantee to result in a total operating cost no higher than the FZC model.* □

Proof: Since the RLS model is a more demanding version of the FZC model, all feasible solutions to RLS are feasible for FZC. With its additional constraints, the RLS model yield a total operating cost higher than the FZC model. □

5.2.3 Increasing the Number of Depots and Vehicles

Let us now comment on the computational implications by tracing how the RLS model expands as the size of the problem grows. Clearly, we increase the number of constraints significantly by adding additional depots. Let us say we increase the depots by $|I'|$. Equations (3) and (4) in the Part I chapter are going to increase by $|I'|$. In other words, the new number of constraints for Eqs. (3) and (4) will be $|I|+|I'|$. Equation (5) in the Part I chapter is going to increase by $|H''|\times|I'|$. This means we have a new set of vehicular constraints for each new depot. The number of constraints in Eq. (6) remains the same, because it depends only on the vehicle fleet. Subtour-breaking constraint (7) is going to increase significantly in the following fashion. Let Cr $(|I|, |I|-1)$ denotes the combination of $|I|$ choose $|I|-1$. If we add $|I'|$ depots to the problem, then the number of constraints becomes

$$\begin{aligned}&\mathrm{Cr}\left(|I|+|I'|,|I|+|I'|\right)+\mathrm{Cr}\left(|I|+|I'|,|I|+|I'|-1\right)\\&+\mathrm{Cr}\left(|I|+|I'|,|I|+|I'|-2\right)+\ldots+\mathrm{Cr}\left(|I|+|I'|,1\right)\end{aligned} \tag{5.12}$$

Beyond that, we multiply each combination by the number of vehicles. Equation (5.8) remains the same since it is based on the vehicle fleet alone. Equation (5.10) is going to increase by $|I'|$. In other words, the new number of constraints for Eq. (5.10) will become $|I|+|I'|$. Similarly, Eq. (5.11) is going to increase by $|I'|$. Equation (5.9) will increase by $|H''|\times|I'|$ and Eq. (5.12) by $|I'|$.

Suppose that the total number of depots is $|I'_{new}|$ after adding $|I'|$ depots to the original problem. Then, we have $|I'_{new}\setminus 1|\,|I'_{new}|\,|H''|$ constraints for Eq. (13) in the Part I chapter. We can define z_{ij} for two different situations in Eq. (14). If $i=j$, then we will add $|I'|$ additional nodes. If $i\neq j$, then $|I'_{new}\setminus 1|\,|I'_{new}|$ constraints are in place. Equation (15) is composed of four subconstraints. It is going to increase by 4 $|I'|$. Equation (16) is composed of two subconstraints. It is going to increase by 2 $|I'|$. Eq. (17) and (18) will increase by $|I'|$. Equation (19) is based only upon the number of vehicles and remains unchanged. The new number of constraints for Eq. (20) will be $|I'_{new}\setminus 1|\,|I'_{new}|$.

We can trace the impact of adding more vehicles to the problem as well. Let $|V'|$ denote the additional vehicles added into the original model. Equations (5), (6), (7), and (19) in the Part I chapter are going to increase by $|V'|$. Equation (7) is going to increase by $|V'|$-fold with every combination. When we think of multi-item inventory, we add one more index to the delivery variables, and add a newsvendor cost-function for each item. The new delivery variable will be z_{ijk}, denoting item k going from i to j. The common resources will be the vehicle-routing constraints and vehicle-capacity constraints. As a decomposition scheme, every item can be analyzed independently (Bard et al. 1998). But every possible solution must measure up to the common resources. When we satisfy the common resources, we reach the optimal solution. It is conceivable that generalized Benders' decomposition would work under these circumstances, albeit at an increased computational cost.

PROPOSITION 3. *When the number of depots $|I|$ increases, the number of constraints in the RLS model increases in the order of max $1\leq k\leq |I|$ {Cr $(|I|, |I|-k)$} and $(|I|-1)\,|I|$. But the number of Benders' cuts increases only in the order of $|I|$. This suggests an increasing return to scale in computational efficiency when generalized Benders' decomposition is used.* □

Proof: In a regular RLS model, there are normally more depots $|I|$ than the number of fleet types $|H|$, each with a different capacity and range, i.e., $|I| > H''$. It is clear from the analysis in Sect. 2.3 that the most dominant increase in constraints in the RLS model over the FZC model is in subtour-breaking Eq. (7) in the Part I chapter, where the constraints are increased in the order of Eq. (12), in which the largest term is $\max_{1 \le k \le |I|} \{Cr(|I|, |I| - k)\}$, where Cr(A, B) denotes the combination of "A choose B." Also, the other dominant set of constraints is Eq. (14) for pickups and deliveries, where it grows in the order of $(|I| - 1)|I|$. Meanwhile, it is clear that the increase in Benders' cuts is only in the order of $|I| - 1$, according to Eq. (3). These linear cuts (3) are based on solving the TSP and Delivery-Allocation subproblems, the latter of which is a small mathematical program with the number of variables in the order of $|I|^2$. This suggests that Benders' decomposition, building upon cuts, achieves an increasing return to scale in computational efficiency. It is computationally more efficient than a competing MIP solution, particularly in dealing with nonlinear constraints and objective function. The nonlinear MIP algorithm also has to deal with a number of constraints in the order of $\max_{1 \le k \le |I|} \{Cr(|I|, |I| - k)\}$ and $|I - 1||I'|$. In comparison, the computational requirements of Benders' cuts are modest, in no small part due to linearization of the constraints and the small size of the Delivery-Allocation sub problem. □

5.2.4 Computational Experiences

Several problems of different sizes were solved, including one with a total of 124 variables and 117 constraints. Fifty-two of the variables are binary, one discrete, and the rest of them continuous. Binary variables are the allocation variables (y_{ij}^{h}), vehicle-routing variables (x_{ij}^{h}) and switch on–off variables related to either sending or receiving items (y_i). The inventory allocation-delivery variable z_{ij} is discrete.

Generalized Benders' Decomposition has the potential to tackle complex and nonlinear programs, making it an attractive procedure for a large class of problems. Based on the computational experiments performed in this research, however, an even better shortcut was found, as expounded by Propositions 4 and 5.

Proposition 4. *For the special case of a linear objective function in Eq. (1), with the remaining nonlinear constraints in place, the RLS model can be solved by regular Benders' partitioning.* □

Proof: Taking advantage of a linear objective function, a better solution is to use the basic partitioning procedure of Benders' to solve the RLS model. If we fix the y vector, Eq. (8) in the Part I chapter is linearized; the problem becomes an MIP instead of a nonlinear program. The MIP can then be simply decomposed into a TSP and Delivery-Allocation subproblem. Taking this fixed-y MIP, we can solve the dual of its relaxed LP. Although the dual will have a large number of variables, most of them will be zero. We then need to calculate the solution to the newsvendor problem given the y-vector used to create the MIP. With the solution to these two subproblems we can define the Benders' cut using the general formula $z \ge f$

$(\mathbf{y})+(\mathbf{b}-\mathbf{By})\,\boldsymbol{\lambda}$. Here $f(\mathbf{y})$ is a function of the binary variables y, and $\boldsymbol{\lambda}$ is the solution to the dual relaxation of the MIP, and B is a matrix that corresponds to the coefficients of the **y** variables in the original problem. We can append this cut to and the vehicle-capacity constraints, substituting in our solution of the newsvendor problem for the z_{ij} values. Solving this integer program will give us our next **y**-vector. The Benders' cut generated by this new y-vector will be appended to the master problem and the vehicle-capacity constraints will be updated by the new newsvendor solution. The whole process starts over. The solution will provide a new upper bound on the original problem, and each solution to the relaxation of the master problem provides a lower bound. The algorithm can terminate either at the optimal point by checking that the lower and upper bounds are equal or at some tolerance set by the user. □

Proposition 5. *In comparison to generalized Benders, the regular Benders' partitioning algorithm as described in Proposition 4 converges in a fewer number of steps.* □

Proof: In the computational experience with both the generalized and regular Benders' decomposition, we realize that the master problem had multiple optimal points at some cuts (as illustrated in Sect. 2.1, a phenomenon common with many integer programs). To address this, we simply use branch-and-bound to explore multiple optima. Each optimal **y**-vector is used to create a new cut that is separately appended to the master problem. Each of these master problems can be solved and compared to the current best solution to decide if we should continue to evaluate that master problem. With the double bounding procedure described in the Proof to Proposition 4, Benders' regular partitioning algorithm can terminate within a user-specified error bound. In comparison with generalized Benders, this double-bounding procedure is more efficient; it converges in fewer steps. □

5.3 Summary, Conclusions and Recommendations

The literature suggests that one achieves savings in terms of delivery cost and inventory cost if inventory and vehicle routing are combined in a single model. Introducing repair and lateral resupply in the formulation further reduces the cost.

Through a lucid example and most importantly through five propositions, this observation is substantiated by theoretical and computational results. It stands up to mathematical reasoning that when generalized Benders' decomposition increases the cuts in the RLS model, total operational cost is reduced. This observation is substantiated by available computational results. Theoretical proofs and our preliminary computational experiences suggest that such cost reduction can be substantial.

Sensitivity analysis on the number of parameters on the final model size yields interesting insights. The computational time can be a huge hindrance if one increases the depots in the model. It would only be appropriate to apply generalized Benders decomposition to the RLS problem, so that one can run the model in a shorter computational time in comparison to regular LP-relaxation. Potentially, generalized

Benders decomposition also allows us to include several commodities to be delivered (instead of a single item type). We can also include exponential distributed demands in inventory problems and Poisson distributed demands in repair problems (Gallego and Moon 1993)—on top of the uniformly distributed ones illustrated in our example. For the case of a linear objective function—a result of a uniformly distributed demand—even better computational efficiency is obtained through the regular Benders' partitioning algorithm. Having accomplished all the above and in spite of the five propositions, more computational results beyond our examples and limited computational experience should be obtained to further substantiate the claim on improved computational efficiency. Hooker (2007) found that logic-based Benders decomposition can improve substantially on the state-of-the-art for the solution of planning and scheduling problems. This is a fruitful direction to explore.

While a distinction is clearly made between repair and inventory, the actual repair process has not been modeled in this chapter. It is not clear that such an undertaking would be straightforward, since it would introduce another stochastic variable in the midst of a huge mixed-integer program (Stadtler 2005). Clearly, the z_{ij} variable in the upper limit of the integral in Eq. (2) in the Part I chapter would now be a random variable (instead of a deterministic variable), since it includes the repaired items as shown in the equation $z_{ij} = \Sigma_h [x_{ij}^h(u) + x_{ij}^h(d)]$. Now there are really two issues. The first is how to integrate Eq. (2). After this is addressed, how does one solve the resulting stochastic program?

Acknowledgements The authors like to acknowledge the valuable inputs from M. Arostegui, M. Niklas, J. Stewart, and J. Weir, for their contribution during the conduct of this study. They also benefited from the insightful comments of reviewers. The study was conducted under the sponsorship of the Air Force Materiel Command at Wright-Patterson AFB while the first author was stationed at the Base and while the second author was a faculty member of the Air Force Institute of Technology. Obviously, the authors alone are responsible for the document as presented. The views expressed here do not represent those of the organizations the authors are/were affiliated with.

References

Bard, J.F., Huang, L., Jaillet, P., Dror, M.: A decomposition approach to the inventory routing problem with satellite facilities. Transp. Sci. **32**, 189–203 (1998)

Chan, Y.: Location, Transport and Land-Use: Modelling Spatial-temporal Information. Springer, Heidelberg (2005)

Gallego, G., Moon, I.: The distribution free newsboy problem: review and extensions. J. Oper. Res. Soc. **44**, 825–834 (1993)

Hooker, J.N.: Planning and scheduling by logic-based benders decomposition. Oper. Res. **55**, 588–602 (2007)

Kaihara, T.: Multi-agent based supply chain modelling with dynamic environments. Int. J. Prod. Econ. **85**, 263–269 (2003)

Melo, M.T., Nickel, S., Saldanha da Gama, F.: Dynamic multi-commodity capacitated facility location: a mathematical modeling framework for strategic supply chain planning. Comput. Oper. Re. **33**, 181–208 (2005)

Sahinidis, N.V., Grossmann, I.E.: Convergence properties of generalized benders decomposition. Comput. Chem. Eng. **15**, 481–491 (1991)

Stadtler, H. Supply chain management and advanced planning—basics, overview and challenges. Eur. J. Oper. Res. **163**, 575–588 (2005)

Wang, Y., Cohen, M.A., Zheng, Y.S.: A two-echelon repairable inventory system with stocking-center-dependent depot replenishment lead times. Manage. Sci. **46**, 1441–1453 (2000)

Chapter 6
A Transportation Planning Tool for Supporting Military Actions in Natural Disaster Relief Operations

Vasileios Zeimpekis

6.1 Introduction

Over the past few years, there has been a growing interest in the design and operations of relief distribution networks (Ichoua 2011). This is due to the increasing number of natural disasters occurring worldwide, as well as due to the worrying and catastrophic impacts they both have on human lives and global economy (Jenkins 2007).

Figure 6.1, depicts a natural disaster summary for a time period of more than 100 years (1900–2011). As it can be seen, the number of people reported killed has been drastically reduced from over 200,000 to less than 50,000 victims. However, the total number of reported disasters has been tremendously increased from 100 to 450, and the total number of people reported affected, from less than 100,000 to more than 500,000 victims respectively.

Natural disasters are a significant cause of dislocation and disruption in the lives of people and communities. Figure 6.2, shows the extensive damage that has suffered the world economy in the last decade due to natural disasters occurred. The year with the greatest losses is 2011, with a cost over $ 350 billion. Furthermore, the same figure depicts the corresponding increase/decrease in estimated losses (in annual basis), compared to the previous year (starting from year 2003).

Figure 6.3 depicts the reported human casualties in the last decade due to natural disasters. The deadliest year of the decade is 2010, with 306,766 losses.

In order to cope with the continuous growth and severity of natural disasters, the support of military forces is usually needed. Indeed, although the armed forces are supposed to be called upon to intervene and take on specific tasks only when the situation is beyond the capability of civil administration, in practice, they usually play a pivotal role in a major disaster. This is due to the fact that armed forces are

V. Zeimpekis (✉)
Design, Operations and Production Systems Lab, Department of Financial & Management Engineering, University of the Aegean, 41 Kountouriotou Street, 82100 Chios, Greece
e-mail: vzeimp@fme.aegean.gr

V. Zeimpekis et al. (eds.), *Military Logistics,* Operations Research/Computer Science Interfaces Series 56, DOI 10.1007/978-3-319-12075-1_6

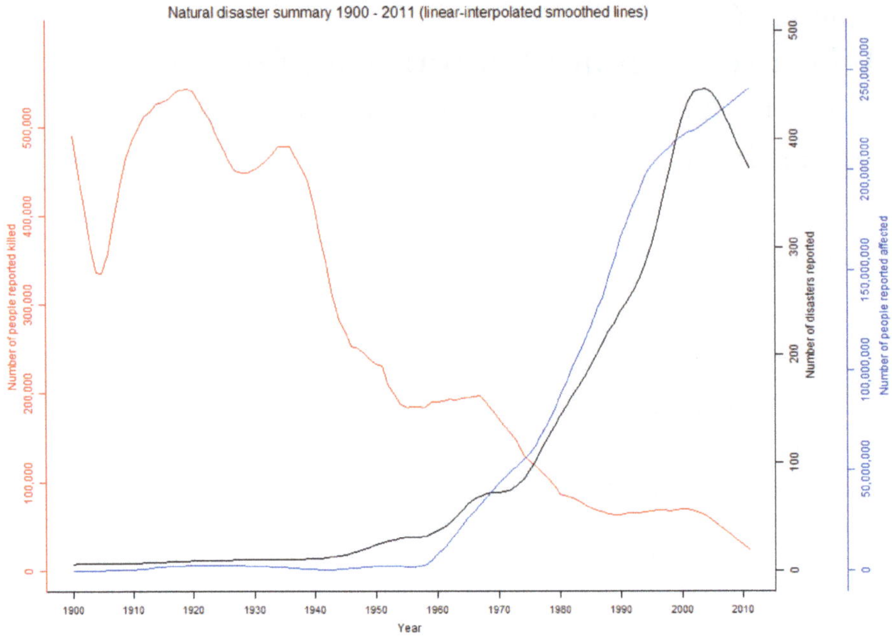

Fig. 6.1 Natural disaster summary 1900–2011 (linear-interpolated smoothed lines). (Source: EM-DAT 2014)

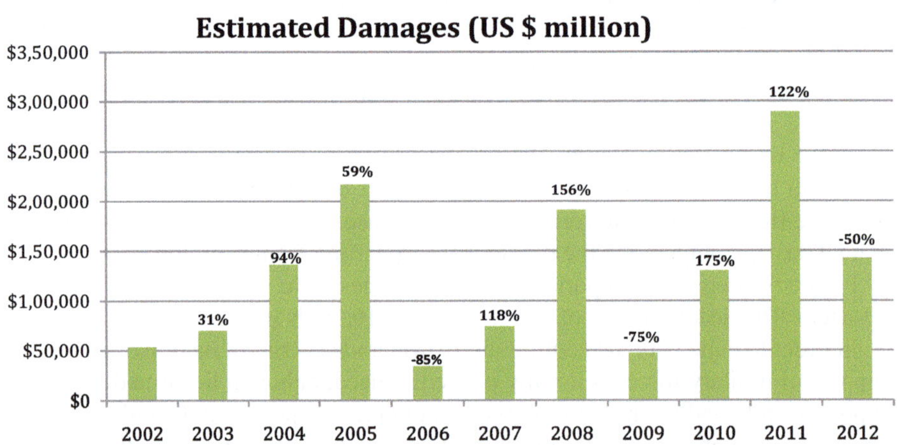

Fig. 6.2 Estimated damages (US $ million) due to natural disasters during the last decade. (Source: EM-DAT 2014)

trained to react in emergencies, and are the biggest rescue and succor providing organizations, capable of moving swiftly to any part of a country, in the shortest possible time (Kemball-Cook and Stephenson 1984; Kapucu 2011). The major types of assistance they provide can be categorized as follows: (a) command and control,

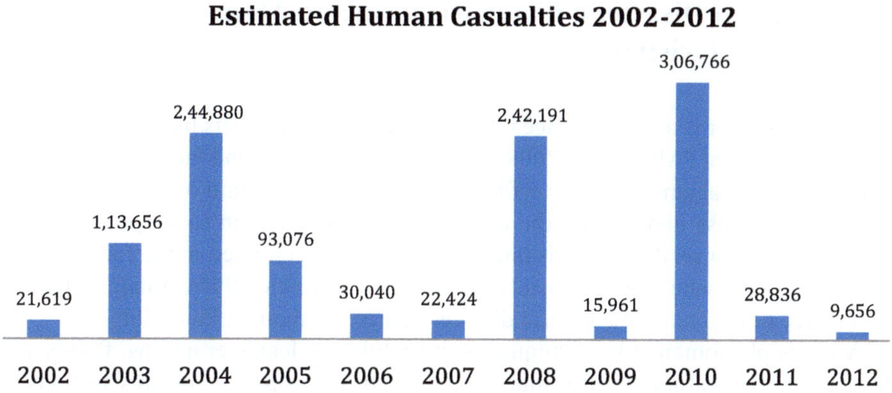

Fig. 6.3 Estimated human casualties worldwide due to natural disasters during the last decade. (Source: EM-DAT 2014)

(b) logistics support, (c) transportation of relief material, (d) setting up and running or relief camps, (e) medical aid, and, (f) construction and repair/restoration of roads and bridges (Kapucu 2011).

Transportation of relief material is one of the most significant processes as it should take place immediately after a disaster occurs. While commercial freight transport operations typically focus on minimizing costs, moving relief material is more concerned about satisfying demand for emergency supplies and saving lives (Ardekani and Hobeika 1988). This task is particularly challenging given that emergency managers must operate under strict budget restrictions. Moreover, humanitarian relief chains take place in a highly dynamic disruption-prone environment where a timely response is vital and resources are scarce (Larson et al. 2005). Furthermore, disasters are generally low probability high impact events. Therefore there is typically not enough historic data that can be used to estimate their probabilistic distributions in order to better prepare for their fatal strikes (Ichoua 2011).

The aim of this chapter is to present the design, implementation and testing of a web tool that supports armed forces in freight transport planning during natural disaster relief operations. The proposed system identifies optimal trips for transferring relief material by taking into consideration trip duration, transportation cost, and risk. The chapter is organized as follows. The main types of natural disasters are described initially followed by their main characteristics. Subsequently the role of military forces in disaster relief operations is presented and the major types of assistance are analyzed. Then the design and implementation of the proposed system is described. Results from initial system testing are presented, showing reductions in administrative and transport cost as well increase in operational service. The chapter ends with conclusions from system usage as well as with future implications.

6.2 Natural Disasters: Categorization and Main Characteristics

A natural disaster is a consequence when a natural hazard affects humans and/or the built environment (Altay et al. 2009). Human vulnerability and lack of appropriate emergency management, leads to financial, environmental and/or, human impact. The resulting loss depends on the capacity of the population to support or resist the disaster: their resilience. This understanding is concentrated in the formulation: "disasters occur when hazards meet vulnerability" (Blaikie 1994). A natural hazard will hence never result in a natural disaster in areas without vulnerability.

Various phenomena like earthquakes, landslides, volcanic eruptions, floods and cyclones are all natural hazards that kill thousands of people and destroy billions of dollars of habitat and property each year. In any case, natural hazards can strike in unpopulated areas and never develop into disasters. However, the rapid growth of the world's population and its increased concentration often in hazardous environments has escalated both the frequency and severity of natural disasters. With the tropical climate and unstable land forms, coupled with deforestation, unplanned growth proliferation, nonengineered constructions which make the disaster-prone areas more vulnerable, tardy communication, poor or no budgetary allocation for disaster prevention, developing countries suffer more or less chronically by natural disasters.

The Center for Research on the Epidemiology of Disasters (CRED) distinguish five major categories of natural disasters (Table 6.1)

Apart from the general categorization of natural disasters shown above, the latter can also be classified based on the time they occur. To this end, disasters can be categorized as follows: (a) sudden onset and (b) slow onset as shown in Table 6.2.

Sudden-onset disasters, such as cyclones, earthquakes, tsunamis, volcanic eruptions and flooding, have been and remain frequent, feared and deadly. The number

Table 6.1 Categories of natural disasters. (Below et al. 2009)

Disaster group	Disaster type
Geophysical	Earthquakes
	Volcanic eruptions
	Mass movement (dry)
Hydrological	Flood
	Mass movement (wet)
Meteorological	Storm
Climatological	Extreme temperature
	Drought
	Wild fire
Biological	Epidemic
	Insect infestation
	Animal stampede

Table 6.2 Categorization of natural disaster based on the time they occur. (Van Wassenhove 2006)

Disasters	Natural
Sudden-onset	Earthquake
	Hurricane
	Tornadoes
Slow-onset	Famine
	Drought
	Poverty

of sudden-onset disasters has increased significantly since 1950, the severity of hurricane-strength cyclones has grown, and the total population affected per event has been increasing (Femia and Werell 2001).

Slow-onset is called an emergency that emerges gradually over time, often based on a confluence of different events (Kovács and Spens 2009). Most discussion of slow-onset disasters concentrates on one hazard: drought. It can take months or sometimes years for the results of drought to become disastrous, in the form of severe water and food shortages and, ultimately, famine. Drought is not the only relevant hazard, though. Pollution of the environment can also be considered a slow-onset disaster, particularly in cases of growing concentrations of toxic wastes, which may build up over years. Human activities that degrade the environment and damage ecosystems—deforestation for instance—also contribute to disasters. Their cumulative impact may not be felt for decades, although the hazards that they make more likely, such as flash-floods and landslides, may be sudden-onset events. Rapid onset natural disasters account for 3 % of disaster relief activities (Kovács and Tatham 2009).

Figure 6.4 depicts the countries with the highest frequency of Natural Disasters in the last decade. China is first in the rank with 293 reported cases, followed by the

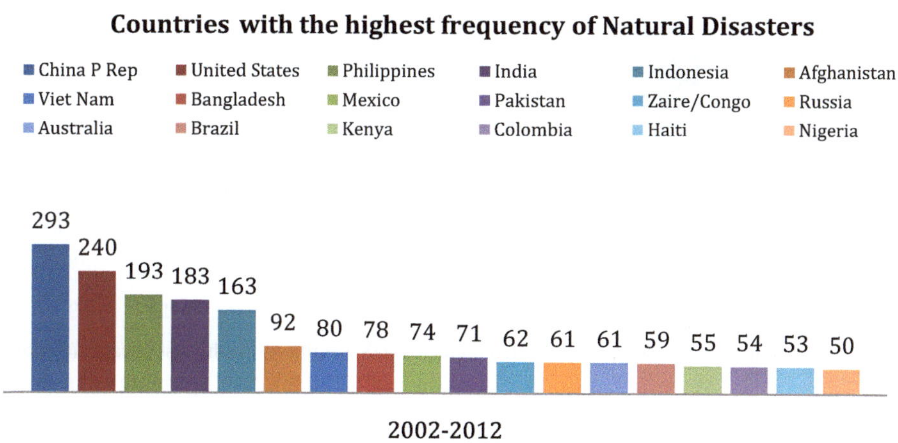

Fig. 6.4 Countries with the most natural disasters during the last decade. (Source: EM-DAT 2014)

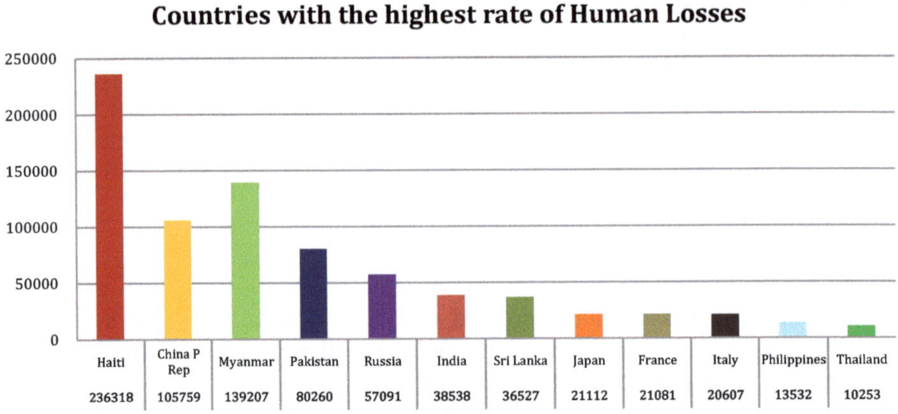

Fig. 6.5 Countries with the highest rate of human losses due to natural disasters during the last decade. (Source: EM-DAT 2014)

U.S. that reported 240 cases. Philippines, India and China are following with 193, 183 and 163 reported cases respectively.

In terms of human losses (Fig. 6.5), the top ranked is Haiti with 236,318 victims, followed by Myanmar and China with 139,207 and 105,759 fatalities respectively.

Figure 6.6 presents the countries with the highest rate of estimated economic damages due to natural disasters the last decade. As it can be seen, Philippines and China, are the top ranked with estimated damages of 1715.7 and US$ 820.8 billion respectively.

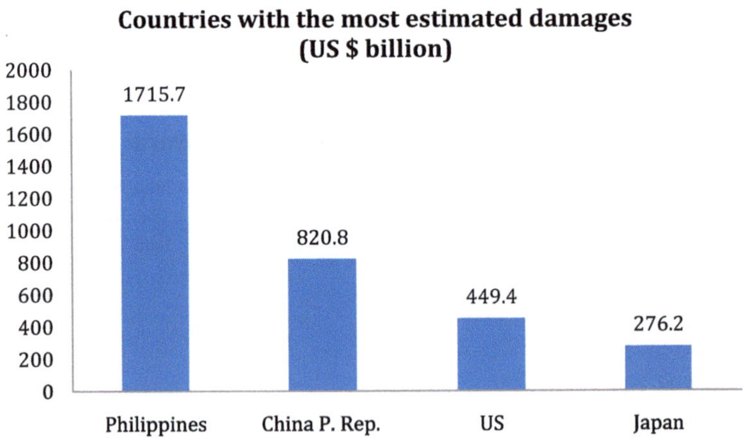

Fig. 6.6 Countries with the most estimated damages (US $ million) for the last decade. (Source: EM-DAT 2014)

6.3 The Role of Military Forces in Disaster Relief Operations

Based on the different types of disasters and requests for assistance, Schrader (1993) defines three response sectors the military is capable of assuming during a disaster mission: (a) special skills corresponding to assistance of response operations, (b) communication in terms of disaster command and control and, (c) organized forces providing general support in a number of actions.

The military's primary skills and capabilities in disaster response are comprised of its transportation advantages (transportation ships, off-road vehicles, etc.), as well as technical experience in urban search and rescue, mobile hospitals, personnel and technology of surveillance and reconnaissance, radiation monitoring, situation assessment, and damage assessment (Kapucu 2011). The military is also the first force that acquires updated equipment and trained personnel in response to establishing communication in disasters (Schrader 1993). During a disaster, federal, state and local governments are quick to call for the military's help and support, availing themselves of the advantages attached to military operations and response. According to Kapucu (2011), these benefits include: manpower with specific qualifications, skills and expertise, strategic and rapid mobilization, updated technology and a variety of equipment (helicopters, aircraft, earth-moving machinery, respirators, medical supplies, power and lighting equipment, under-water capability, etc.) that most emergency organizations are unable to acquire. Moreover, the military's relative autonomy and efficient bureaucratic structure with hierarchical rules; which are effective in command, coordination, and control of manpower, authority, and regulations, is beneficial in providing effective response actions (Anderson 1970; Schrader 1993; US House of Representatives 2006; Sylves 2008). In addition to these advantages, the military assists in sheltering, the construction of temporary housing and restoration of minimal critical infrastructure (water, electric, sanitation, communication infrastructure, etc.) (Schrader 1993; Miskel 2006).

As mentioned previously, the transportation of relief material (consumables such as water, medication, etc., as well as nonconsumables such as tents, torches, etc.) is one of the most important processes during the post response phase as it should take place immediately after a disaster occurs. However, in most cases the planning of freight transport in an area affected from a disaster is not made in a systemic fashion, resulting usually in high administrative and transport cost and inferior service (e.g. time delays, out of stock materials, etc.). The following section presents a web tool that may support military forces by optimizing freight transport planning operations.

6.4 Transportation Planning Tool: System Design and Implementation

The proposed tool may support military forces in seeking near optimal fright transport solutions taking into account trip cost, transport durations and risk. The following sections describe in detail the system design and implementation.

6.4.1 Web Tool Users

The key users that play a significant role in the operation of such tool are the following:

- **Military forces (demand side):** Military forces may usually outsource the transportation of freight. To this end, they seek usually for either a forwarder or a carrier to transport their relief material.
- **Forwarder (supply side):** Forwarders provide turn-key solutions to its customers (e.g. army forces) in transport execution. They contract freight carriers and act as intermediaries (i.e. they plan the trip and they find suitable carriers to execute it).
- **Carriers (supply side):** Carriers provide transportation services either at a national or an international level. Typical carriers include 3PL/4PL companies, as well as road, train, and ship carriers.

6.4.2 Operating Scenarios

The proposed tool supports two operating scenarios

- **Case 1—Military Forces—Forwarders:** In this case, the demand side user (i.e. military forces) seeks and collects offers by forwarders. Forwarders are providing the cost, duration and details of the trip and the shipper uses the platform to determine the most preferable offer with regard to various criteria, including cost, trip duration, and risk.
- **Case 2—Military forces—Carriers:** In this case, army forces must organize by themselves the transportation of their load. For that reason, they request offers from multiple carriers, each of which usually supports a single leg (link) of the full trip. The tool by taking into consideration inter-hub handling time (i.e. unloading/loading) as well as user-defined earliest pick-up time and latest delivery time, it generates various options based on carriers' offers. The shipper (i.e. military officer) may determine the most preferable offer with regard to various criteria, including cost, trip duration, and risk.

6.5 Design and Operational Characteristics

The transportation network used in the web tool is defined by a series of intermodal hubs for each country and follows the hub and spoke model. The first leg of the trip between the origin and the closet intermodal hub is performed by road transport. Subsequently, the last leg (intermodal hub closest to the destination and the final destination) is performed also by road transport. The in-between trip is performed either by ship and/or by train transportation (Fig. 6.7).

Based on the intermodal hub and spoke model, two transportation networks were formulated according to the type of transport as follows:

- Accompanied RoRo-RoLa (Intermodal transport): In this case, appropriate hubs that usually are ports for RoRo/ferries or rail stations for RoLa service are included.
- Unaccompanied (Multimodal transport): In this case, hubs that can manage containers (i.e. container terminals) are included.

The intermodal network information is described in the tool by an appropriate matrix. There are four matrices, each for different type of transport. The columns and rows of each matrix are the corresponding intermodal hubs. That is, for the matrix corresponding to unaccompanied ship transport the hubs are the ones that support this mode of transport. For each cell of the matrix (i.e. for each pair of the hubs), the following information is available: (a) Distance by the equivalent mode, (b) Typical trip duration, (c) Typical cost for two types (20" & 40") of container, and, (d) Risk factor (i.e. how risky a hub is in terms of product loss & damage, and time deviation in handling processes).

Each transport leg in the web tool is associated with a set of values that determine its overall performance. These factors are namely: trip cost, trip time and risk. For simplicity, we have modeled all factors as additive terms in two more general categories: "Generalized time" and "Generalized cost". Trip time and cost can be easily defined under these two categories. Risk on the other hand is analyzed as time-risk and cost-risk.

The web tool, based on the user's given trip details, identifies the possible options (i.e. routes) by using the aforementioned network described and a *k*-shortest path algorithm (Liu and Ramakrishan 1999). In that way the options provided are sorted according to the user's preferences.

The platform's front-end and back-end functions are described as follows:

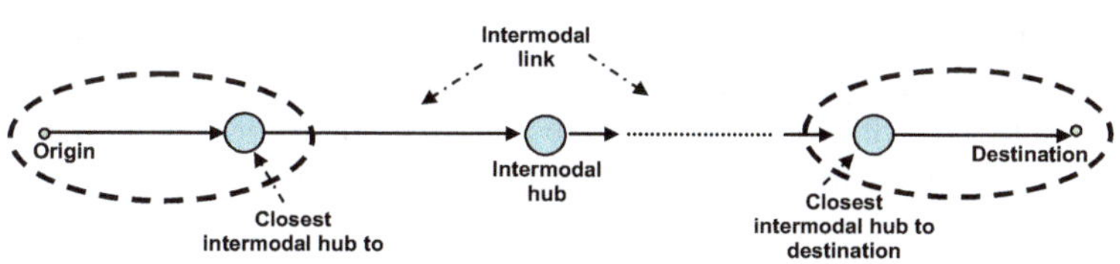

Fig. 6.7 A transport route using the hub and spoke model

- **Front-end functions:** These functions are used by shippers and forwarders and include three steps:
- *Step A—Planning:* In this step, the shipper or forwarder identifies various good alternatives to transport a load from an origin to a destination. The main factors that are taken into consideration in order to evaluate the alternatives are: cost, trip duration, risk, CO_2 footprint
- *Step B—Quoting-Booking:* After the shipper or forwarder has selected its preferred alternative, it requests quotes (from forwarders or carriers).
- Step C—Trip Execution/Tracking: The shipper/forwarder uses a unique ID number in order to track/monitor the status of its load during its trip from the origin to the destination.
- **Back-end functions:** These functionalities are used by forwarders, carriers and the platform administrator in order to provide all the necessary information needed for trip planning, quoting and execution.

6.5.1 Implementation

Figures. 6.8a, 6.8b, 6.8c, and 6.8d present the main front-end function of the web tool. Initially, the user inserts the following information (Fig. 6.8a): (a) Origin & destination (country & city), (b) Origin & destination Hub, (c) Earliest pickup day & latest delivery, (d) Maximum cost (optional), (e) Number and type of containers, (f) Total cargo value, (g) Unaccompanied or Accompanied (RoRo-RoLa) trip and, (h) "Cost vs duration preference" (weighting factors). As far as the last ("h") input is concerned, it must be mentioned that the path's overall performance is determined through a linear combination of its total time and total cost calculations. Assuming that the users might not be familiar with entering numeric coefficients, we designed this module as friendly as possible by using a "volume bar". The volume bar for the weights entry is a simple application component every computer user is familiar with. It looks exactly like the volume bar used for the regulation of sound volume on a personal computer and has a set of volume degrees.

The user may choose the preferred option (Fig. 6.8b) by taking into account the details of each trip (i.e. Hubs used, Legs, Mode, Approximate duration and cost). For the case of duration and cost, the user may have a detailed analysis of all factors that have been taken into consideration for the calculation.

In case there is more than one carrier that provides a transportation service for a certain leg of the trip (for instance in this case there are three carriers that serve the first leg), the user may choose for quoting multiple carriers (Fig. 6.8c)

After selecting the specific carriers for each leg, the system sends an email to each of them requesting a quote. The user should enter its email address in this point so as the system to notify them when there is at least one completed trip offer. At the same time the shipper/forwarder receives a Booking_ID (Fig. 6.8d).

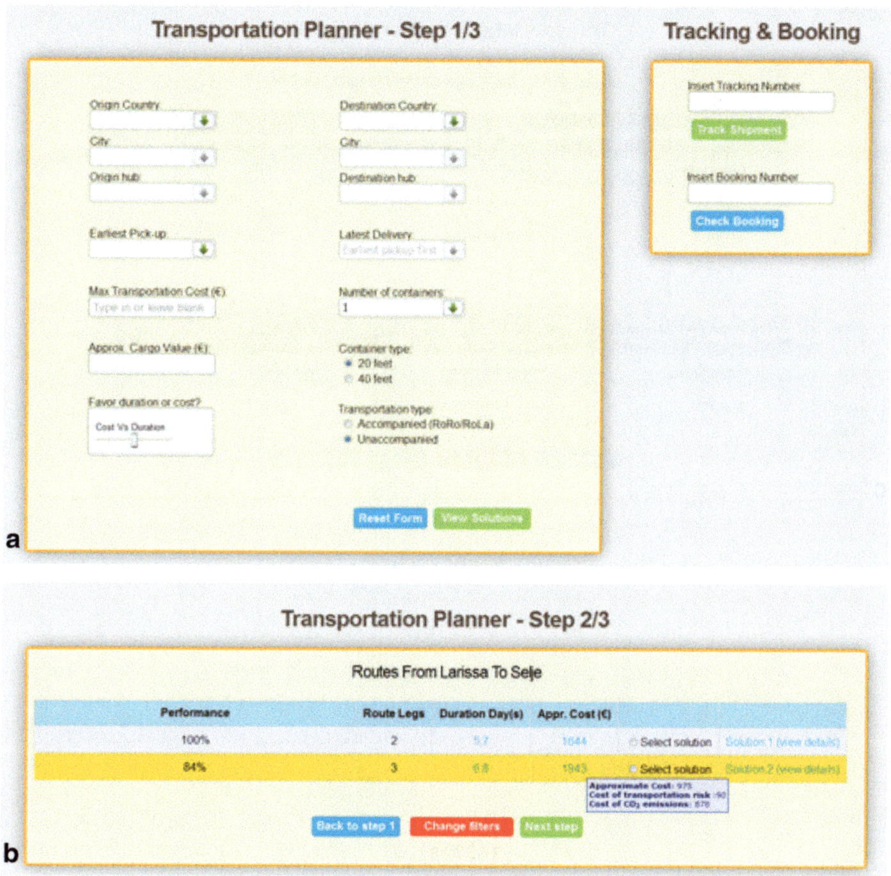

Fig. 6.8 **a** Trip data insertion form, **b** Trip options categorized based on performance, **c** Carrier(s) selection (per leg), and **d** Confirmations and Booking_ID

6.6 Transportation Planning Tool: System Testing

The web tool was tested in a series of real-life scenarios in order to evaluate its performance. Two types of tests were conducted as described below:

- **Test type A:** Trip planning and execution with and without the web tool use: This test main aim was to evaluate whether the web tool could improve the performance of freight transport in terms of administrative cost and time (i.e. the process of identifying/quote/book a trip). In order to do that, 15 tests were conducted in various cases both with and without the use of the tool.

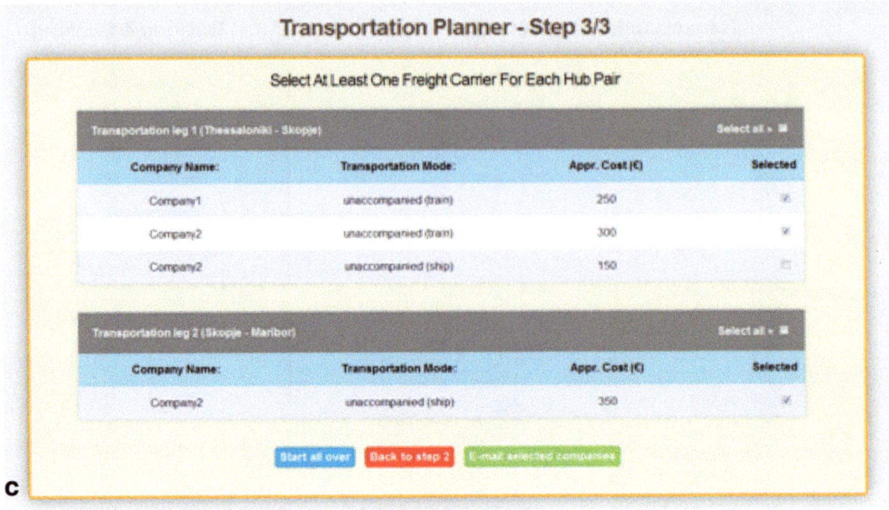

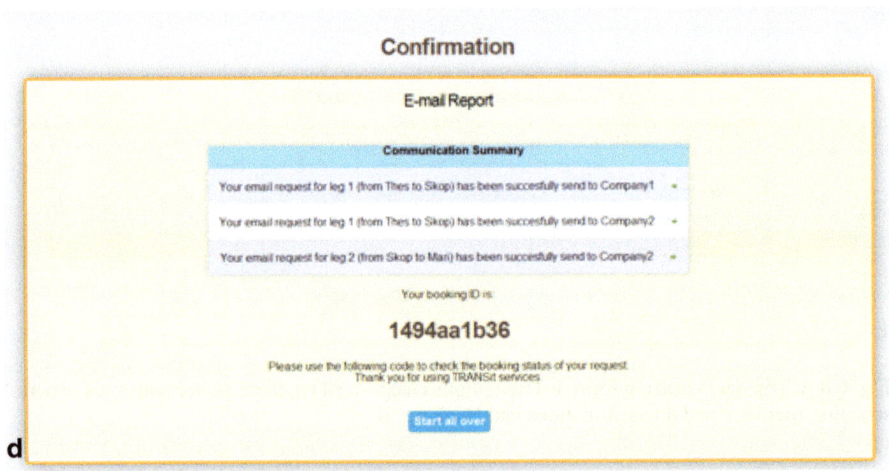

Fig. 6.8 (continued)

- **Test type B:** Trip planning via the web tool (to be) vs current methodology for planning trips (as is): In this test, we evaluated whether the web tool could provide a better trip plan (in terms of cost, trip duration and risk) when compared to the current way of planning a freight transport. Again, 15 different scenarios were evaluated.

The results from the initial testing of the web tool are depicted in Figs. 6.9 and 6.10 respectively. More specifically, Fig. 6.9 depicts the average cost and time with and without the use of the web (platform) tool for Test type A. As it can be seen, the administrative cost and time needed to plan a trip were decreased by 76 and 63 % respectively.

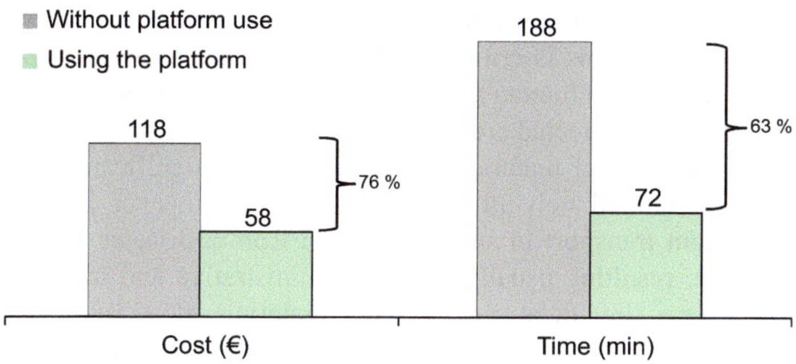

Fig. 6.9 Testing results for Test type A

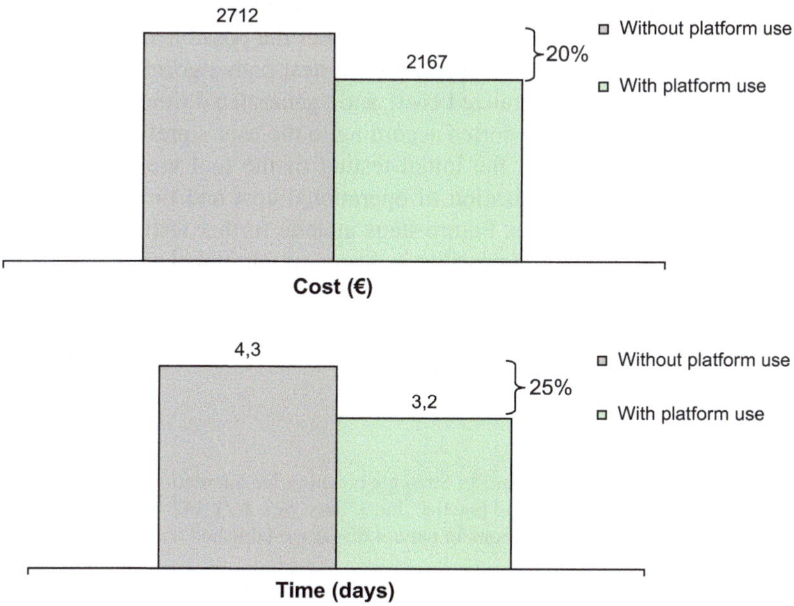

Fig. 6.10 Testing results for Test type B

Figure 6.10 depicts the average cost and time with and without the use of the web platform for Test type B. As it can be seen, the trip planning cost and time were decreased by 20 and 25 % respectively.

6.7 Conclusions

A worldwide increasing trend in natural disaster numbers has been reported by various organizations and research centers especially the last decade. In order to cope with the continuous growth and severity of natural disasters, the support of military forces is usually needed. Indeed, the involvement of the armed forces in disaster response and relief actions is critical as their role is primarily in response to the immediate requirement of human resources and technical equipment for rescue and relief operations of the affected area.

Transportation of relief material is one of the most significant processes as it should take place immediately after a disaster occurs. However, in most cases the planning of freight transport in an area affected from a disaster is not made in a systemic fashion, resulting usually in high administrative and transport cost and inferior service (e.g. time delays, out of stock materials, etc.). To this end, the aim of this chapter was to present the design, implementation and testing of a web tool that supports armed forces in freight transport planning during natural disaster relief operations. The proposed system identifies optimal trips for transferring relief material by taking into consideration trip duration, transportation cost and risk.

The web tool functionalities focus on transportation planning activities of relief material. More specifically, the web tool identifies the possible options (i.e. routes) by using the hub-and-spoke model and a *k*-shortest path algorithm. In the shortest path computations, the "generalized cost" and "generalized time" are used. In that way, the options provided are sorted according to the user's preferences.

The results obtained from the initial testing of the tool are very encouraging showing a significant minimization of operational cost and time when compared to current planning operations. Future steps include further testing of the web tool in various scenarios as well as possible inclusion of additional parameters for more cost effective solutions.

References

Altay, N., Prasad, S., Sounderpandian, J.: Strategic planning for international disaster relief logistics: implications for research and practice. Int. J. Serv. Sci. **2**(2), 142–161 (2009)

Anderson, W.A.: Military organizations in natural disaster established and emergent norms. Am. Behav. Sci. **13**, 415–422 (1970)

Ardekani S.A., Hobeika A.: Logistics problems in the aftermath of the 1985 Mexico City earthquake. Transp. Q. **42**, 107–124 (1988)

Below, R., Wirtz, A., Guha-Sapir, D.: Disaster category classification and peril terminology for operational purposes. Common accord, Center for Research on the Epidemiology of Disasters (CRED) and Munich Reinsurance Company (Munich RE), Universite Catholique de Louvain (UCL), No. 264, Munich, Germany (2009)

Blaikie, P.E.A.: At Risk: Natural Hazards, People's Vulnerability, and Disasters. 1st edn. Routledge, London (1994)

EM-DAT: Natural disaster summary—the international disaster database. Centre for research on the epidemiology of disasters—CRED. http://www.emdat.be/natural-disasters-trends (2014). Accessed 18 Aug 2014

Femia, F., Werell, C.: Double Whammy: sudden and slow-onset disasters for Pacific Island States Center for climate and security. http://climateandsecurity.org/2011/09/26/double-whammy-sudden-and-slow-onset-disasters-for-pacific-island-states/ (2011). Accessed 12 July 2014

Ichoua, S.: Relief distribution networks: design and operations. In: Minis, I., Zeimpekis, V., Dounias, G., Ampazis, N. (eds.) Supply Chain Optimization, Design and Management: Advances and Intelligent Methods. IGI Global Publishing (2011) ISBN: 978-1-61520633–9

Jenkins, W.O Jr.: Homeland security: preparing for and responding to disasters, homeland security and justice issues, before the subcommittee on homeland security. House Committee on Appropriations. GAO-07-395T. http://www.gao.gov/cgi-bin/getrpt?GAO-07-395T (2007). Accessed 10 June 2014

Kapucu, N.: The role of the militray in disaster response in the U.S. Eur. J. Econ. Polit. Stud. **4**(2), 7–33 (2011)

Kemball-Cook, D., Stephenson, R.: Lessons in logistics from Somalia. Disasters. **8**, 57–66 (1984)

Kovács, G., Spens, K.: Identifying challenges in humanitarian logistics. Int. J. Phys. Distrib. Logist. Manage. **39**(6), 506–528 (2009)

Kovács, G., Tatham, P.: Humanitarian logistics performance in the light of gender. Int. J. Product. Perform. Manage. **58**(2), 174–187 (2009)

Larson, R.C., Metzger, M.D., Cahn, M.F.: Emergency response for homeland security: lessons learned and the need for analysis. http://www.sdcorp.net/public/Pub_Emergency_Response_Homeland_Security.pdf (2005). Accessed 8 June 2014

Liu, G., Ramakrishnan, K.G.: A*Prune: an algorithm for finding K shortest paths subject to multiple constraints. http://citeseerx.ist.psu.edu/ viewdoc/download?doi=10.1.1.20.8011&rep=rep1&type=pdf (1999). Accessed 10 June 2014

Miskel, J.F.: Disaster Response and Homeland Security: What Works, What Doesn't. Praeger Security International, Westport (2006)

Schrader, John Y.: The Army's Role in Domestic Disaster Support: An Assessment of Policy Choices. RAND Corporation, Santa Monica (1993) AD-A 282 311

Sylves, R.T. Disaster Policy and Politics: Emergency Management and Homeland Security. CQ Press, Washington D.C. (2008)

US House of Representatives Failure of Initiative: Final Report of the Select Bipartisan Committee to Investigate the Preparation for and Response to Hurricane Katrina. US Government Printing Office, Washington D.C. (2006)

Van Wassenhove, L.N. Humanitarian aid logistics: supply chain management in high gear. J. Oper. Res. Soc. **57**(5), 475–489 (2006)

Chapter 7
Using Plane Tessellation Algorithms to Optimize Resource Allocation

Suchisman Sandipan Gangopadhyay

7.1 Introduction

Voronoi diagrams divide a plane into cells based on how close those parts of the plane are to a set of points, called sites. Every point within a cell is closer to the site within that cell that to any other point (See Fig. 7.1). The lines that divide cells are formed by points that are equidistant from two sites, and vertices are equidistant from three or more points (Deza and Deza 2006). One of the most well-known applications of the Voronoi diagram was its use by John Snow to find the source of the 1854 Cholera outbreak in London (Johnson 2006). (See Fig. 7.2) By dividing the city based on which parts were closest to different water pumps, he was able to find that most of the infected lived close to one particular pump. Today, these diagrams can be used in a range of logistical applications from figuring out taxi-cab deployments in a city taking into account street structures (Eugene 1987) (See Fig. 7.3) to optimization of military resources in forward bases.

The rest of this chapter explains strategies in the use of these diagrams in the optimal allocation of military resources, the modification of the diagrams using weights and the criteria to be used in their selection, the methods and their application in real world scenarios.

7.2 Using Weights to Modify a Voronoi Diagram

To further expand the use of Voronoi diagrams, each site could be given a weight. This weight would modify the distance between some point and that site (Edelsbrunner 1987). Additive weightage, for instance, would subtract the weight from the distance between a site and some point. Due to this, even if a point is closer to one site than

S. S. Gangopadhyay (✉)
University of Illinois at Urbana Champaign, Urbana, IL, USA
e-mail: suchismangang@gmail.com

V. Zeimpekis et al. (eds.), *Military Logistics,* Operations Research/Computer Science Interfaces Series 56, DOI 10.1007/978-3-319-12075-1_7

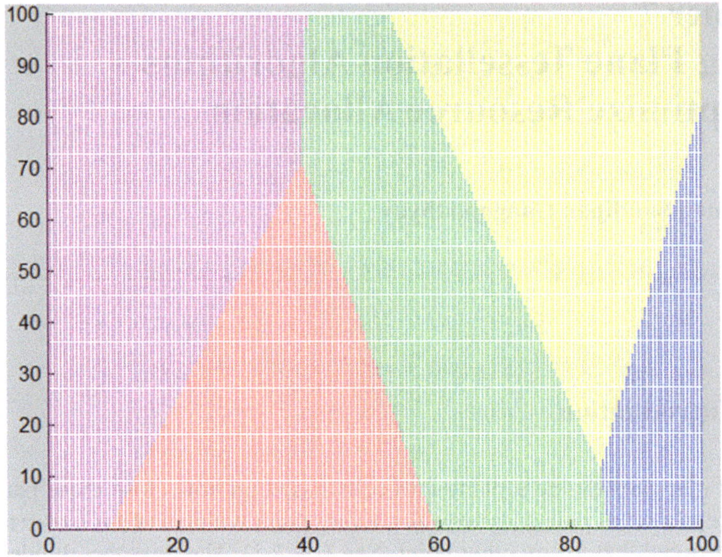

Fig. 7.1 A Voronoi Diagram with each cell being a different color. [Unless otherwise noted, the sites used in the Voronoi diagrams below are: (34, 15, 2), (73, 26, 1), (93, 26, 3), (3, 28, 4), (84, 30, 4)]

Fig. 7.2 This is the map John Snow used to find the source of the 1854 cholera outbreak in London

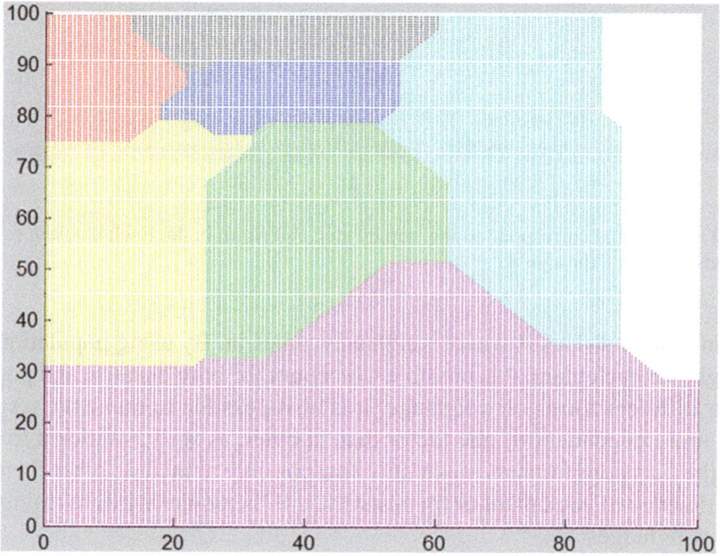

Fig. 7.3 This Voronoi diagram creates sites based on Manhattan distance rather than regular distance. The sites for this diagram are: (13, 86), (34, 67), (26, 82), (53, 18) (23, 74), (78, 78), (95, 81), and (24, 97)

another, it may still belong to the cell of the farther site if that site's weightage is higher. The weight can modify the distance in different ways. For instance, instead of being subtracted from a distance, the weight could be divided from that distance instead. Each site could also be assigned multiple weights, allowing for the Voronoi diagram to take into account more than one criterion.

7.3 Using Weighted Voronoi to Optimize Resource Deployment

At first glance, Voronoi diagrams have little to do with resource deployment. The link between the two comes from a simplification of the resource allocation problem (Jaiswal 1997). A simple way to look at allocating resources to some form of central hubs (i.e. train stations, military bases, power plants, etc.) is to divide the resources in the ratio of the land each hub serves. From this simplification, it is easy to use Voronoi Diagrams to divide the zones that each of these hubs would preside over (Holmberg 2001. Each cell of the Voronoi diagram would represent the portion of land the hub in the middle of the cell administers. The ratios of the cells could be used as the ratio of the resources allocated. This method naturally has many drawbacks, the biggest being that it fails to account for issues other than distance (Sharifzadeh and Shahabi 2006). Using the example of a power plant, not only does how much land the power plant provides service to matter, but also the population

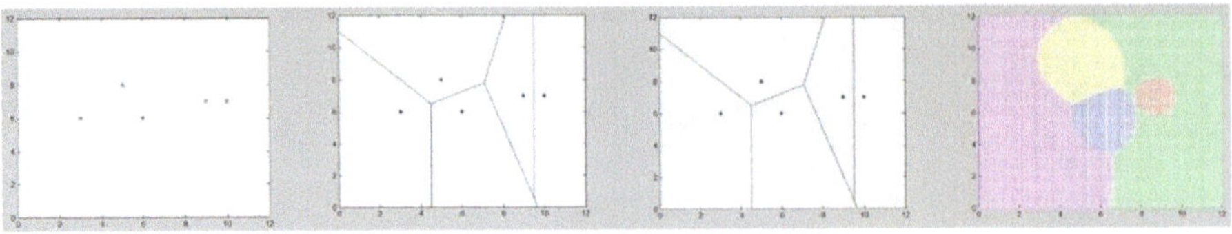

Fig. 7.4 These figures correspond to the step by step algorithm in 4a. Each diagram respectively corresponds to steps 1 through 4

density in that land. This is where weightage comes in. By using population density as a weight for each plant, it is possible to account for both distance and population. By using different forms of weightage, it is also possible to make the resource allocation more dependent of one factor than another, as well as tailor it to get very close to the decisions humans make. It is also possible to include other factors, such as the efficiency of each plant or the resistance of the power wires by using them as separate weightages.

7.3.1 Method

1. Plot the points of hubs to allocate resources to as points on a Cartesian plane
2. Create a Voronoi diagram for the above
3. Choose criteria that would influence the distribution for resources
4. Use the Voronoi cells created in step 2 to find quantitative data about the criteria deemed important in step 3 (See Fig. 7.4)
5. Create a new weighted Voronoi diagram which uses the numbers found in 4 as weights
6. Distribute resources based on the ratio of the cells of the weighted Voronoi diagram created in step 5

7.3.2 An Example—Planning Troop Deployments to Forward Military Bases with Insurgent Activity

Let us assume we are planning the deployment of troops to military bases in territory rife with insurgents. In this case, the amount of land the base administers is an important factor in how many troops to send there, but so is the amount of insurgent activity happening in that land (US Department of State 2009). A way to account for this would be to find the density of insurgent activity in the land each base presides over and use it as a multiplicative weight.

For this situation a step by step method that implements the approach described above in breaking the plane into cells with sizes corresponding to the relative distribution of resources across the sites, would be:

1. Plot the coordinates of the bases on a Cartesian plane
2. Create a Voronoi Diagram for the points generated in step one
3. Count the incidents of insurgent activity in each of the cells created in step and divide the number by the area of the corresponding cell
4. Use these densities as multiplicative weights to create a new, weighted Voronoi Diagram
5. Deploy troops in the same ratio as the ratio of the sizes of the new Voronoi cells

7.4 Determining the Optimal Weightage Strategy

Different applications of weighted Voronoi diagrams will have different weighting needs. In the case of military bases, a resource such as food will be more based on the number of people at a base, gasoline will be more based on the size of the region a base administers, while a resource like ammunition will be based much more on the concentration of insurgent activity—these have been difficult to automate and plan for stateside, leading to stockpiling at foreign shores and ports (Scott et al. 2000). There are many ways to weight a Voronoi diagram, with the most common using additional weightage. Multiplicative weightage is stronger than additional and exponential weightage is stronger than multiplicative. Each weightage has its own unique properties. When a weightage that is somewhere in between two other weightages is necessary, it is possible to modify the weightages by adding, multiplying, or raising each weight to a constant. Each type of weightage reacts differently to this sort of modification.

7.4.1 Additive Weightage Strategy and its Application

This method of weightage is only slightly dependent on weightage and is overall more dependent on distance. To use this weightage simply subtract a site's distance to a point by the weight that site has. (See formulae 1 and 2) Additive weightage can be thought of as making a Voronoi diagram for disks rather than points, with the larger disks having a bigger cell surrounding them. An additively weighted Voronoi diagram is like a regular Voronoi diagram but with curved walls. (See Fig. 7.5) This is convenient for resource allocation because unlike other types of weightages, it is fine to use zero and negative numbers as weights. An example of when to use additive weightage is the deployment of gasoline to military bases, with weightage being the number of insurgents in a base's area of administration. A resource like gasoline is primarily based on the area a base watches over, but is still affected by insurgent activity. To get the strength to be more accurate for the situation, it is possible to use a constant to modify the weightages.

$$\sqrt{(x-a)^2+(y-b)^2}$$

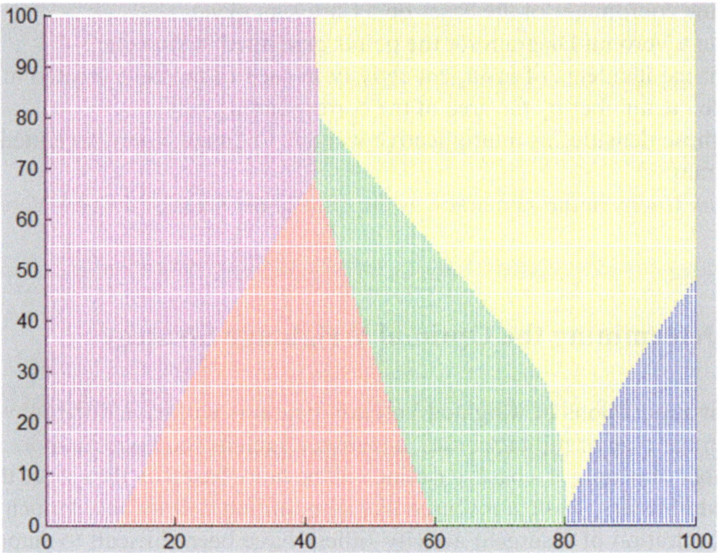

Fig. 7.5 A Voronoi diagram with additive weightage

Formula 1 For all formulae, x and y are the coordinates of a point on a Cartesian plane. a, b, and α are the x and y coordinates and the weight of a site, respectively. k is a constant which would be unchanged no matter the site. The distance formula

$$\sqrt{(x-a)^2+(y-b)^2}-\alpha$$

Formula 2 Distance Formula with Additive Weightage

7.4.1.1 Method to Modify Additive Weightage

Additively weighted Voronoi diagrams can be modified by using some mathematical operator on all of the weights (See formula 3). Adding or subtracting all the weights by some number has no effect (See formula 4), so the simplest way to modify an additively weighted Voronoi diagram is to multiply the weights of every site by a coefficient. (See formula 5). If the coefficient is greater than one, the weightage will become stronger. If the coefficient is between one and zero, the weightage will become weaker. (See Fig. 7.6) Multiplying the weights by a negative coefficient makes it so that sites with higher weightage have smaller cells around them, useful when dealing with a factor that is inversely proportional with how much resources an area should get. Raising every weight by some constant effects an additively weighted Voronoi diagram the same way as multiplying weights, albeit with different strength. (See formula 6) When above zero, an exponent will have stronger effects than a coefficient. When less than zero, this is reversed.

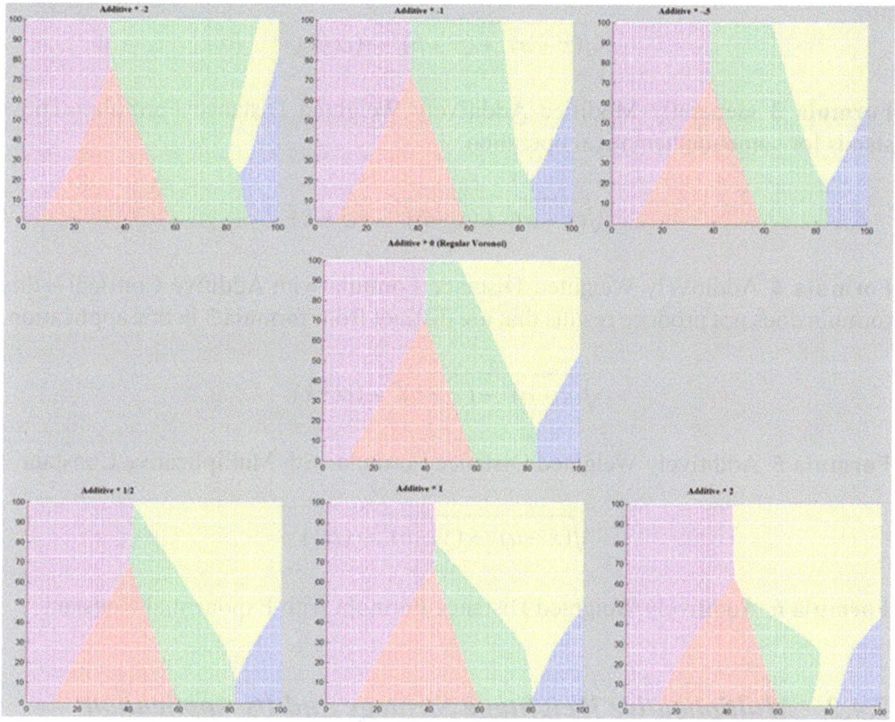

Fig. 7.6 Additively Weighted Voronoi diagrams with the weights multiplied by different constants

7.4.1.2 Example to Apply Additive Weightage

Take the case of distributing gasoline to military bases. To solve for this scenario using an additively weighted Voronoi diagram, steps that implement the approach described above in breaking the plane into cells with sizes corresponding to the relative distribution of resources across the sites:

1. Repeat the steps 1 through 3 in 4.b
2. Attribute these densities to the appropriate sites
3. Create a new Voronoi diagram, this time comparing distance subtracted by the weight of a site as opposed to unmodified distance (See formula 2)
4. Distribute gasoline in the same ratio as the ratio of the sizes of the new Voronoi cells

After getting the results, you may think that they are too dependent on insurgent activity. To fix this, one can modify the weightages:

1. Multiply the weights of each site by a number between 0 and 1 (See formula 5)
2. Using the new weights, follow steps 5 and 6 from the above section.

You can redo the above steps until you find a weightage that works in this instance.

$$\sqrt{(x-a)^2+(y-b)^2}-(\alpha \bullet k)$$

Formula 3 Generally Modified Additively Weighted Distance Formula—The · stands for some mathematical operation.

$$\sqrt{(x-a)^2+(y-b)^2}-(\alpha + k)$$

Formula 4 Additively Weighted Distance Formula with Additive Constant—this formula does not produce results that are distinct from formula 2 in this application.

$$\sqrt{(x-a)^2+(y-b)^2}-(\alpha * k)$$

Formula 5 Additively Weighted Distance Formula with Multiplicative Constant

$$\sqrt{(x-a)^2+(y-b)^2}-(\alpha^k)$$

Formula 6 Additively Weighted Distance Formula with Exponential Constant

7.4.2 Multiplicative Weightage Strategy and Its Application

This method of creating a Voronoi diagram is equally dependent on weight as it is on distance. To use it, divide the distance from a site to a point by that site's weight. (See formula 7)

$$\sqrt{(x-a)^2+(y-b)^2}\,/\,\alpha$$

Formula 7 Distance Formula with Multiplicative Weightage

A multiplicatively weighted Voronoi diagram features curving, sometimes circular structures. (See Fig. 7.7) In this sort of diagram, it is possible for a cell to fit completely inside another cell. One must be careful when choosing a weightage, because negative and zero weights create cases in the Voronoi which do not match up well with real life scenarios. If all sites are negatively weighted, then the Voronoi diagram will make cells based on which site is the farthest away, a zero weightage would not work with this algorithm. While a case where only negative weightages are used may exist in real life, mixing negative and nonnegative weightages results in problems because the sites with nonnegative weights will get no resources. A scenario that may work well with this type of weightage is deploying troops to military bases using the number of insurgents in the area each base presides over as weightages. In this case, both distance to cover and numbers of insurgents are major factors. To adjust the strength, it is again possible to modify the weightages by a constant.

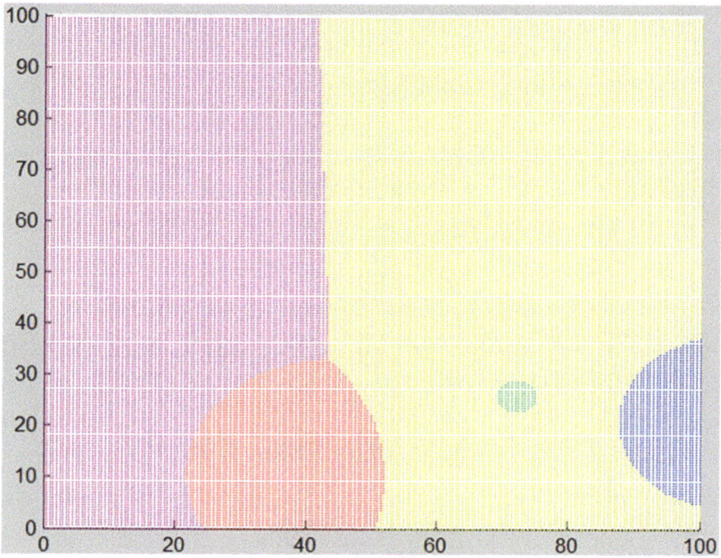

Fig. 7.7 A Voronoi diagram with multiplicative weightage

7.4.2.1 Method to Modify Multiplicative Weightage

Modifying multiplicative weightage: By adding a positive constant to all weightages, the strength of the multiplicative weightage decreases. (See Fig. 7.8 and formula 9)

$$\sqrt{(x-a)^2+(y-b)^2}\;/\;(\alpha \bullet k)$$

Formula 8 Generally Modified Multiplicatively Weighted Distance Formula

$$\sqrt{(x-a)^2+(y-b)^2}\;/\;(\alpha + k)$$

Formula 9 Multiplicatively Weighted Distance Formula with Additive Constant

Naturally, using a negative constant would strengthen the power of the weightage, but this is not recommended because if any weight becomes zero or negative, then the results will be skewed (See Fig. 7.11). Multiplying all the weights with a positive number has no effect on the strength of the diagram, whereas multiplying the weights by a negative coefficient attributes the most resources to sites with the smallest weights and administrative areas (See Fig. 7.9 and formula 10). Multiplying all the weights by zero does not work using this algorithm. Raising all the weights by a value greater than one increases the strength of the weightage. Raising the weights by a value between 1 and 0 results in the weightage becoming weaker (See Fig. 7.10 and formula 11).

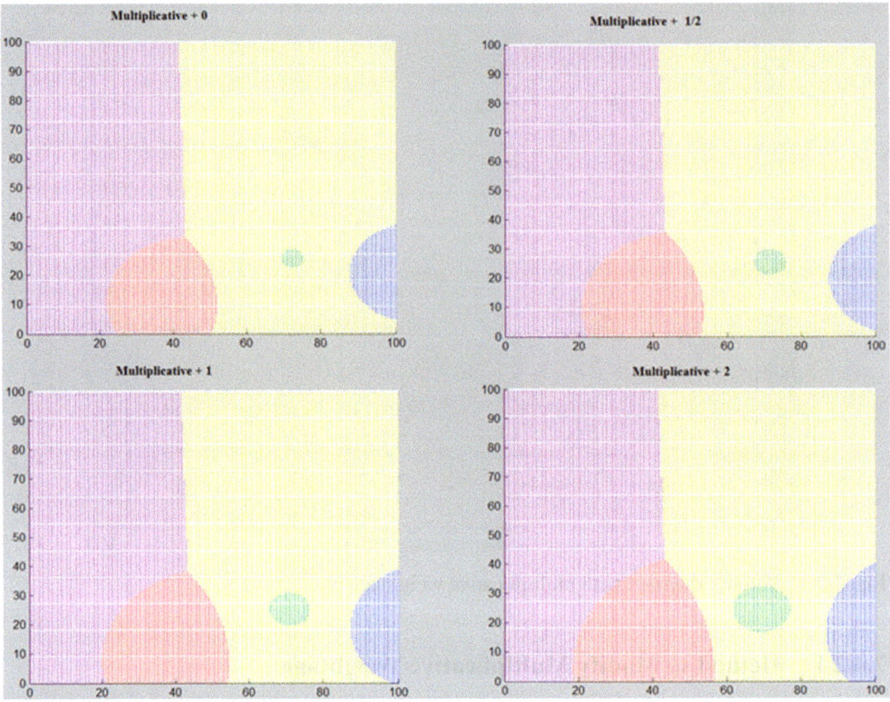

Fig. 7.8 Multiplicatively Weighted Voronoi diagrams with the weights added to different constants

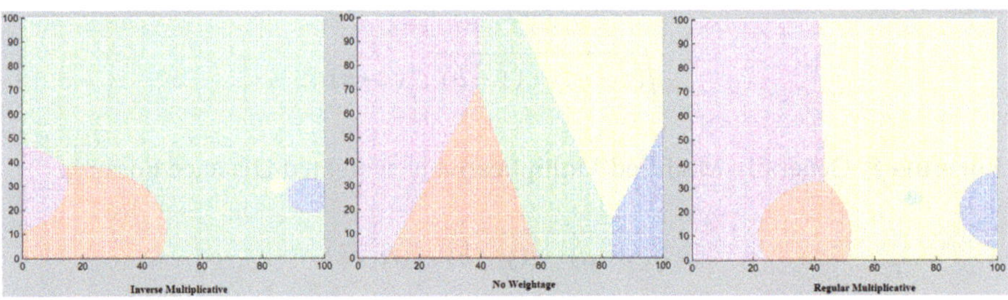

Fig. 7.9 A multiplicatively weighted Voronoi diagram and its inverse. Note that the inverse diagram gives bigger cells to sites which have a small cell in the original Voronoi diagram

$$\sqrt{(x-a)^2+(y-b)^2}\,/\,(\alpha * k)$$

Formula 10 Multiplicatively Weighted Distance Formula with Multiplicative Constant—if a positive constant is used, the results will be indistinguishable from those of formula 7 in this application. If a negative constant is used, the resulting diagram will be the inverse of a regular multiplicatively weighted Voronoi diagram.

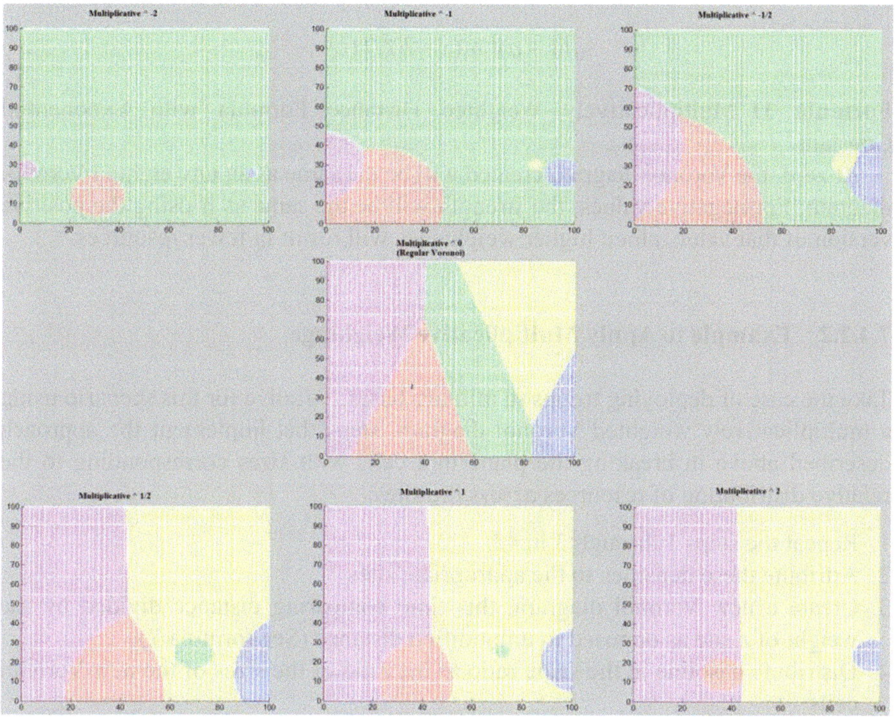

Fig. 7.10 Multiplicatively Weighted Voronoi diagrams with the weights raised by different constants

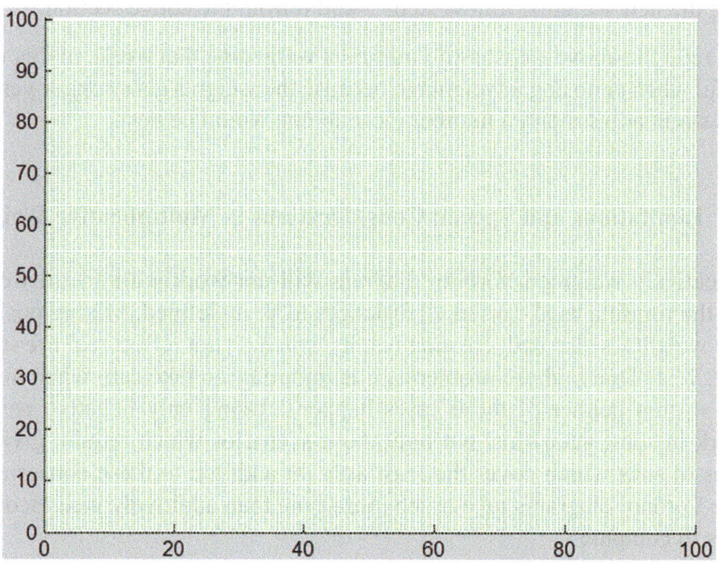

Fig. 7.11 A multiplicatively weighted Voronoi with one site having a negative weight. This site is the only one to have a cell

$$\sqrt{(x-a)^2+(y-b)^2}\,/\,(\alpha^k)$$

Formula 11 Multiplicatively Weighted Distance Formula with Exponential Constant

At zero, the Voronoi diagram created will be the same as an unweighted Voronoi diagram. For negative values, the strength will be the same as if using the positive version of that value, albeit higher weightages will result in fewer resources.

7.4.2.2 Example to Apply Multiplicative Weightage

Take the case of deploying troops to military bases. To solve for this scenario using a multiplicatively weighted Voronoi diagram, steps that implement the approach described above in breaking the plane into cells with sizes corresponding to the relative distribution of resources across the sites:

1. Repeat the steps 1 through 3 in 4.b
2. Attribute these densities to the appropriate sites
3. Create a new Voronoi diagram, this time comparing distance divided by the weight of a site as opposed to unmodified distance (See formula 7)
4. Distribute gasoline in the same ratio as the ratio of the sizes of the new Voronoi cells

After getting the results, you may think that they are too dependent on distance. To fix this, one can modify the weightages:

1. Raise the weights of each site by a number above 1 (See formula 11)
2. Using the new weights, follow steps 5 and 6 from the above section.

You can redo the above steps until you find a weightage that works in this instance. Be careful when choosing a weightage because the weights get stronger very quickly. For a slight adjustment, a number close to one would be best.

7.4.2.3 Limitations and Special Considerations in Multiplicative Weightage

Multiplicatively weighted Voronoi diagram will not work with a zero weightage, because the formula used caused all distances to be undefined. Mixing positive and negative weights is also bad, creating results which do not reflect real life scenarios. (See Fig. 7.11) Due to these problems, it is important to take care when modifying weights so that neither of these cases happens. Using only negative weightages may work in some scenarios, but only those scenarios which require giving more resources to sites which cover the least area. In addition to these concerns, multiplicative Voronoi diagrams take much more time than additively weighted Voronoi diagrams to compute.

7.4.2.4 Exponential Weightage Strategy and its Application

A Voronoi diagram with this type of weightage is more dependent on the weight that it is on distance. To use this weightage, raise the distance from a site to a point by the inverse of the site's weight. (See Fig. 7.12 and formula 12)

$$\sqrt[\alpha]{(x-a)^2+(y-b)^2}$$

Formula 12 Distance Formula with Exponential Weightage

Like a multiplicatively weighted Voronoi diagram, it is possible for a cell to be completely consumed in another, but when two sites are very close together the cell of the stronger site may seem to fit within the other cell, in reality the cell of the stronger point continues outside of that of the site with the smaller weightage (See Fig. 7.13). An exponentially weighted Voronoi diagram also changes based on the scale of the diagram, so it important to ensure that the units of the weightages are consistent with the units of distance. Like a multiplicatively weighted Voronoi diagram, the mixing of positive and negative weights should not be mixed. As is the case with multiplicatively weighted Voronoi diagrams, negative weightages results in sites with smaller cells getting more resources. A case where an exponentially weighted Voronoi may prove useful is the distribution of ammunition to military bases using the number of insurgents as a weightage. In this case, the number of insurgents is the driving force behind the ammunition distributed, but distance still plays a part. Like the other kinds of Voronoi diagrams discussed here it is possible to adjust the strength.

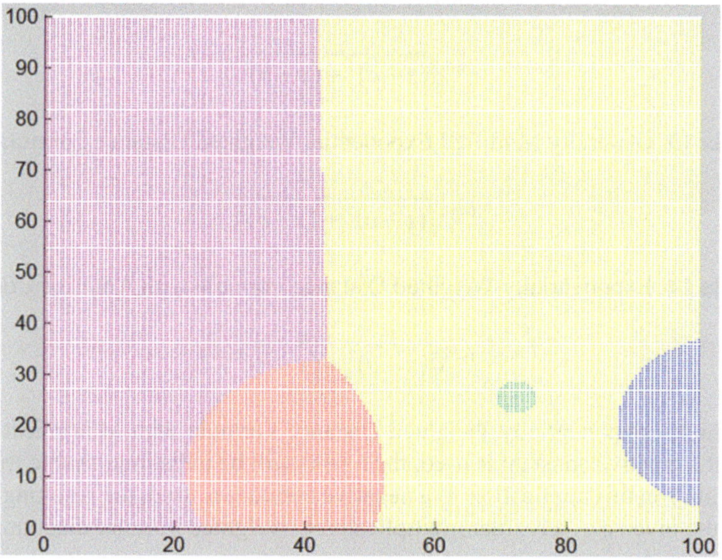

Fig. 7.12 An exponentially weighted Voronoi diagram

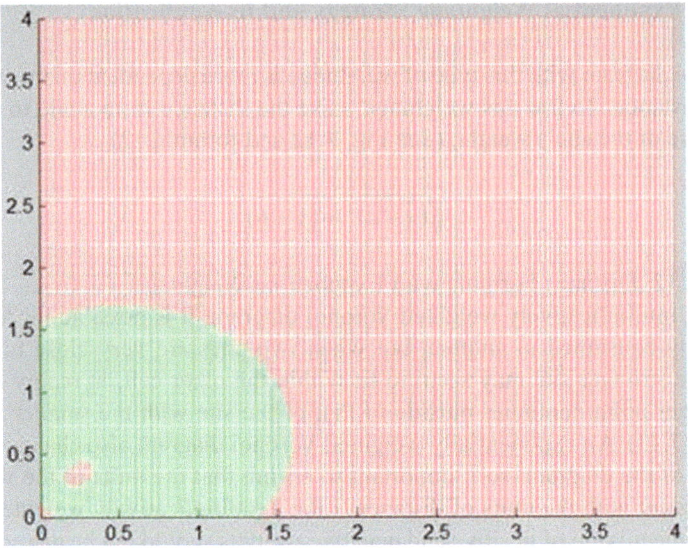

Fig. 7.13 A unique formation of cells present in some exponentially weighted Voronoi diagrams. There are only two sites in this picture. Both *red* areas are due to the same site

7.4.2.5 Method to Modify Exponential Weightage

Modifying Exponential Weightage: Exponential weightage works exactly like multiplicative weightage does. To modify an exponentially weighted diagram, please see the paragraph on modifying multiplicatively weighted diagrams above. (See Figs. 7.14 and 7.15 and formulae 13, 14, 15 and 16 for reference)

$$\sqrt[(\alpha \cdot k)]{(x-a)^2+(y-b)^2}$$

Formula 13 Generally Modified Exponential Weighted Distance Formula

$$\sqrt[(\alpha + k)]{(x-a)^2+(y-b)^2}$$

Formula 14 Exponentially Weighted Distance Formula with Additive Constant

$$\sqrt[(\alpha * k)]{(x-a)^2+(y-b)^2}$$

Formula 15 Exponentially Weighted Distance Formula with Multiplicative Constant—if a positive constant is used, the results will be indistinguishable from those of formula 7 in this application. If a negative constant is used, the resulting diagram will be the inverse of a regular multiplicatively weighted Voronoi diagram.

$$\sqrt[(\alpha^k)]{(x-a)^2+(y-b)^2}$$

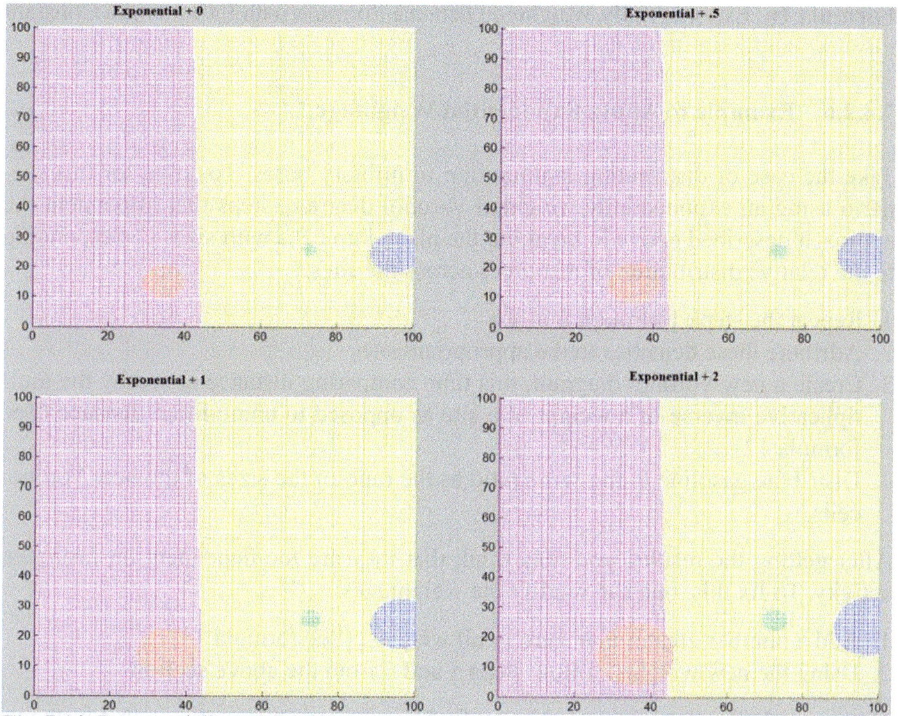

Fig. 7.14 Exponentially weighted Voronoi diagrams with the weights added to different constants

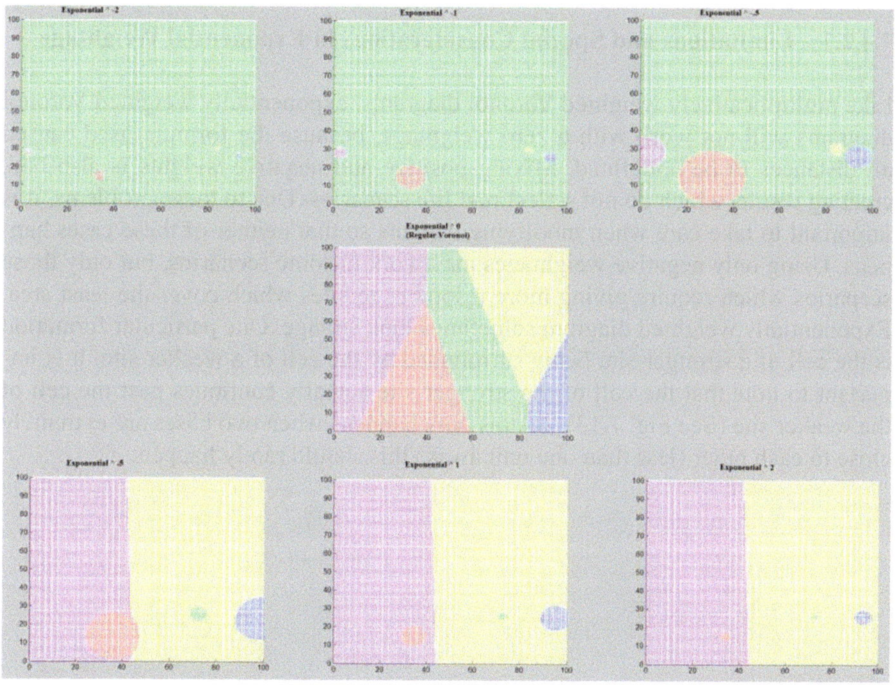

Fig. 7.15 Exponentially weighted Voronoi diagrams with the weights raised by different constants

Formula 16 Exponentially Weighted Distance Formula with Exponential Constant

7.4.2.6 Example to Apply Exponential Weightage

Take the case of distributing ammunition to military bases. To solve for this scenario using an exponentially weighted Voronoi diagram, steps that implement the approach described above in breaking the plane into cells with sizes corresponding to the relative distribution of resources across the sites:

1. Repeat the steps 1 through 3 in 4.b
2. Attribute these densities to the appropriate sites
3. Create a new Voronoi diagram, this time comparing distance raised by the multiplicative inverse of a weight of a site as opposed to unmodified distance (See formula 12)
4. Distribute gasoline in the same ratio as the ratio of the sizes of the new Voronoi cells

After getting the results, you may think that they are too dependent on insurgent activity. To fix this, one can modify the weightages:

1. Add a number greater than zero to all weights. (See formula 14)
2. Using the new weights, follow steps 5 and 6 from the above section.

You can redo the above steps until you find a weightage that works in this instance.

7.4.2.7 Limitations and Special Considerations in Exponential Weightage

Like multiplicatively weighted Voronoi diagrams, exponentially weighted Voronoi diagrams will not work with a zero weightage, because the formula used caused all distances to be undefined. Mixing positive and negative weights is also bad, creating results which do not reflect real life scenarios. Due to these problems, it is important to take care when modifying weights so that neither of these cases happens. Using only negative weightages may work in some scenarios, but only those scenarios which require giving more resources to sites which cover the least area. Exponentially weighted diagram sometimes look strange. One particular formation is the cell of a stronger site being surrounded by the cell of a weaker site. It is important to note that the cell of the stronger site actually continues past the cell of the weaker site (See Fig. 7.13). As this only happens when two bases are extremely close to each other (less than one unit away) this should rarely happen.

7.5 Conclusion and Contribution

This approach to resource allocation at forward military bases enables a highly visual representation of various factors beyond the area covered by each base such as enemy activity and geographical constraints. This opens up an alternative to calculating and depicting resource allocation.

7.6 Suggestions for Further Research

Very little work has been done in finding an efficient method to create exponentially weighted Voronoi diagrams, so these diagrams take the longest to make. More efficient methods for exponentially weighted Voronoi will have significant applications not only in logistics, but diverse applications such as cell phone tower connection models, optimization of radiation chemotherapy sites, etc.

Tessellation solutions with weapon assignment decision support and assess the objectives (Roux and van Vuuren 2007). Further, a decision analysis aiming at multiple-objectives (e.g., optimal allocation of munitions, fuels and troops) methods and explore new methods for assessing weights like in (Ewing et al. 2006).

This approach can be compared with the outcome with the assignment problem (Gardenfors et al. 1973) for the optimal distribution of personnel.

The described method will be limited by the capability to model specific factors uniformly inside a cell. Each of the weighting strategies (additive, multiplicative and exponential) is uniform. In reality, weightage of points inside the cells may differ based on dissimilarities of insurgent activity of different areas within the same cell, based on factors that are not being modeled. Since each cell is obtained from the intersection of half-spaces, they will not be convex polygons or areas. This leads to distorted Voronoi diagrams, unable to accommodate solutions as the ones described.

7.7 MatLAB Program Samples

7.7.1 MatLAB—Weight Dist Code

```
function [ WDist ] = WeightDist( x,ix,y,iy,ia )
   %UNTITLED3 Summary of this function goes here
   %  Detailed explanation goes here
   %WDist = abs((x-ix))+abs((y-iy));
   WDist = (((x-ix)^2+(y-iy)^2)^(.5))^(1/(ia^2));
end
```

7.7.2 MatLAB—Weighted Voronoi Code

```
function [areas] = WeightVoroN(sites)

   hold off;
   hold on;
   k = size(sites,1);
   colors = ['r' 'g' 'b' 'm' 'y' 'c' 'w' 'k'];

   minx = 0;
   maxx = 100;

   miny = 0;
   maxy = 100;

   stepx = (maxx - minx)/200;
   stepy = (maxy - miny)/200;
   a = minx:stepx:maxx;
   b = miny:stepy:maxy;

   areas = [0 0 0 0 0 0 0 0];

   for x = a
      for y = b
         ix = sites(1,1);
         iy = sites(1,2);
         ia = sites(1,3);
         zMax = WeightDist(x,ix,y,iy,ia);
         maxIndex = 1;
         i = 0;
         while i<k
            i = i+1;
            ix = sites(i,1);
            iy = sites(i,2);
            ia = sites(i,3);
            z = WeightDist(x,ix,y,iy,ia);
            if (z < zMax)
               zMax = z;
               maxIndex = i;
            end
          end
          plot(x,y,colors(maxIndex));
          areas(maxIndex) = areas(maxIndex)+1;
     end
   end
  end
```

References

Deza, E., Deza, M.: Dictionary of Distances, pp. 255, 256. Elsevier Science, Amsterdam (2006)

Edelsbrunner, H.: 13.6 Power Diagrams, Algorithms in Combinatorial Geometry, EATCS Monographs on Theoretical Computer Science 10, pp. 327–328. Springer-Verlag, Berlin (1987)

Eugene, F.K.: Taxicab Geometry. Dover, New York (1987). ISBN 0-486-25202-7

Ewing, P.L., Tarantino, W., Parnell, G.S.: Army base realignment and closure military value analysis. Decision analysis. Decis. Anal. Inf. **3**(1), 33–49 (2006)

Gardenfors, P.: Assignment problem based on ordinal preferences. Manage. Sci. **20**(3), 331–340 (1973)

Holmberg, K.: Encyclopedia of Optimization, pp. 609–616. Springer, New York (2001)

Jaiswal, N.K.: Military Operations Research: Quantitative Decision Making. Kluwer, Boston (1997)

Johnson, S.: The Ghost Map: The Story of London's Most Terrifying Epidemic—and How it Changed Science, Cities and the Modern World, pp. 195–196. Riverhead Books, New York (2006). ISBN 1-59448-925-4

Roux, J., van Vuuren, J.: Threat evaluation and weapon assignment decision support: a review of the state of the art. J. Oper. Res. Soc. S. Afr. **23**(2), 151–187 (2007)

Scott, B.F., Rainey, Lt Col James C., et al. The logistics of war, Air Force Journal of (2000)

Sharifzadeh, M., Shahabi, C.: Computer Science Department, University of Southern California. Additively weighted voronoi diagrams for optimal sequenced route queries (2006)

US Department of State.: US Government Counter Insurgency Guide, pp. 26 (2009)

Chapter 8
A Metaheuristic Reconstruction Algorithm for Solving Bi-level Vehicle Routing Problems with Backhauls for Army Rapid Fielding

Athanassios Nikolakopoulos

8.1 Introduction

Long-term stockpiles of material causes serious shortcomings during military operations, while achieving superior logistical efficiency mandates that the military moves to a rapid and reliable transportation process that provides time-definite delivery to users. The objective is to define optimal allocations of required flows of personnel and materiel within the geographic area of operation. A theatre distribution system is comprised of facilities, installations, methods, and procedures designed to receive, store, maintain, distribute, and control the flow of materiel between exogenous inflows to that system and distribution to end-user activities and units within the theatre (Crino et al. 2004). Such a distribution system may be efficiently represented by a network where the associated physical components are categorized as nodes, modes, and routes. Improved logistics support at all levels has been characterized as a major priority and immediate need for the military services. A large variety of military logistical problems are tackled in the recent literature (Brigantic and Mahan 2004), ranging from the planning of munitions distribution (Clark et al. 2004) to airlift mission monitoring and scheduling, the solution of theatre distribution vehicle routing and scheduling problem (Wilkins et al. 2004) and unmanned aerial vehicle routing (O'Rourke 1999).

In military logistics, the Army fielding process secures that new and used equipment is optimally circulated among warehouses, military units and theatre of operations or exercise (Carier 2007). For the theater distribution planning specific

A. Nikolakopoulos (✉)
National Technical University of Athens, School of Chemical Engineering,
9 Heroon Polytechneiou str., 15780 Zografou Campus Athens, Greece
e-mail: nikolako@mail.ntua.gr

Hellenic Military Academy, Sector of Mathematics and Engineering,
Leoforos Varis Koropiou, Vari Attikis, Athens, Greece

V. Zeimpekis et al. (eds.), *Military Logistics,* Operations Research/Computer Science Interfaces Series 56, DOI 10.1007/978-3-319-12075-1_8

requirements include prescribing routing and scheduling plans that optimize the utilization of theater assets while satisfying end user demand and time requirements (Kaminski 1995).

Responsiveness, flexibility and efficiency are key objectives in this forward and reverse operation, especially because theater level operations face a race against a growing deficit. Minimization of the use of transport media, personnel and time resourses is of utmost importance for improving the supply chain management system and equipment fielding operations. The progress of information and communication technologies along with industry partnership has allowed the transition of the Army to a requirement-based system where needs can now be ordered and shipped forward and backward in a "just in time logistics" procedure. Distribution planning proves to be of particular importance due to the benefits it offers to the overall process. The integration of forward and reverse flows of products and materials offers additional savings of material, personnel, vehicles, fuel and time resources.

The present paper, addresses Vehicle Routing Problems with Backhauls and Time Windows (*VRPBTWs*) where military units are divided into two sets, one with delivery (line-haul units) and another with backhaul demands (backhaul units). Additional precedence constraints are imposed, which require that in each route pickup units can be served only after all deliveries have been completed. Finally, time windows restrict the duration of each route and the time the service of each unit begins. The optimization problem is formulated as a bi-level optimization model. The objective of the leader's problem is the minimization of the required number of vehicles while the objective of the follower's problem is the minimization of the total duration of the routes. First a mixed integer programming formulation of the problem is given and tested for the solution of instances of moderate size. The objective function is a critical feature of the model that permits the transformation of the bi-level problem into a classical MILP problem. Since the Capacitated VRPs (*CVRPs*) are NP-hard problems, the *VRPBTWs* are NP-hard in the strong sense. Thus, only small instances of these problems can be tackled successfully by exact methods. The major volume of work directed to the solution of *VRPBTWs* is based on heuristic techniques. A literature review on both exact and heuristic methods will be provided in the next section.

The present work uses a new metaheuristic algorithm for the solution of *VRPBTWs*. Initial solutions are produced by a simple construction heuristic. Current solutions are partially destroyed using six different heuristics. The first two heuristics accelerate the progress of the leader's objective while the last four promote the improvement of the follower's objective. The two objectives are incorporated in a properly scaled aggregated objective function. New solutions are produced by the construction heuristic after applying one of the six alternative heuristics, which remove a subset of customers from the current complete solution. A variation of the Threshold Accepting (*TA*) method (Dueck and Scheuer 1990) with adaptive threshold list (Nikolakopoulos and Sarimveis 2007) and gradually reinforced Local search (Sarimveis and Nikolakopoulos 2005) is used for improving the solutions.

At the occasion of the production of better solutions the Local search is intensified for a predetermined number of iterations and then relaxed for escaping from local optima. The proposed method has proven to be competitive for the solution of a number of problems proposed in (Gélinas et al. 1995), with favorable results in many of them compared to the results of the most recent heuristic methods that have been proposed in the literature in (Gélinas et al. 1995; Thangiah et al. 1996; Potvin et al. 1996; Zhong and Cole 2005; Reimann et al. 2002; Ropke and Pisinger 2006).

The rest of this chapter is organized as follows: Section 8.2 reviews literature of exact and heuristic techniques, used for the solution of *VRPBTWs*. Section 8.3 presents a formal definition of the *VRPBTW* along with the mixed integer programming formulation of the problem. Section 8.4 describes the proposed heuristic method. Section 8.5 presents the procedure and results for tuning the algorithm parameters. Section 8.6 reports computational results on benchmark instances and the chapter ends with conclusions in Sect. 8.7.

8.2 Literature Review

Solution of *VRPBTWs* was firstly attempted by utilizing branching techniques for Branch and Bound methods based on column generation for solving a set partitioning formulation of the problem (Gélinas et al. 1995), by branching on the resource variables (time or capacity) instead of the network flow variables. A substantial reduction of the explored number of nodes and the required computational time was achieved by this method. Problems with up to 100 nodes were solved to optimality. The objective was the minimization of the total travelling times. In the work of Thangiah et al. (1996) a new heuristic algorithm was proposed for the solution of *VRPBTWs* and tested on the instances introduced in (Gélinas et al. 1995). The new algorithm was based on a parallel insertion heuristic of Kontoravdis and Bart (1992) for the production of the initial solutions and λ-interchanges or 2-*opt* exchanges local search methods for the improvement of the solutions. The primary objective was the minimization of the number of vehicles, while the secondary objective was the minimization of the travelling times. Solutions on problems with up to 100 nodes were within 2.5 % of the known optimal solutions on average. In (Potvin et al. 1996) a greedy route construction heuristic was used, which inserts customers one by one into the routes using a fixed a priori ordering of customers. Next, a genetic algorithm was adopted to identify an order that produces good routes. A Tabu Search algorithm was proposed in (Duhamel et al. 1997) and solutions were produced for the instances of Gélinas et al. (1995). Initial solutions were produced using a modification of the simple insertion heuristic. The first objective was the minimization of the number of vehicles, as in the work of Thangiah et al. (1996), but as a second objective they considered the minimization of the summation of travelling, service and waiting times and not just the travelling times. An Ant system algorithm was proposed in (Reimann et al. 2002) where initial solutions were produced by an extension of the Solomon's heuristic, while local search used the 3-opt and 4-opt operators proposed in (Osman 1993). The objective was to minimize the fleet size, and given a fleet size, to minimize operating costs. Hasama et al. (1999) use Simulated Annealing and model the state of solution as a sequence of characters. New states of solution are generated by exchanging the position of two characters or reverse the direction of a partial string. Label matching algorithms were developed in (Cheung and Hang 2003) and the *VRPBTW* was formulated as a set-partitioning problem. Recently a cluster-first routing-second method was proposed (Zhong and Cole 2005), which starts from an infeasible initial solution and then drives the search towards strong feasibility. The objectives are the minimization of the number of routes and secondly the minimization of the total distance of all the routes. The most recent work for the solution of *VRPBTWs* is that of Ropke and Pisinger (2006), who proposed a large neighborhood search heuristic. The objective in their work is also bi-criteria.

8.3 Problem Definition

In the capacitated *VRPBTW*, a homogeneous fleet V with $K_{avl} = |V|$ vehicles of equal capacity Q is available. A set N of n customers, $N = \{1, 2\ldots, n\}$, must be served. There is a pickup p_i or a delivery d_i request for every customer $i \in N$. If $p_i > 0$ then $d_i = 0$ and if $d_i > 0$ then $p_i = 0$, i.e. a customer can have only delivery or only pickup demand. The delivery service in a vehicle route must precede the pickup service. The total service of the customer lasts st_i units of time. The complete directed graph induced by the customers is $G = (N^+, A)$, where $N^+ = N \cup \{0, n+1\}$ is the set of vertices and A is the set of arcs. The depot is represented by the vertex 0 and $n+1$. A is the set of directed arcs that connect any pair of vertices, except that no arc terminates in vertex 0, and no arc originates from vertex $n+1$. A traveling cost $c_{i,j}$ and time $t_{i,j}$ corresponds to each arc $(i, j) \in A$ (assumption in this work: a unit of travel distance corresponds to a unit of travel cost), while a time window $[e_i, l_i]$ is assigned to each vertex $i \in N^+$. This is in fact a time restriction, meaning that the time T_i at which service to customer i, begins, must lie within the respective time window. If a vehicle reaches the customer at time $T_r < e_i$ then it waits for a time period equal to $e_i - T_r$ until the service begins. The time windows $[e_0, l_0] = [e_{n+1}, l_{n+1}]$ corresponding to the depot actually pose constraints on the time where a vehicle can leave/arrive to the depot. Zero delivery demands, pickup demands and service times are assigned to nodes $\{0, n+1\}$, that is, $d_0 = d_{n+1} = p_0 = p_{n+1} = st_0 = st_{n+1} = 0$. The primary objective is the minimization of the required number of vehicles. This is realized by letting some of the vehicles to remain at the depot and contribute zero cost. These vehicles do not serve any customers and their routes are represented by the arc $(0, n+1)$ to which zero travelling cost and time are assigned: $c_{0,n+1} = t_{0,n+1} = 0$. The secondary objective is the minimization of the total traveling cost. In a feasible solution each customer is serviced exactly once (p_i, $d_i \leq Q$, $\forall\, i \in N$ and no split delivery is permitted), every route originates at vertex 0 and ends at vertex $n+1$, and the time windows and capacity constraints are satisfied.

The set of customers N comprises of two subsets of customers. The first subset *LH* contains customers which have only delivery demand (line-haul customers) and the second subset *BH* contains only customers with pickup demand (backhaul customers).

Thus: $N = LH \cup BH$, $p_i = 0, \forall i \in LH$ and $d_i = 0, \forall i \in BH$. Furthermore, the backhaul customers cannot be served in a route before the service of the linehaul customers is completed.

8.3.1 Mixed Integer Programming Formulation for the VRPBTW

The next four sets of variables are considered in the problem:

$$x_{k,i,j} = \begin{cases} 0 \text{ if } \textit{vehicle } k \text{ does not drive from vertex } i \text{ to vertex } j \\ 1 \text{ if vehicle } k \text{ drives from vertex } i \text{ to vertex } j \end{cases}, \ \text{(i, j)} \in \text{A and k} \in \text{V},$$

$D_{k,\,i}$ The load, to be delivered, on the vehicle *k* when leaving from customer *i*.
$P_{k,\,i}$ The picked up load on the vehicle *k* when leaving from the customer i.
$T_{k,\,i}$ The starting time of the service of vehicle *k* at customer *i*.

The *VRPBTW* can then be formally described as the following multi-commodity network flow model with time window priority and capacity constraints:

$$Min \left\{ 10^{a*} \left(\sum_{k \in V} \sum_{i \in V} x_{k,0,i} \right) + \sum_{k \in V} \sum_{i \in N*} \sum_{j \in N^*} c_{i,j} x_{k,i,j} \right\} \tag{8.1}$$

$$\text{s.t.} \sum_{k \in V} \sum_{j \in N^+} x_{k,i,j} = 1, \quad \forall i \in N \tag{8.2}$$

$$\sum_{i \in N^+} x_{k,i,j} = \sum_{i \in N^+} x_{k,j,i}, \quad \forall k \in V, \quad \forall j \in N \tag{8.3}$$

$$\sum_{j \in N^+ \setminus \{0\}} x_{k,0,j} = 1, \quad \forall k \in V \tag{8.4}$$

$$\sum_{i \in N^+ \setminus \{n+1\}} x_{k,i,n+1} = 1, \quad \forall k \in V \tag{8.5}$$

$$x_{k,i,j} = 0, \quad \forall k \in V, \quad \forall i \in BH, \quad \forall j \in LH \tag{8.6}$$

$$D_{k,i} + P_{k,i} \le Q, \quad \forall i \in N^+, \quad \forall k \in V \tag{8.7}$$

$$D_{k,n+1} = 0, \quad \forall k \in V \tag{8.8}$$

$$D_{k,0} = \sum_{i \in N} \sum_{j \in N} x_{k,i,j} d_i, \quad \forall k \in V \tag{8.9}$$

$$P_{k,0} = 0, \quad \forall k \in V \tag{8.10}$$

$$P_{k,n+1} = \sum_{i \in N} \sum_{j \in N} x_{k,i,j} p_i, \quad \forall k \in V \tag{8.11}$$

$$D_{k,i} - d_j - D_{k,j} \le (1 - x_{k,i,j}) Q^{*1}, \quad \forall (i,j) \in A, \quad \forall k \in V \tag{8.12}$$

$$D_{k,j} + d_j - D_{k,i} \le (1 - x_{k,i,j}) Q^{*2}, \quad \forall (i,j) \in A, \quad \forall k \in V \tag{8.13}$$

$$P_{k,i} + p_j - P_{k,j} \le (1 - x_{k,i,j}) Q^{*3}, \quad \forall (i,j) \in A, \quad \forall k \in V \tag{8.14}$$

$$P_{k,j} - p_j - P_{k,i} \le (1 - x_{k,i,j}) Q^{*4}, \quad \forall (i,j) \in A, \quad \forall k \in V \tag{8.15}$$

$$T_{k,i} + x_{k,i,j}(st_i + t_{i,j}) - T_{k,j} \le (1 - x_{k,i,j}) T^{*}, \quad \forall (i,j) \in A, \quad \forall k \in V \tag{8.16}$$

$$e_i \left(\sum_{j \in N^+} x_{k,i,j} \right) \le T_{k,i} \le l_i \left(\sum_{j \in N^+} x_{k,i,j} \right), \quad \forall i \in N^+, \forall k \in V \tag{8.17}$$

$$E \le T_{k,i} \le L, \quad \forall i \in \{0, n+1\}, \forall k \in V \tag{8.18}$$

$$D_{k,i} \ge 0, \quad \forall i \in N^+, \quad \forall k \in V \tag{8.19}$$

$$P_{k,i} \ge 0, \quad \forall i \in N^+, \quad \forall k \in V \tag{8.20}$$

$$x_{k,i,j} \in \{0,1\}, \quad \forall (i,j) \in A, \quad \forall k \in V \tag{8.21}$$

The objective function (8.1) minimizes the number of vehicles and the total cost of the routes, giving priority to the attainment of the first goal. The number of used vehicles is computed by the term $\left(\sum_{k \in V} \sum_{i \in N} x_{k,0,i} \right)$, because for each used vehicle there is exactly one route from vertex 0 ("the driving-out depot") to one vertex in N, while for unused vehicles there is no route from vertex 0 ("the driving-out depot") to any vertex in N. The exponent a^* of the multiplier in the first term of the objective function is chosen in a way that a feasible solution with fewer vehicles is preferred over any solution with more vehicles regardless of the corresponding total travelling costs, i.e. total travelling cost is used to choose a solution only among solutions which use the same number of vehicles.

In particular, since the total traveling cost C_{tot} cannot exceed $C_{max} = (K_{av} + n)c_{max}$, where c_{max} is the maximum cost of traveling between any pair of vertices of the graph, a^* is computed as follows:

$$a^* = \arg_a\left\{\min(10^{a-1}), 10^{a-1} > C_{\max}\right\}, a \in \mathbf{Z}^+ \tag{8.22}$$

This way C_{tot} coexists with the number of vehicles K in a joint objective function (8.1), named from now on *obj*, i.e. the number of used vehicles is $K = \left\lfloor obj / 10^{a^*} \right\rfloor$ and the total traveling cost is $C_{tot} = obj - K \cdot 10^{a^*}$. The coefficient 10^{a^*} works as a weight multiplier and $UB = 10^{a^*}(K+1)$ is an upper bound to the candidate solutions.

Constraint (8.2) restricts the assignment of the service of each customer to exactly one vehicle. The set of equalities (8.3–8.5) pose flow constraints, requiring that when a vehicle leaves the depot, it must return to it and additionally, if a vehicle reaches a customer it must leave the customer and continue its route. According to constraints (8.6) no transition from backhaul to line-haul customers is permitted in a route, giving priority to the service of line-haul customers. According to the capacity constraint (8.7), when a vehicle leaves a customer, the total load must be less than or equal to the capacity Q. When a vehicle leaves the depot to serve a set of customers it has to be sufficiently loaded with delivery goods in order to meet all the requests. Furthermore, when a vehicle returns to the depot, it must be loaded with all the goods it has picked up from customer, but no delivery goods can still be loaded on the truck. These requirements are enforced by constraints (8.8–8.11). The delivery load of a vehicle k which visits vertex j after i, has to be decreased by the quantity of goods demanded by customer j (constraint sets (8.12) and (8.13)). Accordingly, the pickup load is increased by the quantity picked up from customer j (constraint sets (8.14) and (8.15)). Constraints (8.16–8.18) describe the relation between flow variables and the times that vehicles start servicing the customers. Constraint sets (8.12–8.15) and (8.16) comprise the subtour elimination constraints. The constant values Q^{*1}, Q^{*2}, Q^{*3}, Q^{*4} and T^* must be at least $(Q-d_j)$, Q, Q, $(Q-p_j)$ and $(L-E)$ respectively, otherwise feasible solutions could be potentially cut off.

Small VRPBTW instances with up to ten customers are solved to optimality in large amount of time (~10 h). Thus the need for an efficient heuristic is obvious.

8.4 Description of the Proposed Method

The flowchart of the proposed algorithm is presented in Fig. 8.1. The first step is the preparation of data to meet the precedence constraints. Then, the initial solution with objective function value obj_{new} and threshold list are produced using the *Insertion Heuristic* as described in Sect. 4.4. The procedure for producing the threshold list is described in Sect. 4.4. The current solution is assigned the value obj_{new}. The current solution is partially destroyed using one of the six destruction heuristics described in Sect. 4.3 and a new solution is produced using the *Insertion Heuristic.*

- If the new solution is improving on the current solution the algorithm performs intense local search for a prescribed number of iterations. Then the procedure of destroying and reconstructing the solution is repeated.
- If the new solution is not improving, and if the difference of the new and the current solution is less than the current threshold T the current solution is assigned the value obj_{new} and the procedure is repeated.
- If the difference of the new and the current solution is larger than the current threshold T a new solution is produced and the procedure is repeated.

The algorithm terminates when a maximum number of iterations is reached.

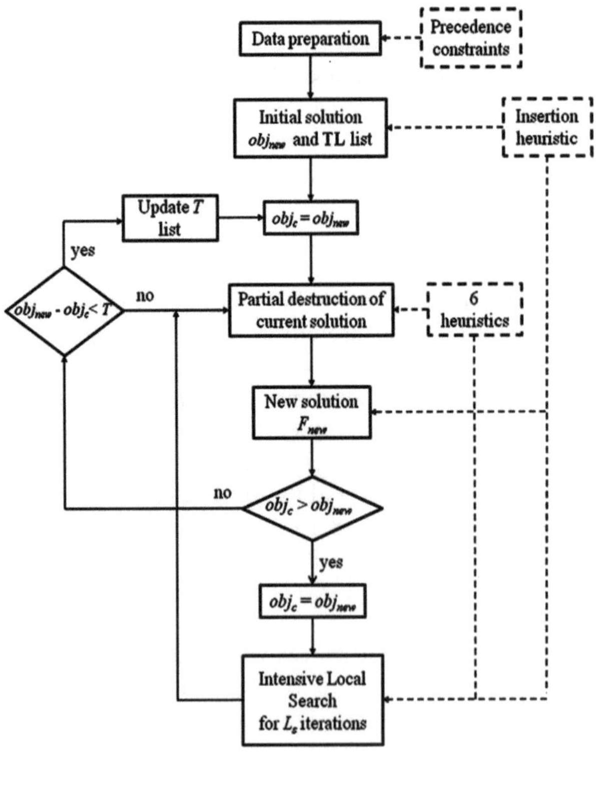

Fig. 8.1 Flowchart of the proposed algorithm

8.4.1 Objective Function

As mentioned before, the primary objective is the minimization of the total number of vehicles, while the minimization of the total distance (cost) traveled by all vehicles is considered as the secondary objective. A candidate solution to this problem assigns N_k customers to each vehicle k in a particular order. The route of the vehicle k can thus be represented as an elementary path in G:

$$M_k = \{0 \equiv m_{k,0}, m_{k,1}, m_{k,2} \ldots, m_{k,N_k}, m_{k,N_k+1} \equiv n+1\},$$

where $m_{k,1}, m_{k,2}, \ldots, m_{k,N_k}$ are distinct elements of the set N. The path starts from the depot and returns to it and is feasible if it satisfies the *path constrains*:

$$\sum_{l=1}^{i} p_{m_{k,l}} + \sum_{l=i+1}^{N_k} d_{m_{k,l}} \leq Q \quad i = 1, \ldots, N_k \tag{8.23}$$

$$e_{m_{k,i}} \leq T_{m_{k,i}} \leq l_{m_{k,i}} \qquad i = 1, \ldots, N_k \tag{8.24}$$

where $T_{m_{k,i}} = \max\left\{e_{m_{k,i}}, T_{m_{k,i-1}} + t_{m_{k,i-1}, m_{k,i}} + st_{m_{k,i-1}}\right\}$ is the starting time of the service at node $m_{k,i}$. A feasible solution for the problem is a set of K disjoint feasible elementary paths starting and ending at the depot, where all customers are served exactly once. The aggregated objective function is formulated as follows:

$$obj = 10^{\alpha^*} K + \sum_{K=1}^{K} \sum_{i=0}^{N_k} c_{m_{k,i}, m_{k,i+1}} \tag{8.25}$$

The term K in (8.25) is obviously equal to the number of used vehicles, while the term $\sum_{K=1}^{K} \sum_{i=0}^{N_k} c_{m_{k,i}, m_{k,i+1}}$ stands for the total traveling cost in a feasible solution. Priority to the attainment of the first goal is given by assigning a proper value to the parameter α^*. This value is obtained as discussed in the previous section by equation (8.22).

8.4.2 Initial Solution—Insertion Heuristic

The data should be appropriately pre-processed before implementing the algorithm. In particular, for *VRPBTW* problems, the cost of traveling from backhaul to line-haul customers is set to: $c_{BH,\,LH} \leftarrow c_{BH,\,LH} + M$, where $M = 10^{\alpha^*}$. This action ensures that the line-haul customers will always be served before the backhaul customers.

The rationale behind the insertion heuristic is simple: Given a list containing all the customers, a schedule of vehicle routes is constructed by inserting one by one the customers in the feasible position corresponding to the least additional cost.

Priority is given to already existing routes, but if there is no feasible position, a new route is created for serving the customer. A representation of the complete solution to the problem is

$$Routes = \left\{u_{1,0}, u_{1,1}, \ldots, u_{1,veh_1+1}, u_{2,0}, u_{2,1}, \ldots, u_{2,veh_2+1}, \ldots u_{K,0}, u_{K,1}, \ldots, u_{K,veh_K+1}\right\}$$

where K is the total number of used vehicles, $veh_k = N_k$ is the number of customers served by vehicle k ($k = 1, \ldots, K$), $u_{k,0}$ and u_{k,veh_k+1} for $k = 1, \ldots, K$ denotes the depot, and $u_{k,i}$ for $i = 1, \ldots, veh_k$ denotes the ith customer assigned to vehicle k.

More analytically, the insertion heuristic used for the construction of the initial solution consists of the following steps:

Step 1 Generate a random permutation of all customers: $CO = \{v_1, v_2, \ldots, v_N\}$.

Step 2 Initial route: Set $i = 1$, $veh_1 = 0$. Create the first route: $K := 1$. Insert v_1 in route $K = 1$ and set $veh_1 = veh_1 + 1$. Route 1 is $R_1 = \left\{u_{1,0}, u_{1,1}, u_{1,veh_1+1}\right\}$, where $u_{1,0}$ and $u_{1,2}$ denote the depot and $u_{1,1}$ is v_1.

Step 3 Insertion of the next customer. Set $i = i + 1$.

Compute $\mathbf{D}_{k,j} = c_{u_{k,j}, v_i} + c_{v_i, u_{k,j+1}} - c_{u_{k,j}, u_{k,j+1}}$, $k = 1, \ldots, K$ and $j = 0, 1, \ldots, veh_k$.

Find $(k_1^*, j_1^*) = \underset{k,j}{\operatorname{argmin}}(\mathbf{D}_{k,j})$ and create the set E: $\left\{(k_1^*, j_1^*)\right\}$

If the path $\left\{u_{k_1^*,0}, \ldots, u_{k_1^*, j_1^*}, v_i, u_{k_1^*, j_1^*+1}, \ldots, u_{k_1^*, veh_{k_1^*}+1}\right\}$, is feasible (the constrains (8.23) and (8.24) are not violated), insert node v_i in route k_1^* after node $u_{k_1^*, j_1^*}$ and set $veh_{k_1^*} = veh_{k_1^*} + 1$.

Otherwise consider E as the set of infeasible positions and check feasibility of the new path for the next

$$(k_2^*, j_2^*) = \underset{k,j}{\operatorname{argmin}}(\mathbf{D}_{k,j}) \; and \; \{k, j\} \notin E$$

If the path is feasible, insert customer v_i in route k_2^* after node $u_{k_2^*, j_2^*}$ and set

$$veh_{k_2^*} = veh_{k_2^*} + 1.$$

Else $E := E \cup \left(k_2^*, j_2^*\right)$ and continue with the next minimum cost position. If no insertion is possible create a new route $K := K + 1$ to serve customer v_i and set $veh_K = 1$ and $E := \varnothing$.

Step 4 Stopping criterion. If $i < N$ go to ***Step 3***.

Else Stop. The complete feasible initial solution $Routes_{int}$ with number of vehicles $K_{int} = K$, total distance cost td_{int} and total aggregated cost obj_{int} is formulated.

Note 1 The pre-processing of the data combined with Step 3 shall never allow the insertion of a backhaul customer before a line-haul customer.

8.4.3 Proposed Scheme for Producing a New Solution

The new solution production scheme consists of the next steps:

1. Remove a set of customers *DCO* from current solution $Routes_c$ with K_c routes. The remainder of the current solution is $DRoutes_c$, which is always feasible regarding time and capacity constraints.
2. Set $i=0$, $CO := DCO$ and consider $DRoutes_c$ as an incomplete schedule. Produce the new solution $Routes_{new}$ with K_{new} number of vehicles using the *Insertion Heuristic* from ***Step 3*** of the previous algorithm. Set $Routes_c \equiv Routes_{new}$ and $K_c = K_{new}$.

Six different heuristics are used for removing the set of customers *DCO*:

1. Remove all the customers of two randomly chosen routes of $Routes_c$
2. Remove all the customers of the first (in the representation of the solution) k_r routes of $Routes_c$, where k_r is a random integer number $\in [1, K_c]$.
3. Chose at random a customer *i* and remove the customers, whose distance from *i* is at most $\delta_* c_{0,i}$, where $c_{0,i}$ is the distance (cost) from the depot to customer *i*.
4. Chose at random a customer *i* and remove the customers with delivery demand d_c that satisfies $\delta_* d_i \leq d_c \leq (\delta + 1)_* d_i$, where d_i is the delivery demand of customer *i*.
5. Chose at random a customer *i* and remove the customers with pickup demand p_c that satisfies $\delta_* p_i \leq p_c \leq (\delta + 1)_* p_i$, where p_i is the pickup demand of customer *i*.
6. Chose at random a customer *i* with midpoint of time window:
7. $mp_i = \dfrac{l_i + e_i}{2}$ and remove the customers for which the time window midpoint

$mp_c = \dfrac{l_c + e_c}{2}$ satisfies $\delta_* \, mp_i \leq mp_c \leq (\delta + 1)_* \, mp_i$.

In the last four heuristics δ is a random number $\in [0, 1]$ generated from a normal distribution.

Note 2 The first two heuristics accelerate the progress of the primary objective while the last four help the improvement of the secondary objective. Each iteration of the solution improving algorithm, which is presented next, utilizes only one removal heuristic. The probability of applying each removal heuristic will be discussed later along with the description of the solution improving algorithm. The idea behind the first two choices is that when a solution is disintegrated by removing customers from one or more routes, the removed customers have the opportunity to be redistributed and served by the remaining routes. This way, the reduction in the number of vehicles is more likely to happen. The idea applies more successfully in the early stages of the search procedure, where customers of the initially created routes have less possible positions to be inserted in. The idea behind the last four heuristics is that customers with distance, demand or time window proximity are more likely to be successfully relocated, as far as the goal of minimizing the total cost of the routes is concerned, while capacity and time constraints are still satisfied.

8.4.4 *The Solution Improving Algorithm*

The algorithm begins with an initial solution, which is updated in successive iterations. It accepts even nonimproving solutions as long as they lay under a specific limit (threshold). When a new best is found the algorithm performs persistent local search. More analytically:

Preliminary step Create the initial threshold list **TL**:

The total distance cost of the initial solution $Routes_{int}$ is td_{int}. By the proposed scheme for producing a new solution we generate L–1 additional solutions. The L distance costs corresponding to the solutions that have been generated so far are sorted in a ascending order, $td_{i+1} > td_i, \quad i = 1,\ldots, L-1$. The threshold accepting vector is produced next, whose elements are computed as follows:

$$\mathbf{TL}_i = td_i - td_1, \quad i = 1,\ldots, L.$$

The Threshold accepting algorithm follows the next three steps:

Step 1 Initialize:

$Routes_c$:= $Routes_{int}$, obj_c:= obj_{int}, td_c:= td_{int} and K_c:= K_{int} where index c indicates the current values of the variables.

Set number of iterations $it = 0$ and $Ls = Ls_o$.

Step 2 Set $it = it + 1$.

Produce new solution: $Routes_{new}$ with obj_{new}, td_{new} and K_{new} using the *scheme for producing a new solution* described earlier.

Calculate $Dif = obj_{new} - obj_c$.

If $Dif < \mathbf{TL}_L$, then $Routes_c := Routes_{new}$, $obj_c := obj_{new}$ $td_c := td_{new}$ and $K_c := K_{new}$ (the new solution becomes the current solution)

If $Dif > 0$, then $\mathbf{TL}_L := Dif$ and sort the elements of **TL** in an ascending order.

Else $Routes_{best} := Routes_{new}$, $obj_{best} := obj_{new}$, $td_{best} := td_{new}$ and $K_{best} := K_{new}$

Set $\mathbf{TL}_L := 0$ for the next $round(\alpha_{ls} \cdot it)$ iterations, where $\alpha_{ls} \in [0, 1]$.

Endif

Endif

Step 3 If $it = it_{max}$ the algorithm stops and $Routes_{best}$ with obj_{best}, td_{best} and K_{best} is the best solution found by the algorithm. Otherwise return to Step 2.

Note 3 The proposed method accepts deteriorating solutions regarding the secondary goal of minimizing the total travelling cost (flexible), but not with respect to the primary goal of minimizing the number of vehicles. This happens because it is always true that TL_L < Dif when a new solution uses more vehicles than the current solution.

8.5 Algorithm Tuning

The influence of the six removal heuristics on the performance of the proposed algorithm was examined by measuring the success rate of each heuristic on a number of tests. The following procedure is used for tuning the probabilities of applying each of the six heuristics:

Step 1 Initialize: set equal probabilities p_i for applying each heuristic *i*.

Step 2 Run the algorithm for the maximum number of iterations it_{max}, keeping record of the total improvement of the objective function value achieved separately by each heuristic; TI_i.

Step 3 Set $p_m{}^* = TI/TI_i$ where TI is the total improvement of the objective function value.

- If $\sum (p_m^* - p_m)^2 \leq \varepsilon$ stop; p_m^* are used for applying each heuristic
  m= i, ii, iii, iv, v, vi.
- Else and go to Step 2.

The p_m^* s converge at p_i^* =0.17, p_{ii}^* =0.33, p_{iii}^* =0.25, p_{iv}^* =0.03, p_v^* =0.05 and p_{vi}^* =0.17.

Heuristics (i) and (ii) prove to be more successful in the early stages of the search, where the number of vehicles can be easily reduced because the customers of the destroyed routes can be relocated in the remaining routes. Regarding removal heuristics (iii)–(vi), (iii) is the most powerful while small variations were observed between (iv) and (*v*), and overall these two heuristics exhibit weak efficiencies. The performance of the algorithm was also tested individually for each move, by utilizing each time only one heuristic type for performing local search. A considerable increase in the convergence time was observed that often exceeded 100 %. More specifically, by using only one of the moves (i)–(ii) the algorithm is often trapped at suboptimal solutions, while when utilizing only one of the heuristics (iii)–(vi), the algorithm is not able to address successfully the primary objective.

Note 4 In Step 2 of the solution improving algorithm, when a new overall better solution is found ($Dif < 0$), a gradually reinforced ($Ls = \alpha_{ls} * it$) persistent local search is conducted. The value of α_{ls} was set after testing to 0.05. This local search tries to exploit the nearest neighbors of the best solution $Routes_{best}$ in order to find an even better one without allowing deteriorations of the current solution ($\mathrm{TL_L} := 0$).

8.6 Computational Results

The MatLab (Mathworks 2009) programming language was used for coding the algorithm and a 3.2 MHz Pentium 4 processor was used for all computational experiments. For our computational experiments the length of the Threshold list L is set to $|N|$.

The proposed method was tested on solving 15 *VRPBTW* instances with 100 customers, proposed in (Gélinas et al. 1995). In this work the set of problems was solved, by running ten times the algorithm for each instance. The instances of Gélinas et al. (1995) are based on the *R*1 series developed in (Solomon 1987) for *VRPTWs*. Test problems are constructed by randomly choosing 10, 30 and 50 % of the 100 customers of Solomon's problems and inverting their delivery to pickup demand and the distance data are truncated to one decimal place. Results for these problems are reported in (Gélinas et al. 1995; Thangiah et al. 1996; Reimann et al. 2002; Ropke and Pisinger 2006; Duhamel et al. 1993; Hasama et al. 1999). It must be noted that the results of Gélinas et al. (1995) are the optimal solutions to the problem of minimizing the total travelling time (or traveled distance assuming that a unit of travel distance corresponds to a unit of travel cost) and do not consider the minimization of the number of vehicles. In that sense, the results of the proposed method are not directly comparable to the results of (Gélinas et al. 1995). Also the results of the proposed method are not directly comparable to the results of (Zhong and Cole 2005, Reimann et al. 2002; Ropke and Pisinger 2006), because in (Zhong and Cole 2005, Reimann et al. 2002; Ropke and Pisinger 2006) unlike the original data of (Gélinas et al. 1995) the distances are represented using doubles. Table 8.1 summarizes the results produced by the proposed method and the best results found in the literature. The first column contains the names of the instances and the second denotes the percentage of backhaul customers in the total number of customers. The six next columns report the best solutions found in the literature (Gélinas et al. 1995; Thangiah et al. 1996; Potvin et al. 1996; Zhong and Cole 2005; Reimann et al. 2002; Ropke and Pisinger 2006) regarding the number of utilized vehicles and the total distance. The last five columns report the best and worst results produced by the proposed method and the average computational times. For each instance, bold fonts denote the best results in terms of number of vehicles or travelling time without taking into account the priority of the first objective. It is shown that larger number of vehicles can often require less travelling time than smaller number of vehicles (see for example the results of (Ropke and Pisinger 2006) and the proposed algorithm for instance R101 with 50 % backhauls). Compared to the other algorithms, the proposed method produces better solutions in the number of vehicles in four instances but lower total cost of routes in only one. Regarding the first objective the algorithm proves successful by finding the least number of vehicles for 11 instances. The proposed method uses reasonable time resources with average computing time *av. time* = 128.33 s. Note that the computation times are not directly comparable since tests are run on different systems and different coding languages.

8.7 Conclusions

The present work examined vehicle routing problems with backhauls and time windows in the context of forward and reverse logistics of military operations. Two goals were set for the problems. The primary goal was the minimization of the number of vehicles and the second was the minimization of the total travelling

Table 8.1 Comparative results on VRPBTW instances with 100 customers of Gélinas et al. (1995)

		Results (Gélinas et al. 1995)	Results (Thangiah et al. 1996)	Results (Potvin et al. 1996)	Results (Zhong and Cole 2005)	Results (Reimann et al. 2002)	Results (Ropke and Pisinger 2006)	Proposed method				
Instance	%BH	td_{best} [K_{best}]	td_{best} [K_{best}]	td_{best} [K_{best}]	td_{best} [K_{best}]	td_{best} [K_{best}]	td_{best} [K_{best}]	K_{best}	td_{best}	K_{worst}	td_{worst}	$time_{av}$ (s)
R101	10	1767.9	1842.3 [24]	1815.0 [23]	1848.04 [24]	1831.68 [22]	1818.86 [22]	21	1786	21	1852.7	125
	30	1877.6	1928.6 [24]	1896.6 [23]	2034.61 [24]	1999.16 [23]	1959.56 [23]	22	1881.9	23	1890	233
	50	1895.1	1937.6 [25]	1905.9 [24]	2057.05 [25]	1945.29 [24]	1939.1 [24]	22	1980.9	24	1935.9	87
R102	10	1600.5	1654.1 [20]	1622.9 [20]	–	1677.62 [19]	1653.19 [19]	19	1637.9	20	1706.2	210
	30	1639.2	1764.3 [21]	1688.1 [20]	–	1754.43 [22]	1750.7 [22]	20	1760.8	21	1734	98
	50	1721.3	1745.7 [21]	1735.7 [21]	–	1782.21 [22]	1775.76 [22]	19	1726.8	19	1753.6	105
R103	10	–	1371.6 [15]	1343.7 [16]	–	1348.41 [16]	1387.57 [15]	15	1446	16	1520	201
	30	–	1477.6 [16]	1381.6 [15]	–	1395.88 [16]	1390.33 [15]	15	1490.3	18	1647.6	68
	50	–	1543.2 [16]	1456.6 [17]	–	1467.66 [17]	1456.48 [17]	16	1455.2	16	1455.2	215
R104	10	–	1220.3 [13]	1117.7 [12]	–	1205.78 [11]	1084.17 [11]	11	1233.4	12	1312.4	65
	30	–	1302.5 [13]	1169.1 [12]	–	1128.3 [12]	1154.84 [11]	12	1273	12	1296.6	114
	50	–	1346.6 [13]	1203.7 [13]	–	1208.46 [12]	1191.38 [11]	12	1264.7	12	1327.1	125
R105	10	–	1553.4 [17]	1621.0 [17]	1590.54 [17]	1544.81 [16]	1561.28 [15]	16	1544.9	16	1617.2	97
	30	–	1706.7 [18]	1652.8 [16]	1667.92 [17]	1592.23 [16]	1583.3 [16]	16	1616	16	1722.3	103
	50	–	1657.4 [18]	1706.7 [18]	1699.88 [19]	1633.01 [17]	1710.19 [16]	16	1655.3	16	1655.3	79
Average results		–	1603.46 [18.27]	1554.47 [17.8]	–	1567.66 [17.67]	1561.11 [17.27]	16.8	1583.54	17.47	1628.4	128.33

cost. A mixed integer programming formulation is presented that clearly identifies the problem. A metaheuristic heuristic algorithm was proposed for the solution of *VRPBTWs*. Initial solutions are produced by a simple construction heuristic. New solutions are produced by the construction heuristic after applying one of the six alternative heuristics, which remove a subset of customers from the current complete solution. A variation of the TA method with adaptive threshold list and gradually reinforced Local search is used for improving the solutions. For minimizing the number of vehicles required the proposed method has proven to be competitive for the solution of a number of problems, with favorable results in many of them compared to the results of the most recent heuristic methods that have been proposed in the literature. However, it is not as successful for minimizing the total travelling time.

References

Brigantic, R.T., Mahan, J.M. (eds.): Defense Transportation—Algorithms Models and Applications for the 21st Century. Elsevier, Amsterdasss2004)

Carier, J.D.: The Army rapid fielding initiative. Syst. Inf. Eng. Des. Symp. IEEE. 1–4 (2007)

Cheung, R.K., Hang, D.D.: Multi-attribute label matching algorithms for vehicle routing problems with time windows and backhauls. IIE Trans. **35**(3), 191–205 (2003)

Clark, S.J., Barnhart, C., Kolitz, S.E.: Large-scale optimization planning methods for the distribution of United States army munitions. Math & Comp Mod **39**, 697–714 (2004)

Crino, J.A., Moore, J.T., Barnes, J.W., et al.: Solving the theater distribution vehicle routing and scheduling problem using group theoretic tabu search. Math & Comp Mod 39:599–416 (2004)

Dueck, G., Scheuer, T.: Threshold accepting: a general purpose optimization algorithm appearing superior to simulated annealing. J. Comput. Phys. **90**, 161–175 (1990)

Duhamel, C., Potvin, J.Y., Rousseau, J.M.: A tabu search heuristic for the vehicle routing problem with backhauls and time windows. Transport Sci. **31**, 49–59 (1997)

Gélinas, S., Desrochers, M., Desrosiers, J. Solomon, M.M.: A new branching strategy for time constrained routing problems with application to backhauling. Ann. Oper. Res. **61**, 91–109 (1995)

Hasama, T., Kokubugata, H., Kawashima, H.: A heuristic approach based on the string model to solve vehicle routing problem with various conditions, Preprint for World Congress on Intelligent Transport Systems, No.3027, Toronto, Canada (1999)

Kaminski P.G.: The revolution in defense logistics, In Keynote Address of the USAD for Acquisition and Technology, Alexandria, VA (1995)

Kontoravdis, G., Bard, J.F.: Improved heuristics for the vehicle routing problem with time windows. Technical Report, Operations Research Group, Department of Mechanical Engineering, The University of Texas, Austin, USA (1992)

Mathworks: MatLab version (7.8.0347) R2009a, February 12, 2009, License number: 54126 (2009)

Nikolakopoulos, A., Sarimveis, H.: A threshold accepting heuristic with intense local search for the solution of special instances of the traveling salesman problem. Eur. J. Oper. Res. **177**, 1911–1929 (2007)

O'Rourke, K.P.: Dynamic unmanned aerial vehicle (UAV) routing with a Java encoded reactive tabu search metaheuristic. Master's Thesis, Air Force Institute of Technology, USA (1999)

Osman, I.H.: Metastrategy simulated annealing and tabu search algorithms for the vehicle routing problem. Ann. Oper. Res. **41**, 421–451 (1993)

Potvin, J., Duhamel, C., Guertin, F.: A genetic algorithm for vehicle routing with backhauling. Appl. Intell. **6**, 345–355 (1996)

Reimann M., Doerner, K., Hartl, R.F.: Insertion based ants for vehicle routing problems with backhauls and time windows. In: Dorigo, M., Caro G.Di., Sampels, M. (eds.) Ant Algorithms, pp. 135–147. Springer, Berlin (2002)

Ropke, S., Pisinger, D.: A unified heuristic for a large class of vehicle routing problems with Backhauls. Eur. J. Oper. Res. **171**, 750–775 (2006)

Sarimveis, H., Nikolakopoulos, A.: A line up evolutionary algorithm for solving nonlinear constrained optimization problems. Comp. Oper. Res. **32**, 1499–1514 (2005)

Solomon, M.: Algorithms for the vehicle routing and scheduling problem with time window constraints. Oper. Res. **35**, 254–265 (1987)

Thangiah, S.R., Potvin, J.Y., Sun, T.: Heuristic approaches to vehicle routing with backhauls and time windows. Comp. Oper. Res. **23**, (11) 1043–1057 (1996)

Wilkins, D.E., Smith, S.F., Kramer, L.A., et al.: Airlift mission monitoring and dynamic rescheduling. Math & Comp Mod **39**, 141–155 (2004)

Zhong, Y., Cole, M.H.: A vehicle routing problem with backhauls and time windows: a guided local search solution. Transport. Res. E-Log. **41**, 131–144 (2005)

Chapter 9
Reliability Study of Military Operations: Methods and Applications

Ioannis S. Triantafyllou

9.1 Introduction

One of the most important issues in military operations is how to plan a realistic and appropriate tactic in order to face off effectively every kind of difficulties that come along. Defensive and offensive strategies, transposition systems, operations assurance, telecommunication networks or logistics planning are some of the affairs that should be taken care of in order to build the required substratum for successful results. In order to adjust properly the aforementioned elements, a reliability analysis of the corresponding systems may offer essential conclusions and information. This approach has already attracted some research interest in the last few years. For example, Sven Guzman et al. (2012) applied reliability methods to model multistate network flow problems, Grosselin (2012) used parametric statistical analysis to decrease the probability of a catastrophic launch failure of a satellite, while Anderson-Cook et al. (2007) proposed a Bayesian reliability model in order to improve the operational level of missile systems.

Reliability characteristics of a military tactic are of considerable interest in the analysis and forming procedure of a strategy. The main terminus of a martial plan is to accomplish its aim. However, since the success of a tactic cannot be affirmed before its implementation, it is of great concern to determine the probability for a plan to come true. For a detailed presentation and analytical perusal of the art of war strategy, the interested reader is referred to the survey of General Carl von Clausewitz (1909). A reliability study of military scenarios, which includes the calculation of reliability function and the signature vector of the applied structure, offers a detailed analysis of their crucial features and thus it contributes to the stepping-stone of a military planning.

I. S. Triantafyllou (✉)
Department of Statistics and Insurance Science, University of Piraeus,
80 Karaoli and Dimitriou Str., 18534 Piraeus, Greece
e-mail: itrantal@unipi.gr

V. Zeimpekis et al. (eds.), *Military Logistics*, Operations Research/Computer Science Interfaces Series 56, DOI 10.1007/978-3-319-12075-1_9

In the sequel, let us introduce some important concepts and notations of the Statistical Reliability Theory, which will be proved useful in next sections of the Chapter. First of all. let T be the lifetime of a reliability system of order n and $T_1, T_2, \ldots, T_n$ the lifetimes of its components. If we assume that $T_1, T_2, \ldots, T_n$ are independent and identically distributed (i. i. d.) according to a common underlying distribution, the Signature of the system is defined as the probability vector $\mathbf{s}(n) = (s_1(n), s_2(n), \ldots, s_n(n))'$ with

$$s_i = s_i(n) = P(T = T_{i:n}),\ i = 1, 2, \ldots, n \tag{9.1}$$

where $T_{1:n} \leq T_{2:n} \leq \ldots \leq T_{n:n}$ are the order statistics of the sample $T_1, T_2, \ldots, T_n$ while $P(T = T_{i:n})$ denotes the probability that the system fails upon the $i-th$ failure of its components. It can be verified that, in the i. i. d. case, the coordinates $s_i(n)$ of the signature depend only on the system structure and not on the (common) distribution of T_i (Samaniego (1985)).

Let us next denote by $n!$ the number of ways of rearranging n distinct elements, while C_i corresponds to a minimal cut set consisting of i failed components. In other words, C_i is a set of i components, the failure of which guarantees the failure of the whole system while simultaneously every $(i-1)$ of them do not. The quantities $n! \cdot s_i$ can be calculated by examining the minimal cut sets of the system and counting how many among the $n!$ equally likely permutations of $T_1, T_2, \ldots, T_n$ result in a minimal cut set failing upon the occurrence of $T_{i:n}$.

The signature of a system is closely related to many well-known reliability concepts, a fact turning it to a very important tool for investigating the performance of a coherent structure and comparing structures between each other (Triantafyllou and Koutras (2008a); Eryilmaz et al. (2011)). For example the reliability polynomial of a structure, which is related to the probability that the system is still functioning, can be easily expressed in terms of the Signature, stochastic ordering for systems' lifetimes is often made feasible by simply comparing their signatures etc. For a detailed and up-to-date presentation of the signature of coherent systems and their applications, the interested reader is referred to the excellent survey of Samaniego (2007).

In Sect. 9.2, we establish recurrence relations for the evaluation of signatures of some well-known reliability structures, while several numerical results are additionally provided. In Sect. 9.3, we apply the general results of the previous section, in the military area. More specifically, we present four different scenarios of military operations, which are appropriately paralleled with the reliability systems mentioned earlier and interesting conclusions about their success in practice are deduced.

9.2 General Results for Consecutive-Type Systems

Over the past three decades, a substantial research effort has been spent on the study of characteristics of consecutive type reliability systems (Triantafyllou and Koutras (2008b); Eryilmaz and Zuo (2010); Kuo and Zuo (2003)). This can be attributed to the fact that, such systems have been used to model and establish optimal designs of telecommunication networks, oil pipeline systems, vacuum systems in accelerators, spacecraft relay stations etc.

A linear consecutive-k-out-of-n: F system $C(k,n)$ consists of n components that are linearly ordered, the system failing if and only if at least k consecutive components fail. This system has been subject of substantial research interest for many years and a lot of generalizations have been suggested in order to accommodate more flexible operation principles. For example, the m-consecutive-k-out-of-n: F system $C(m,k,n)$ $(n \geq mk)$, which was first introduced by Griffith (1986), fails if and only if there exist at least m nonoverlapping runs of k consecutive failed components (for a recent contribution on the subject see Eryilmaz et al. (2011)). Additional interesting generalizations of the classical consecutive-k-out-of-n: F structure include the r-within-consecutive k-out-of-n: F system (Griffith (1986); Triantafyllou and Koutras (2011)). A r-within-consecutive k-out-of-n: F system consists of n (linearly arranged) components and fails if and only if there exist k consecutive components which include among them, at least r failed ones $((1 < r \leq k \leq n))$. Moreover, the so-called (n,f,k) system (or combined f-out-of-n: F and consecutive-k-out-of-n: F system) involves two common failure criteria. More specifically, the (n,f,k) system consists of n components (ordered in a line or a circle) and fails if, and only if, at least f failed components or at least k consecutive failed components exist. It is worth mentioning that the configuration of an (n,f,k) system was first introduced by Tung (1982) as an application to a complex infrared detecting system and since then it has attracted considerable research attention. For a survey on the consecutive-k-out-of-n: F systems and their generalizations the interested reader may refer to Eryilmaz (2010) or to the excellent monograph by Kuo and Zuo (2003).

In this section, we study reliability characteristics of the aforementioned structures and we prove general results concerning their signatures. The formulas, which are established in the following propositions, constitute pioneer research work and indicate one of the main contributions of the Chapter. More specifically, we present some details for the application of a generating function approach to the (n,f,k) system, and focusing on the special case of a $(n,f,2)$ system we discuss techniques for evaluating its signature vector and reliability function. In addition, some recurrence relations for the coordinates of the signature vector of a linear consecutive-k-out-of-n: F and a r-within-consecutive k-out-of-n: F system are also established for specific design parameters.

Let us now consider an (n,f,k) system, where $f > k$; we recall that for the case $f \leq k$ the (n,f,k) system coincides with the well-known f-out-of-n: F structure and its reliability properties have been extensively studied in the past. As already mentioned, the system consists of n components and fails if, and only if, at least f failed components or at least k consecutive failed components exist. Figure 9.1 illustrates the failure criterion of the (n,f,k) structure for specific values of its design parameters. Note that a grey-filled box indicates a failed component, while a blank box indicates a working one.

The next proposition offers a recursive scheme for the coordinates of the signature vector of a $(n,f,2)$ system. The proof of Proposition 9.1 is based on the

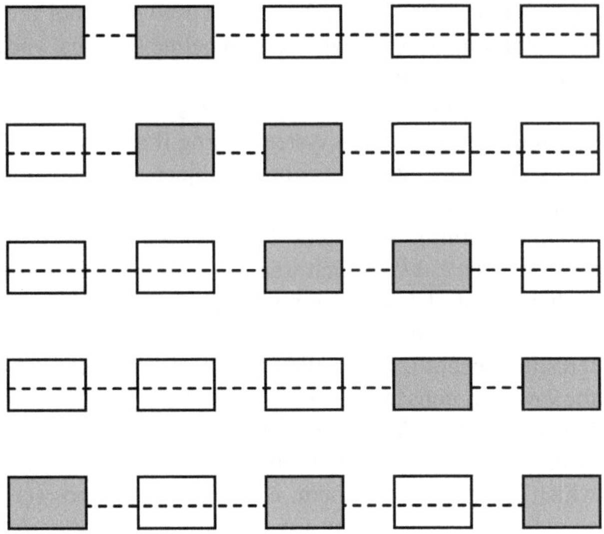

Fig. 9.1 The (n, f, k) system for $n = 5, f = 3, k = 2$

generating function of the reliability polynomial R_n, e.g. a power series whose coefficients encode information about the polynomial R_n that is indexed by the natural numbers $n \geq 1$.

Proposition 9.1 The coordinates $s_i(n)$ of the signature vector of a $(n, f, 2)$ system consisting of n independent and identically distributed components satisfy the following recurrence relation

$$\begin{aligned}
\sum_{j=0}^{f+1}\binom{f+1}{j}(-1)^j\Bigg(& i\binom{n-j-2}{i}s_i(n-j-2)-(i-1)\binom{n-j-3}{i-1}s_{i-1}(n-j-3) \\
& -3i\binom{n-j-3}{i}s_i(n-j-3) \\
& +3i\binom{n-j-4}{i}s_i(n-j-4)+2(i-2)\binom{n-j-5}{i-2}s_{i-2}(n-j-5)s_{i-2}(n-j-5) \\
& +3(i-1)\binom{n-j-5}{i-1}s_{i-1}(n-j-5)-i\binom{n-j-5}{i}s_i(n-j-5) \\
& -(i-2)\binom{n-j-6}{i-2}s_{i-2}(n-j-6)-2(i-1)\binom{n-j-6}{i-1}s_{i-1}(n-j-6) \\
& -(i-2)\binom{n-j-7}{i-2}s_{i-2}(n-j-7)-(i-3)\binom{n-j-7}{i-3}s_{i-3}(n-j-7)\Bigg)=0,
\end{aligned} \tag{9.2}$$

where $\binom{a}{b}$ denotes the number of ways of selecting b objects out of a distinct elements.

Proof. We first recall that, for any coherent system, the double generating function of $i\binom{n}{i}s_i(n),\ 1\le i\le n,$ is given by

$$\sum_{n=1}^{\infty}\sum_{i=1}^{n} i\binom{n}{i}s_i(n)\,t^i x^n = tx\frac{\partial R\left(x(1+t);\frac{1}{1+t}\right)}{\partial x} - t(t+1)\frac{\partial R\left(x(1+t);\frac{1}{1+t}\right)}{\partial t}, \tag{9.3}$$

where $R(z;p)=\sum_{n=1}^{\infty}R_n(p)z^n$ is the reliability generating function (Triantafyllou and Koutras (2008b)). Since for a $(n,f,2)$ system, the generating function $R(z;p)$ is given by

$$R(z;p)=\frac{(1-pz)^f-(qz)^2\left\{\sum_{i=0}^{f-3}(pqz^2)^i(1-pz)^{f-i-1}+(pqz^2)^{f-2}\right\}}{(1-z)(1-pz)^f},$$

where $q=1-p$ is the common unreliability of its components (Triantafyllou and Koutras (2014)), we then substitute in (9.3) and we obtain the expression

$$\sum_{n=1}^{\infty}\sum_{i=1}^{n} i\binom{n}{i}s_i(n)\,t^i x^n = \frac{d}{x^2(1-x-tx)^2(1-x-tx^2)^2(1-x)^{f+1}},$$

where

$$\begin{aligned}
d = & -t^4(1-x)^{f+1}x^6 - f(1-x)^3\left(-(tx^2)^f+(1-x)(tx^2)^f\right)\\
& +t^3x^4\left(-(tx^2)^f(2x+f-2)+(1-x)^f x(x^2-1)\right)\\
& +t(x-1)^2\left((1-x)(tx^2)^f\left((f-1)x^2+x+f-2\right)-(tx^2)^f(2fx^2+2x+f-2)\right)\\
& +(tx)^2\left(-(1-x)^2(tx^2)^f(x+f-3)+(x-1)\right)\\
& \left(-2(1-x)^{f+1}x^2-(tx^2)^f(4(x-1)+f(x^2+2)))\right).
\end{aligned}$$

If we introduce the notation

$$c_n(t)=\sum_{i=1}^{n} i\binom{n}{i}s_i(n)t^i, \tag{9.4}$$

then on noting that the coefficients of x^{n+1} of the left hand side should vanish for $n\ge 2f+5$, we may readily verify the following recursive scheme for $c_n(t)$

$$\begin{aligned}
\sum_{j=0}^{f+1}\binom{f+1}{j}(-1)^j\Big(&c_{n-j-2}(t)-(t+3)c_{n-j-3}(t)\\
&+3c_{n-j-4}(t)+(2t^2+3t-1)c_{n-j-5}(t)\\
&-(t^2+2t)c_{n-j-6}(t)-(t^2+t^3)c_{n-j-7}(t)\Big)=0, \qquad n\ge 2f+5.
\end{aligned}$$

We next substitute $c_n(t)$ by (9.4) in the last formula and pick out the coefficients of t^i, $i = 1,2,\dots,n$, on both sides; the recurrence relation ensues by straightforward algebraic manipulations. □

In order to launch the recursive scheme proved in Proposition 9.1, a number of initial conditions would be necessary. These conditions can be effortlessly derived by exploiting again the same equation, now taking into account the coefficients of x^{n+1}, for $n < 2f + 5$ and setting $s_i(n) = 0$, if $i \le 0$, $n \le 0$, $i < k$, $n < f$ or $n < k$ and in the case of obtaining any negative value of $s_i(n)$. It is noteworthy that the main result of Proposition 9.1 holds also true for a $(n, f, 2)$ system with exchangeable components. Therefore, it is feasible to compute reliability function $R_n(t)$ for such systems in the exchangeable case based on equation (9.2) and the following well-known result

$$R_n(t) = \sum_{i=1}^{n} s_i(n) P(T_{i:n} > t), \tag{9.5}$$

where $T_{1:n} \le T_{2:n} \le \dots \le T_{n:n}$ are the order statistics of lifetimes $T_1, T_2, \dots, T_n$ of the components of the structure. It is noteworthy that formula (9.5) has been first introduced by Samaniego (1985) for the i. i. d. case and has been expanded by Navarro and Rychlik (2007) for structures with exchangeable components.

It is worth mentioning that Eryilmaz and Zuo (2010) studied the calculation of signatures of systems involving two common failure criteria and provided an alternative nonrecurrence method for obtaining the signatures of such systems. More specifically, they proved that the signature vector of an $(n, f, 2)$ system is given as follows

$$\mathbf{s} = (p_1(n), p_2(n), \dots, p_{f-1}(n), \sum_{i=f}^{n} p_i(n), 0, 0, \dots, 0),$$

where $p_i(n)$ denotes the $i-th$ coordinate of the signature vector of a consecutive-two-out-of-*n*: *F* system. Since $p_i(n)$ can be easily calculated by the exact formula (see, e.g., Triantafyllou and Koutras (2008a))

$$p_i(n) = \frac{(n-i+1)\binom{n-i+2}{i-1} - i\binom{n-i+1}{i}}{i\binom{n}{i}}, \tag{9.6}$$

it is clear that if we aim at the evaluation of the signature of an $(n, f, 2)$ of a specific structure (and not for a family of structures with different f's and n's) the procedure proposed by Eryilmaz and Zuo (2010) is much faster than the recursive scheme mentioned above.

Let us next consider the well-known linear consecutive-*k*-out-of-*n*: *F* system $C(k, n)$. As already mentioned, the system consists of n components and fails if, and only if, at least k consecutive failed components exist. Figure 9.2 illustrates the

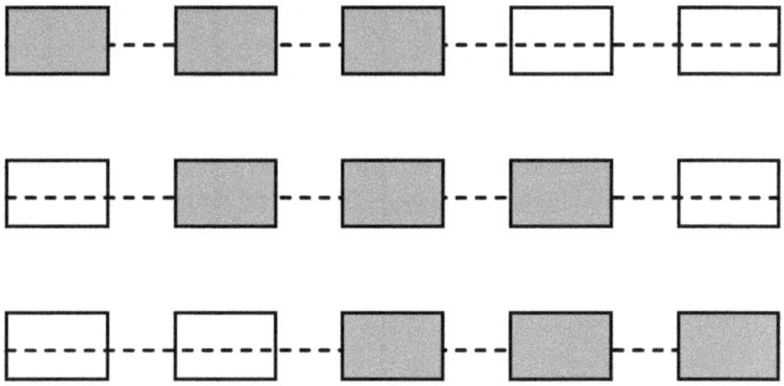

Fig. 9.2 The $C(k,n)$ system for $k = 3, n = 5$

failure criterion of the $C(k,n)$ structure for specific values of its design parameters. Note again that a grey-filled box indicates a failed component, while a blank box indicates a working one.

Proposition 9.2 offers some recurrences for the evaluation of its signatures for the special case $k = 2$.

Proposition 9.2 The coordinates $p_i(n)$ of the signature vector of a $C(k,2)$ system consisting of n independent and identically distributed components satisfy the following recurrence relations

1. $\left(1-\frac{1}{i}\right)(n+1)(2n-3i+4)p_{i+1}(n+1)-(n-2i+3)(2n-3i+3)p_i(n)=0$
2. $(n+1)(n-2i+4)(2n-3i+4)p_i(n+1)-(n-i+2)(n-i+1)(2n-3i+6)\,p_i(n)=0$, for $i = 1,2,\ldots,n$.

Proof. We recall equation (9.6) and the following ensues

$$p_i(n) = \frac{(i-1)(2n-3i+4)(n-i+1)_{i-2}}{(n)_i},$$

where

$$(n)_i = \frac{n!}{(n-i)!}.$$

The results we are looking for, are deduced after straightforward algebraic manipulations. □

Finally, for a r-within-consecutive k-out-of-n: F system $W(r,k,n)$ we prove some recurrence relations for the evaluation of its signatures for the special case $r = 2$. As already mentioned, the system consists of n components and fails if, and only if, there exist k consecutive components which include among them, at least r failed ones. Figure. 9.3 illustrates the failure criterion of the $W(r,k,n)$ structure for specific values of its design parameters. Note that a grey-filled box indicates a failed component, while a blank box indicates a working one.

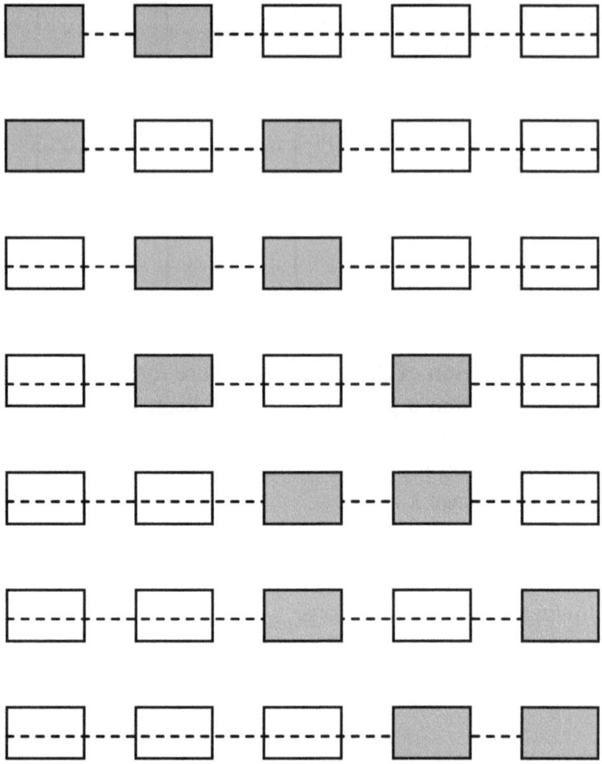

Fig. 9.3 The $W(r,k,n)$ system for $r = 2, k = 3, n = 5$

Proposition 9.3 offers some recurrences for the evaluation of its signatures for the special case $r = 2$.

Proposition 9.3 The coordinates $v_i(k,n)$ of the signature vector of a two-within-consecutive *k*-out-of-*n*: *F* system consisting of *n* independent and identically distributed components satisfy the following recurrence relation

$$\left[(n-i+1)(n-k(i-2)+i-2)_{i-1}-(n-k(i-1)+i-1)_i\right]v_i(k+1,n)$$

$$-\left[(n-i+1)(n-k(i-2))_{i-1}-(n-k(i-1))_i\right]v_i(k,n)=0.$$

Proof. The $i-th$ coordinate of the signature vector of a coherent system can be expressed as (Boland and Samaniego (2004))

$$v_i(k,n)=a_{n-i+1}(n)-a_{n-i}(n), i=1,2,...,n,$$

where

$$a_i(n)=\binom{n}{i}^{-1} r_i(n)$$

and $r_i(n)$ denotes the number of path sets of the structure with exactly i working components. Since for the special case of a two-within-consecutive k-out-of-n: F system, we have (Naus (1968))

$$r_{n-j}(n) = \binom{n-(j-1)(k-1)}{j},$$

we conclude that its signatures take on the following form

$$v_i(k,n) = \frac{(n-i+1)\binom{n-(k-1)(i-2)}{i-1} - i\binom{n-(k-1)(i-1)}{i}}{i\binom{n}{i}}.$$

The recurrence relations are readily concluded after some algebraic manipulations.

□

As an illustration, we apply the recurrences proved in the previous propositions and we provide several numerical results for the signature vector of consecutive-type systems consisting of n independent and identically distributed components for different values of the design parameters. Table 9.1 summarizes the outcomes of the computational procedure that has been followed.

9.3 Reliability Characteristics of Military Operations

In this section, we treat the consecutive-type systems studied earlier, as operational tactics of several defensive or offensive military schemes. Structural properties of these scenarios, such as the signature vector or the reliability function, are discussed in detail and several conclusions concerning the effectiveness of the aforementioned military operations are deduced.

Let us first consider a scheme where a motorcade of n trucks transfers comestibles and accoutrements inside a war area. For security reasons, each truck is obliged to hold a distance of 10 meters from the previous and the following one. However, it is known that if at least $k = 2$ consecutive trucks are taken out, then the necessary bond of the motorcade is lost and the mission is cancelled. The aforementioned scenario is related to the operation of a linear consecutive two-out-of-n: F system, where n denotes the number of its components. If we assume that the autocade consists of $n = 8$ trucks, then the signatures of the corresponding reliability structure are presented in Table 9.1. For example, we observe that the probability that the mission is cancelled upon the third truck being taken out, namely the probability that the consecutive two-out-of-eight: F system fails upon the third total failure of its components, is equal to $p_3(8) = 11/28$.

Table 9.1 The signatures of consecutive-type structures

System	Design parameters	–	*i*							
C(*m*, *k*, *n*)	*m*=2, *k*=2	*n*	1	2	3	4	5	6	7	8
		4	0	0	0	1	–	–	–	–
		5	0	0	0	3/5	2/5	–	–	–
		6	0	0	0	2/5	3/5	0	–	–
		7	0	0	0	2/7	12/21	1/7	0	–
		8	0	0	0	3/14	1/2	2/7	0	0
(*n*,*f*,*k*)	*f*=3, *k*=2	4	0	1/2	1/2	0	–	–	–	–
		5	0	2/5	3/5	0	0	–	–	–
		6	0	1/3	2/3	0	0	0	–	–
		7	0	2/7	5/7	0	0	0	0	–
		8	0	1/4	3/4	0	0	0	0	0
C(*k*,*n*)	*k*=2	4	0	1/2	1/2	0	–	–	–	–
		5	0	2/5	1/2	1/10	0	–	–	–
		6	0	1/3	7/15	1/5	0	0	–	–
		7	0	2/7	3/7	9/35	1/35	0	0	–
		8	0	1/4	11/28	2/7	1/14	0	0	0
W(*r*,*k*,*n*)	*r*=2, *k*=3	4	0	5/6	1/6	0	–	–	–	–
		5	0	7/10	3/10	0	0	–	–	–
		6	0	3/5	2/5	0	0	0	–	–
		7	0	11/21	47/105	1/35	0	0	0	–
		8	13/28	13/28	1/14	0	0	0	0	0

An interesting military scheme that parallels the two-within-consecutive *k*-out-of-*n*: *F* system is described straightforward. Let us consider that *n* gunships, ordered in a line, approach an area-target. According to the plan, the mission is scrubbed whenever at least two gunships, among any consecutive three ones, are shot down. In terms of Reliability Theory, whenever exist at least two failures occur, among any consecutive *k* components, the reliability system fails. If we assume that the mission includes $n = 8$ gunships, then the signatures of the corresponding reliability structure are presented in Table 9.1. For example, we observe that the probability that the mission is cancelled upon the third gunship being shot down, namely the probability that the two-within-consecutive three-out-of-eight: *F* system fails upon the third total failure of its components, is equal to $v_3(3,8) = 1/14$. The aforementioned plan is expected (with probability almost equal to 93 %) to fail before the third total failure of gunship.

In the sequel, we consider a military scheme that parallels to the *m*-consecutive-*k*-out-of-*n*: *F* system. More specifically, let us assume that a defensive ordering, consisting of a total number of *n* strongholds in a line, is under attack. The defenders recognize that once the assaulters manage to defuse at least two couples of consecutive strongholds, the battle is over. In words, if we presume that $n=8$, then it is straightforward that once at least two couples of consecutive components flunk, the two-consecutive-two-out-of-eight: F structure fails. Table 9.1 sheds light on the probabilities that accompany the aforementioned military plan. For example, we can easily conclude that the probability that the defensive ordering, mentioned before, shall fail upon the sixth breaking down of a stronghold, equals to 1/7.

Finally, an additional martial scenario of some interest, that can also be studied as a reliability system is described as follows. Let us assume that a telecommunication network, consisting of $n = 8$ stations ordered in a line, covers up the necessities of the liaison between troops taking part in a military operation. It is known that an even communication level is not fulfilled whenever at least three stations or two consecutive stations are out of order. Based on the entries of Table 9.1 referring to the $(n, f, 2)$ system, we observe that the aforementioned telecommunication network is shut down upon the third failure of a station with probability equal to 3/4.

9.4 Conclusions

In this Chapter, we study some reliability characteristics of well-known structures and deduce several mathematical results that can be applied in military operations. A whole section is dedicated to illustrate how the formulas, that have been previously established, can be proved useful for monitoring a military activity or manipulating troops during a battle. The main purpose that serves this Chapter, is to corroborate the connection between the mathematical study of a reliability system and the military domain, or the necessity that decision making and military tactics should be statistically validated. It is of some research interest for future work to study further reliability structures and adopt their properties in order to shed light on different military operations.

References

Anderson-Cook, C.M., Graves, T., Hamada, M., Hengartner, N., Johnson, V.E., Reese, C.S., Wilson, A.G.: Bayesian stockpile reliability methodology for complex systems. Mil. Op. Res. **12**, 25–7 (2007)

Boland, P.J., Samaniego, F.J.: The signature of a coherent system and its applications in reliability. In Mathematical Reliability: An Expository Perspective. Kluwer, Boston (2004)

Clausewitz, von Carl.: On War, Gutenberg (1909)

Eryilmaz, S.: Review of recent advances in reliability of consecutive-k-out-of-n: F and related systems. Proceedings of the Institution of Mechanical Engineering-Part O. J. Risk Reliab. **224**, 22–237 (2010)

Eryilmaz, S., Zuo, M.J.: Computing and applying the signature of a system with two common failure criteria. IEEE Transactions on Reliability. **59**, 576–580 (2010)

Eryilmaz, S., Koutras, M.V., Triantafyllou, I.S.: Signature based analysis of m-consecutive k-out-of-n: F systems with exchangeable components. Naval Res. Logist. **58**, 344–354 (2011)

Griffith, W. S.: On consecutive–k–out–of–n: failure systems and their generalizations. In: Basu, A.P. (ed.) Reliability and Quality Control, pp. 157–165. Elsevier, Amsterdam (1986)

Grosselin, K.: Bayesian Estimates of the Rideshare Reliability Effect. Mil. Op. Res. **17**, 39–49 (2012)

Kuo, W., Zuo, M. J.: Optimal Reliability Modeling: Principles and Applications. Wiley, N.J. (2003)

Naus, J.: An extension of the birthday problem. Am. Stat. **22**, 27–29 (1968)

Navarro, J., Rychlik, T.: Reliability and expectation bounds for coherent systems with exchangeable components. J. Multivar. Anal. **98**, 102–113 (2007)

Samaniego, F.J.: On closure of the IFR class under formation of coherent systems. IEEE Trans. Reliab. **34**, 69–72 (1985).

Samaniego, F. J.: System Signatures and their Applications in Engineering Reliability, vol. 110, Springer, N. Y. (2007)

Sven Guzman, M., Pohl, E.A., Schneider, K., Rainwater, C.: Application of Reliability Methods to Social Networks. Mil. Op. Res. **17**, 51–58 (2012)

Triantafyllou, I.S., Koutras, M.V.: On the signature of coherent systems and applications. Probability in the Eng. and Informational Sci. **22**, 19–35 (2008a)

Triantafyllou, I.S., Koutras, M.V.: On the signature of coherent systems and applications for consecutive–k–out–of–n: F systems. In: Bedford, T., Quigley, J., Walls, L., Akali, B., Daneshkhah, A., Hardman, G. (eds.) Advances in Mathematical Modeling for Reliability, pp. 119–128. IOS Press, Amsterdam (2008b)

Triantafyllou, I.S., Koutras, M.V.: Signature and IFR preservation of 2-within-consecutive k-out-of-n: F systems. IEEE Trans. Reliab. **60**, 315–322 (2011)

Triantafyllou, I.S., Koutras, M.V.: Reliability properties of (n,f,k) systems. IEEE Trans. Reliab. **63**, 357–366 (2014)

Tung, S.S.: Combinatorial analysis in determining reliability. Proc. Ann. Reliab. Maintainab. Symp. 262–266 (1982)

Index

V. Zeimpekis et al. (eds.), *Military Logistics,* Operations Research/Computer Science Interfaces Series 56, DOI 10.1007/978-3-319-12075-1

MIX
Papier aus verantwortungsvollen Quellen
Paper from responsible sources
FSC® C105338

If you have any concerns about our products,
you can contact us on
ProductSafety@springernature.com

In case Publisher is established outside the EU,
the EU authorized representative is:
Springer Nature Customer Service Center GmbH
Europaplatz 3, 69115 Heidelberg, Germany

Printed by Libri Plureos GmbH
in Hamburg, Germany